THE DICTIONARY OF SACRED AND MAGICAL PLANTS

THE DICTIONARY OF SACRED AND MAGICAL PLANTS

Christian Rätsch

With a Foreword by
Albert Hofmann

Translated by
John Baker

Santa Barbara, California
Denver, Colorado
Oxford, England

ISBN 0-87436-716-6

99 98 97 96 95 94 93 92
10 9 8 7 6 5 4 3 2 1

First published in 1988 by Akademische Druck-u. Verlagsanstalt, Graz/Austria under the title Lexikon der Zauberplanzen aus ethnologischer Sicht.
This enlarged English language edition published by arrangement with Prism Press, 2 South Street, Bridport, Dorset DT6 3NQ, Great Britain.
Published in the United States 1992 by ABC-CLIO, Inc. 130 Cremona Drive, P.O. Box 1911 Santa Barbara, California 93116-1911.
This book is manufactured on acid free paper. Manufactured in the United States of America.

Table of Contents

Foreword

Actually, all plants are magical plants. Each miraculously builds itself up from inorganic matter — water, carbonic acid, nitrogen, and minerals — using only sunlight for energy. The bodies of plants represent stored solar energy, and provide the foundation for both the animal and the human worlds. Yet plants do not give us food, medicines, and vitamins alone, but also substances which are capable of affecting consciousness, the true center of our being.

Plants which contain such substances — which we may call psychovitamins — are magical plants in the more narrow sense. It is these plants which form the subject of the book before you.

Magical plants alter our sensations, and consequently the manner in which we perceive the external world. These changed perceptions result in alterations of consciousness. As our window upon ordinary reality vanishes, a different reality enters our consciousness, a reality which experience tells us is at least as real as our ordinary state — if not more intense, more real. It is easy to see why plants with such uncanny, magical effects came to be used in the practices and ceremonies of magicians, medicine men, shamans and healing priests, and why they also came to play such an important role in the mystery cults.

The use of magical plants reaches far back into human history, and has been demonstrated in all cultures. For the contexts with which they have been associated (witchcraft and magic) are expressions of a very human aspiration — the yearning to gain insight into hidden layers of being, to learn about powers not normally accessible to humans, and to understand the proper ways to utilize these powers.

This dictionary of magical plants provides information about the botanical classifications and pharmacology of many of these plants and about the roles which they have played in history and the manners in which they have been used. As a result, the reader is offered a fascinating and colorful portrait of some of the lesser known facets of the human story. Those readers whose interest in a particular magical plant is stimulated by the text, moreover, will be able to use the comprehensive bibliography in order to access the original literature. In a time like ours, with its one-sided emphasis upon the rational aspect of reality, a book such as this provides a signpost towards the magical, which is just as real as reality itself is magical. It is my hope that this work reaches a broad audience.

Dr Albert Hofmann
Rittimatte 1992

'In herbs may be found the full power of the world. He who knows their secret abilities is omnipotent.'

Indian proverb

Preface

The encounter with a foreign culture is one of the most exhilarating experiences available in the modern world. Such an experience is even more profound when it occurs in conjunction with a glimpse of another reality. Magic is a gateway to other realities. Since prehistory, magic and plants have been closely linked. Shamans ingest plants so that they may leave their bodies and travel into other realities, healers use mushrooms and ayahuasca to help them ascertain disease causes that are not normally perceivable and to unfold their healing powers. Diviners and clairvoyants utilize thornapple, fly agaric, or ololiuqui so that they may behold what is normally hidden or see into the future. Some herbs are said to cause levitation. The enormous amounts of opium consumed by fakirs enable them to become oblivious to pain and increase their stamina. Alchemists make use of secret roots when they brew their elixirs of immortality, and magicians 'bewitch' their victims by means of monkey seeds or henbane seeds. Priests burn incense in order to contact the gods, witches use flying ointments to go on astral journeys, and yogis consume hemp to unite with the god Shiva. The magician-priests of the Andes chew coca until they are able to interpret and understand the omens and other signs of their environs. These magical abilities are pharmacologically supported or expedited by the active ingredients contained in certain plants.

This book represents an attempt to compile a dictionary of some of the many plants which have found use in the ethnographic context of magic. Because people throughout history have utilized an untold number of plants for such purposes, such a work must always remain incomplete. And yet it is my hope that it will help the reader to become more profoundly aware of many of the wonderful things in our world. Future research and experience will expand the picture of magic plants that is sketched herein.

I would like to thank from the bottom of my heart all of those who have supported me in my efforts, especially Claudia Müller-Ebeling, Albert Hofmann, Ralph Metzner, Terence and Kat McKenna, Stan Grof, Herman de Vries, Galan O. Seid, Nirmol and Anupama, Ulrike and Werner, Sigi and Ossi, Dennis Alegre, Hanscarl Leuner, Hartmut Laatsch, Michael

Schlichting, and my heathen family.

The original German text has been substantially revised and expanded for this English edition. New findings have been incorporated and a number of plants added that were not included in the original edition, as were a number of tables. In making these revisions, I have been aided by Dennis McKenna, Antonio Bianchi, Francesco Festi, Jochen Gartz, Marlene Dobkin de Rios, Andrew Weil, William Emboden, Werner Larsen, Christoph Hodel, Nevill Drury, Martin Hanslmeier, and Karl Gratzl. Special gratitude goes to my friend and translator, John Baker.

The study of magical plants is an adventure which takes one far beyond the frontiers of academic science. My wish is that this book may serve as a guide for those who are ready to undertake this adventure.

Dr Christian Rätsch
Hamburg 1992

Translator's Introduction

The task of the translator is to render, as accurately as possible, the ideas expressed in one language into ideas understandable in another. Ideally, none of the translator's own ideas should slip — whether intentionally or otherwise — into the text being produced. Instead, he should serve solely as a channel or medium of expression, performing his job while remaining an objective observer apart from and outside of the realm of ideas that are being translated.

Such an ideal, of course, is impossible to attain, and some aspects of the personality of the translator will inevitably slip into the translated text. In fact, this outcome is unavoidable — and just as the reader must of necessity interpret the text he is reading in terms of his own knowledge and experience, so too will the translator produce a text which will ultimately incorporate his own knowledge and experience as well.

The difficulties involved in translation — in rendering one reality into another — are compounded when the translator is unable to confer with the author of the original text. In such cases, the translator must become more than merely an exchanger of words and phrases; he must also interpret ideas across time and/or space. In the present case, however, it has not been necessary that I assume such a role. For the text of this revised and expanded English edition has been produced through a cooperative effort by the author and myself. First, the author reworked the entire original text, adding, deleting, and revising portions as he saw fit. Then, after I had translated this text, he was able to proof the text and add still further revisions. In this way, we were able to work as a team with one primary goal: to make this edition as accessible as possible to the English speaker.

Despite our cooperation, one word in particular proved extremely difficult to translate. This is the German word *Rausch*, which is typically rendered as 'intoxication'. This English term is used to denote a condition in which a person's faculties are affected by the toxic (i.e. poisonous) effects of some substance. One connotation of the term is that these effects represent an *impairment* of normal functioning, in such a way that perception and cognition are both *adversely* affected. As a consequence, many English speakers might argue that any experiences, insights, etc., obtained while intoxicated must be of less significance than those obtained in 'normal', non-intoxicated states.

The definition of the word *Rausch* in modern German conforms only in part to the current English understanding of intoxication. Traditionally, the concept of *Rausch* has referred to much more than merely the manner in which a substance affects a person — it also signifies the transcendental nature of such states, as the usual ties with everyday reality are loosened and the individual becomes open to experiences outside the domain of normal existence. In such states, the individual is alone with his experiences, and must draw upon what he has previously learned if he is to understand them. In modern societies, where these states are often pursued solely for hedonistic purposes, an individual frequently enters them without any serious training and is forced to interpret his experiences as best he can. If the more unusual of these have not been anticipated — either through individual preparation or cultural training — then they may be interpreted as something fearful or evil. To an outsider, such apparently negative experiences may even seem to provide confirmation of the purported 'toxic' effects of the substances which elicit them.

In contrast, societies which have developed traditional patterns for utilizing plants such as those discussed in this book rarely leave the individual to himself. Extended periods of ritual preparation normally precede the use of such substances, and guides are frequently present during the *Rausch* itself. As a result, a person has a good idea of what to expect in such states, and consequently is much less likely to have negative experiences. As he contacts the ancestors, or journeys to the abodes of the gods, or peers into the body of the person he is attempting to heal, the individual who is experiencing this state knows that he is in contact with a reality much greater than that within which he normally spends his time.

A *Rausch*, in other words, is not an end in itself, but a means to an end. It represents a door, or a vehicle, or a bridge to a realm filled with unknowns — and hence with potential knowledge (this topic is dealt with in some detail in the Introduction). Rendering *Rausch* as intoxication, then, would represent a grave distortion. After consulting with the author, I chose instead to use the somewhat less pejorative term 'inebriation'. While fraught with many of the same associations as intoxication, it does place less emphasis upon the supposedly toxic causes behind the experiences.

American society has an ambivalence about altered states that is not shared by many other cultures, including the Germans. There, the induction of altered states is a tradition which goes back for well over fifteen hundred years. Whether it was to communicate with their gods, celebrate their group identity, or accentuate the pleasurable experiences of love, the Germanic tribes made enthusiastic use of the magical plants which they had available. This attitude, this positive appreciation of extraordinary states, is another aspect implied in the concept of *Rausch*.

Of course, this enthusiasm did not bring with it a blanket approval to use with abandon any or all of the plants which the Germans considered magical. For the concept of *Rausch* also implies respect and reverence for both those substances and procedures which are capable of invoking altered states and the states themselves.

It is curious that the English language, so rich in other ways, should lack a suitable equivalent for *Rausch*. Inebriation is a poor substitute. I, and many others, would be grateful if we could develop new concepts for talking about these states.

This work contains many terms of a technical nature, and since I am not equally fluent in the various domains of science, mistakes can occur. Besides the author, two persons have helped me to catch at least some of my mistakes. Robert Zanger provided a great deal of insightful input into the English version of the Introduction, while Doug Stults read and commented upon the final version of the entire text. I gratefully acknowledge their efforts on my behalf. Their help notwithstanding, any incorrect use or spelling of any term, or any other error, is of course my responsibility.

Dr John Baker
Ventura 1992

Introduction

What is Magic?

'For in consciousness is that which is wonderful, *and with it you reach beyond things.'*

Antonin Artaud

The world is a unity comprised of two poles. All that occurs and all that is experienced arises through the interaction between these two poles. These poles have been given many names: Good and Evil, Light and Dark, Day and Night, Positive and Negative, God and the Devil, Heaven and Hell, Thesis and Antithesis, Being and Nothingness — as well as male and female, true and false, living and dead. The world is manifested through every element which helps to compose its unity. Each element is but *one* aspect of the world and reflects but *one* experience of the world, while the world itself is the expression of and provides access to but *one* aspect of being. And thus, every person is *one* part of the whole. All of the world's mythologies speak of an original, paradisiacal condition, which was static and unitary. When humans appeared, this original condition became impossible. Humans set forth to experience the totality of the world. In doing so, they encountered the benevolent gods and their malevolent counterparts. Man emerged from a static paradise into a world of change. Once out of paradise, there was no return. Yet memories remained, and the quest for a way back began.

Humans long to live in a perfect world, to be whole, healthy, successful, and happy. We want to live, and live well. We dream of a paradise on earth. By living in harmony, in oneness with the stones, plants, animals, and gods, we may be able to realize this dream. Yet there is also another side to the universe, one that is dark, sick, and destructive.

Humans speak of their experience of the world as reality. 'And indeed, each of us is a philosopher, for we each experience the world in a unique manner and make our own personal picture of it in accordance with our uniqueness. Every person must manage in his own unique reality' (Hofmann

1986:13). We all want to be satisfied with our reality. If we are not satisfied, then something must be changed. But in order for reality to be changed, the experience of the world must be changed. Change, however, can only be effected through the actions of the gods and demons, and through magic.

The world is a stream of constant change. All that lives changes and is transformed. Consciousness arises from nothingness, becomes a person by experiencing the world, and ultimately returns to nothingness. Wherever you look, you find change. Change is determined by the laws of the gods; it occurs in a regular manner. And yet change may be controlled. A person who knows the laws of change can make use of them, control them, and thus effect magic. Magic, in other words, entails a conscious attempt to modify a constantly changing world in order to achieve a particular end.

Magic draws upon powers in the universe which are normally not perceivable or controllable. One needs knowledge to harness these powers — knowledge of the internal relationships between things and of the metaphysical effects of things. Traditionally, such knowledge is attained through initiation. Magic is thus a secret knowledge for utilizing the hidden powers of the universe.

There has never been a culture which did not know of magic. Every human society has its stories of magicians, of persons who learn how to harness normally invisible powers and laws and then serve their community by healing the sick, helping the desperate, alleviating need, effecting fertility, and warding off the dark side of the universe. Because there are two sides to the world, however, there are also those who use magic to harm their fellows. They may send disease and death, sow misfortune, bring fertility to a standstill, or cast a shadow over the light side of the universe. Wherever good magicians exist, evil sorcerers exist as well. Benevolent magic and harmful sorcery are but two poles of one unity, reflecting the drama of existence and the game between the gods and the demons. And thus, a person who can effect magic has the power to evoke both good and evil.

What are Magical Plants?

'No "medicines", "talismans", "magical grains", or even poisons will function without the word. If they are not "spoken", they cannot help. In themselves, they have no activity of any kind. It is only the intelligence of the word which frees these powers and makes them effective.'

Jahnheinz Jahn, Mahu

To effect magic, knowledge alone is not enough. A person also needs to perform the proper rituals and use the correct tools. Magic is activated by ritual and directed by means of tools. All human cultures have rituals of magic, and all have developed a number of instruments of magic which are manufactured and employed according to secret traditions or instructions given by the gods and demons.

A person who knows of the inner relationships of things is also capable of recognizing and utilizing the magical powers which lie hidden therein. Magicians see these powers, and they recognize, name, and direct them in accordance with their goals. Since time immemorial, humans have used countless natural and artificial objects as instruments of magic: shells and ammonites, rocks and crystals, plants and animals, food and drink, pictures and sculptures, jewelry and fabrics, weapons and tools, signs and altars (cf. Biedermann 1976; Nemec 1976; Rätsch & Guhr 1989). Many magicians consider plants the primary instruments of magic. Through their knowledge and ritual activity, magicians transform plants into instruments of magic. It is only through knowledge and action, through *cultural use*, that any plant becomes magical. Magical plants are thus the tools of the magician, tools which serve to transform reality. And as we have noted, they can be utilized to produce both beneficial and injurious results.

In this book, we will be considering the anthropological and ethnopharmacological uses of a select group of plants. Anthropology investigates human culture. Ethnopharmacology investigates the cultural use of pharmacologically active substances (cf. Dobkin de Rios 1984; Efron 1967). For this reason, any monograph on magical plants should include a discussion of their pharmacological properties. When magical plants are considered from an anthropological perspective of analytical and comparative research, we find that they may be systemized or classified in certain ways. The classification introduced in this work is a preliminary one, and future research will surely lead to its revision, improvement, and expansion. Some improvements have already been made for this English edition, which includes a consideration of objects found in association with burials.

Magical Drugs and Plants of Prophecy

Plants which magicians ingest or administer in order to obtain insights into normally invisible realities or to discover hidden aspects of being may be termed magical drugs or plants of prophecy (cf. Rätsch 1986b, 1991a; Schultes & Hofmann 1979). Due to their profound effects, such plants have been variously characterized as hallucinogens, psychedelics, entheogens, psychotomimetica, psychodysleptica, or ecstatica.* Albert Hofmann, who discovered LSD and studied the magical drugs of Mexico, has provided what is perhaps the most appropriate definition of the effects of hallucinogens:

> Hallucinogens distinguish themselves from all other psycho-active substances through their extremely profound effects upon the human psyche. They bring about radical psychological changes which are associated with altered experiences of space and time, the most basic categories of human existence. Even the consciousness of one's own corporeality and one's own self may be changed dramatically. Hallucinogens take us to another world, to a type of dream world which is nevertheless experienced as completely real, as even more intense and consequently in some ways more real than the ordinary world of everyday reality. At the same time, if the dosage is not too high, consciousness and memory are retained completely. This is a key distinction between these substances and the opiates and other intoxicants, whose effects are associated with an obscuration of consciousness. Sensory sensations, especially smell, become more sensitive. Objects appear more vivid, their colors more luminous. Often, they seem transparent with a magical luster. The environment takes on new meaning, and objects begin to live. The sense of time is largely disturbed. Often, time appears to stand completely still. One lives timelessly, completely in the Here and Now, and this leads to an incredible intensification of experience.
>
> (Hofmann 1975:12-13).

Most cultures consider plants which are capable of evoking such effects in humans to be divine. Referred to as plants of the gods, they may be administered outside of the magical context during sacred occasions, often in communal ritual circles (cf. La Barre 1970; Müller-Ebeling & Rätsch 1987). Frequently, they are used in the preparation of ritual libations (cf. Huber 1929). Many of the plants which will be discussed in this book belong to this category: **Angel's Trumpet, Ayahuasca, Balche', Borrachero, Ergot, Fly Agaric, Gaise Noru Noru, Guatillo, Haoma, Hemp, Iboga,**

* The term phantastica, introduced by Louis Lewin, is actually more correct. Unfortunately, Lewin included a number of plants in this category which are neither magical drugs nor plants of prophecy.

Jambur, Jurema, Kava-Kava, Koribó, Manaka, Mandrake, Mushrooms, Ololiuqui, Peyote, Salvia Divinorum, San Pedro Cactus, Snuff, Solandra, Soma, Teonanacatl, Thornapple, Tobacco, Villca, Voacanga.

Magical Medicines
Plants which magicians ritually prepare and administer to the ill to treat afflictions brought about by black magic or the gods and demons may be referred to as magical medicines.

Both common plants (such as maize and potatoes) and rarer plants known only to the magician may be used for medicinal purposes. A magical medicine contains magical power. This is incorporated into the plant by means of certain rituals, magical sayings, spells, and charms, and consecration (cf. Schindlbeck 1978). In principle, all plants belong to this category. Still, magicians usually prefer certain ones. The most important of these have been included in this book: **Aloe, Amate, Beans, Benzoin, Canella, Coffee, Date Palm, False Mandrake, Garlic, Ginseng, Lotus, Maize, Mistletoe, Orchids, Rue, Solomon's Seal, Tamarisk, Tulasi, Vervain, Wine.**

Elixirs of Immortality
This category includes plants which are ritually prepared and used as elixirs for preserving youth, increasing longevity, or for attaining immortality. Many magicians and alchemists have searched for elixirs of this type and, according to legend, some have actually found them (cf. Metzner 1986, 1987). Several of the plants described in this book have been used as ingredients in elixirs of immortality: **Fly Agaric, Fo-Ti, Ginseng, Haoma, Ling-Chih, Lotus, Soma, Tea, Water Lily, Wine.**

Love Charms and Aphrodisiacs
Plants which are culturally employed for purposes of awakening love in a particular person and directing that love to another may be characterized as love charms. Often, the plant (whose collection frequently entails complicated rituals) is mixed into the food of the person to be charmed or hidden in his or her dwelling or clothes. With other love charms, persons may ingest a particular plant or plants in order to increase their basic attractiveness to the opposite sex (cf. Aigremont 1987; Gifford 1962; Hirschfeld & Linsert 1930).

In contrast, aphrodisiacs are agents which are ingested or applied to the body in order to awaken sexual desire and to intensify the erotic experience (cf. Müller-Ebeling & Rätsch 1986; Rätsch 1990a)

Fig. 1: Inca magicians brewing a magical drink. This illustration provides an insightful example of the manner in which many Europeans conceived of indigenous belief systems. Here, the kettle typically associated with the witches of Europe has become an implement of the physicians of the New World (Pomo de Ayala, 16th century).

can be grouped together. Many of the plants discussed in this book may be placed into this category: **Aconite, Angel's Trumpet, Artemisia, Beans, Belladonna, Betel, Calamus, Coca, Coffee, Cola, Colorines, Dita, Ephedra, False Mandrake, Fly Agaric, Fo-Ti, Galangan, Garlic, Genista, Ginger, Ginseng, Guaraná, Hemp, Henbane, Iboga, Lakshmana, Lettuce, Mandrake, May Apple, Niando, Nutmeg, Nux Vomica, Orchids, Prickly Poppy, Quebracho, Saffron, Sassafras, Scopolia, Solandra, Thornapple, Vervain, Voacanga, Water Lily, Witches' Ointments, Woodrose, Yohimbe.**

Magical Incenses

Many aromatic plants and plant products (resins, oils, essences) are smoked or burned as incense. The tradition of using incense to purify sacred activities and sites is very ancient. This practice rests upon the belief that fire liberates the spirits which dwell in plants from their mortal shells and, once freed, these then become capable of effecting certain things. Often, they can banish demons or personified illnesses and help a person gain the favor of the gods (cf. Henglein 1985; Vinci 1980). The Magical Papyri of ancient Egypt describe how incenses may be utilized to evoke prophetic demons.

Certain incenses produce altered states of consciousness. These are often inhaled by shamans and diviners so that they may enter into trance and behold that which is normally invisible and hidden. In the course of human history, hundreds of plants have been used as ingredients in incenses. Only a few, typically associated with magic, are discussed in this book: **Aloe, Arbor Vitae, Artemisia, Asafoetida, Bay Laurel, Benzoin, Calamus, Canella, Cedar, Coca, Hellebore, Hemp, Henbane, Juniper, Pichi-Pichi, Poppy, Saffron, Sassafras, Tagetes, Tobacco, Wild Rosemary.**

Amulets and Fetishes

Amulets are objects which contain an invisible, physically non-demonstrable (magical) power which serves the owner in a specific manner. In addition to this passive protective function, amulets also represent an active accumulation of desired conditions. The owner of an amulet will normally carry it at all times or store it in a place constructed especially for this purpose. Amulets may be manufactured by magicians and by 'normal' persons. A countless number of both natural and artificial objects have been used as amulets in human history. Parts of plants (seeds, rinds, roots), which are easily transportable because of their form and qualities, have long been employed for such purposes (cf. Kriss-Rettenbeck & Hansmann 1977; Rätsch & Guhr 1989; Scanziani 1972). Plants which have been used to produce amulets include: **Aloe, Angel's Trumpet, Beans, Betel, Cola,** are easily transportable because of their form and qualities, have long been employed for such purposes (cf. Kriss-Rettenbeck & Hansmann 1977; Rätsch & Guhr 1989; Scanziani 1972). Plants which have been used to produce amulets include: **Aloe, Angel's Trumpet, Beans, Betel, Cola, Colorines, False Mandrake, Ginseng, Juniper, Ling-Chih, Lotus, Maguey, Maize, Mandrake, May Apple, Mistletoe, Nutmeg, Orchids, Peyote, Teonanacatl, Thornapple, Tobacco.**

Fetishes are sacred objects, typically manufactured from a number of items (both natural and artificial) which contain a personal or foreign magical power. This power is the object of the owner's cultic veneration and may be used to his advantage. Fetishes are offered sacrifices, and they are evoked by means of prayer. Most fetishes are carved from wood or roots. Through the act of carving, they become charged with magical power. Many anthropomorphic fetishes feature small boxes worked into the area of the navel. Magical objects from the plant, animal, and mineral kingdoms may be placed inside these boxes (cf. Thiel *et al.*, 1986). Plants which play a role in fetish beliefs include: **Aloe, Amate, Cedar, Ginseng, Iboga, Mandrake, Yohimbe.**

Magical Staffs and Tools

Plants often provide the raw materials which magicians use to ritually manufacture a variety of magical tools, including magical staffs and nets, witches' brooms, divining rods, magical daggers, and bowls and basins for storing magical drugs and similar substances (cf. Gessmann n.d.). Several of the plants treated in this book provide materials for the fabrication of magical devices: **Amate, Cedar, Genista, Haoma, Hemp, Maguey, Mistletoe, Witch Hazel.** The famous Thyrsos staff of Dionysos and his followers, which consisted of a stalk of fennel (*Ferula communis*) and a pine cone (cf. Baumann 1982:60-62), may be included in this category.

Forked Trees

In some societies, it is believed that pulling a person through a natural or artificial hole or gap will separate them from their afflictions. Holes in rock walls and houses are used for this purpose, as are split or crooked trees. Trees whose trunks contain a hole or a split, whether caused by lightning, the actions of a magician, or for no known reason at all, are called 'forked trees' (German = *Zwieselbaum*; cf. Feilberg 1897). The species of tree is unimportant. A person who crawls through a forked tree is said to have entered a new reality.

Poisons and Death Charms

There are a multitude of plants, small amounts of which can cause serious poisoning or even death (cf. Engel 1987; Roth *et al.*, 1984). The 'common' folk has always feared and generally avoided such plants. Persons — whether magicians or not — who made use of such plants were often shunned as poisoners and witches. In most societies, knowledge of the toxic effects of plants belongs to the realm of magic.

Poisons also have an important role to play in religious ordeals (cf. Evans-Pritchard 1976; Lewin 1929). Plants which can be ritually utilized to cause the deaths of others are called death charms (cf. Davis 1985; Resch 1987). Poisons and death charms are often one and the same, and may thus be encompassed within the same group. A number of plants discussed in this book fall into this category: **Aconite, Calabar Bean, Colorines, Ikema, Jequirity, Mushrooms, Nux Vomica.**

Grave Goods

In many cultures, certain objects (often of a personal nature) are placed in the graves of the dead. These are intended to aid the departed during the journey into the afterlife. These goods are usually artifacts, stones, minerals, shells, and ammonites. Food, drugs, and plant amulets are frequently put into the grave as well. Archaeological evidence has shown that the Neanderthals of Shanidar were placing plants (flowers) in the graves of their dead some 60,000 years ago (cf. Rätsch 1991a). The following plants have been used as grave goods: **Beans, Cedar, Coca, Colorines, Ephedra, Guayusa, Hemp, Henbane, Lotus, Maize, Mate, Poppy, Prickly Poppy, San Pedro Cactus, Thornapple, Tobacco.**

Who Uses Magical Plants?

'The history of the world is implied in the circle of this dance between two suns, the one that sets and the one that rises. And when the sun sets, the magicians enter the circle ...'

Antonin Artaud

Magical plants can only be utilized by someone who has the requisite knowledge. Such knowledge comes from many sources. It may be passed on from one generation to the next as tradition. It may be divinely revealed — bestowed upon humans during a dream or vision (either spontaneous or produced by certain magical drugs) — or received during contemplation and meditation. In many societies, magical plants are seen as teachers. The visions which they grant to humans may illustrate the proper way to live, reveal the secret powers of healing herbs or amulets, or initiate contact with beings not normally perceivable. Magical knowledge has its origins in visions of these kinds.

And who are the persons who use magical plants? Usually, they are individuals who have been chosen, whether through foresight, divine revelation, a call from the realm of the spirits, or by other magicians. In acquiring their knowledge of magical plants, they also take on ethical obligations: they are charged with aiding others and helping to keep the community intact. In the anthropological literature, these persons are variously known as shamans, medicine men or women, fetish priests, witch doctors, magical priests, or simply healers.

Others turn to magical plants out of personal interest. In doing so, they may elect the path of priest, herbalist, or diviner, all of which are socially sanctioned and defined. To pursue their paths, they become apprenticed to others who have experience.

Persons whose interests lie in increasing their own personal power often commit themselves to the forces of darkness. In their eyes, magical plants are instruments for furthering their own interests and harming others. Such individuals typically learn alone. In the anthropological literature, they are known variously as witches, black magicians, and sorcerers.

Magical plants, and in particular the less dangerous ones, may also be employed by 'normal' persons. Information concerning the manufacture of many amulets, aphrodisiacs, and love charms is often common knowledge. Similarly, most people know about the effects of poisons. The knowledge of non-specialists, however, is usually very superficial and rudimentary, and it is often incorrect.

How are Magical Plants Used in Psychedelic Rituals of Knowledge?

'The riders shall lay the whip to their horses,
cross the bridges and gallop on!
I build the bridge of heaven and the bridge of earth.
I erect a bridge between this world and the next.
I raise the bridge of the three levels and the
bridge of the seven stars...'

Invocation of a Yao Shaman

Throughout history, many magical plants have been utilized to penetrate into worlds not accessible in everyday life. Cultures differ in the manners in which they explain these worlds, just as they differ in the manners which they use to enter them. Nevertheless, there are certain commonalities in the manners in which these plants are used in most non-Western contexts. These concern the ritual framework surrounding their use, a sacred context which explains why the experiences evoked by some plants are important and even describes the contents of the experiences themselves. Because such rituals are typically conducted in order to gain insight into the universe and to arrive at answers to questions of existential import, it is useful to refer to them as *psychedelic rituals of knowledge*.

A metaphor will help us grasp the meaning of such rituals. This metaphor is the *bridge to the gods*, which is a *path to knowledge*. Like more mundane bridges, the bridge to the gods must be stable and secure. An unstable bridge is too unsafe to walk upon or traverse. A bridge must be crossed with trust and respect. In the same way, a path to knowledge must be traversed with trust and persistence. The ritual context provides a *vehicle* for traversing the path to knowledge, while the magical plant provides the *fuel*. If we wish to completely cross a bridge, our vehicle must be in perfect working order. If it breaks down midway, we will not reach our destination — the gods. When conducting a psychedelic ritual, knowledge concerning the preparation and dosage of the substance to be used is of paramount importance. Otherwise, *unnecessary* accidents may occur.

The concept of *bridge* is fraught with symbolic meaning, and is an image which is often encountered in the ethnographic context (Lemoine 1989). In the West African Iboga cult (**Iboga**), references are made to a 'bridge to the ancestors' (Fernandez 1982). South American shamans traverse a 'bridge of smoke' or a 'bridge of coca' (Martin 1969). Others cross a rainbow bridge to the Milky Way or to Valhalla. These bridges are not visible structures; they are internal paths to spiritual worlds. Yet a bridge is not merely a passage across an abyss to a new shore. A bridge is a way to knowledge which may be entered by means of a certain substance or plant. A bridge is a possibility which enables the searcher for knowledge to come to those who provide knowledge — the gods and the goddesses.

Gods and *goddesses* are beings which can be encountered by any person, albeit not within the visible world. They are beings who act within a world that is normally closed and imperceivable to us. Through magic, a person can control the world by causing the invisible to exert influence upon the visible (Rätsch 1985). The greatest effects are achieved when a person asks the gods to do this. Yet how can one perceive things that are normally invisible? One *sees* more than the world of everyday reality when one ingests a plant with psychedelic effects.

The term *psychedelic* precisely characterizes the intention of traditional rituals of knowledge: the manifestation of hidden dimensions of the psyche. A person who uses a psychedelic, however, should not become fragmented, but more integrated. He should not experience the world as something demonic; instead, his new experience of the world should show him the *proper way to live.*

Magical plants are frequently concerned with that domain of human experience or behavior which the Western world calls religion, religious experience, or mysticism. In the languages of many non-Western societies (e.g. the Mayan language of the Lacandon Indians) the word 'religion' does not exist, nor is there an equivalent concept. Similarly, there is no word for 'belief'. Does this mean that these people have no religion? In a Western sense, in which religion is so often a leisure activity having the character of a hobby and is thus detached from everyday life, they do indeed lack religion. They do not *believe* in gods; they do not *acknowledge* any gods. Instead, they *know* that the gods exist. They also *know* which gods exist, what they look like, and what their personalities are. And they are able to recognize the effects that these gods have upon the world within which they live. What is more, this knowledge is not passively limited to the functions which these gods fulfill in the universe, for they also know how to actively contact them — they know the paths that must be trod in order to meet the gods. This ethnographic fact, which tells us that many societies do not have a religion in a Western sense, but rather a knowledge of divine effects, is the key to understanding psychedelic rituals of knowledge.

There are several types of psychedelic rituals of knowledge. In spite of their apparent differences, all are designed to assist learning. Examining the various types of these rituals makes it possible to determine the structure common to all.

Mysteries

Mysteries are ritual communities or cultic associations which aim at facilitating a shared vision of the gods, knowledge of the gods, or knowledge of true reality. The most famous mysteries are known from antiquity (cf. Meyer 1987); for example, the Eleusinian mysteries (**Ergot**), the mysteries of the cult of Isis and Osiris, the Dionysian mysteries at Pompeii (**Wine**). In these rituals, psychedelics enable the participants to discern the gods and to recognize and understand the influence which they have upon the world (Wasson *et al.*, 1978). The aim of initiation into a mystery is not to heal the sick (although miraculous recoveries often occur), but rather to offer normal, healthy persons the chance to learn something about their station in the world as well as their place in the universe. Mysteries are concerned with providing answers to questions of the greatest import: *Who are we? Where do we come from? Where are we going? What does it all mean?*

Libations

Libations occur collectively within a ritual community (Huber 1929). Cults practising rituals of this type aim at producing a simultaneous and communal altered state of consciousness. In other words, the participants should attain this state together, and should contact the gods as a group. The shift in consciousness aims at attracting the gods to earth and into the circle of participants (**Beer**). The Greek *symposion* (= 'a drinking together'), best known from the writings of Plato, was one type of ritual libation. Here, the leader of the *symposion* determined the amounts of the substances (**wine**, water, herbs) which would be used to produce the drugs that would be given to the group.

Other typical libations include the Indo-European rituals in which **Soma** or **Haoma** were consumed (Flattery & Schwartz 1989). During these rituals, the participants assembled outdoors. It was said, 'man is the temple, and in man we recognize god, and in order to make this possible, we drink soma'. A fire was lit within the circle of participants and the beverage was handed around. The participants then sang about their visions (many of these songs may be found in the *Rig Veda*). The **Mead** carousal of the Germanic tribes had a similar meaning. The group consumed the mead (a brew of honey, water, and such 'bitter herbs' as **Henbane** or **Wild Rosemary**) in order to experience group inebriation, so that the gods would come among the drinkers.

Ritual Circles

A ritual circle is not a ritual intended for a cult community (Müller-Ebeling & Rätsch 1987), but rather a ritual which is attended by only those persons who feel the desire to do so. During the **Peyote** rituals of the North American Indians, the members of a community are not summoned to a religious ceremony. Only those who are actually searching for knowledge and wish to travel the *peyote road* will come to one of the nocturnal peyote meetings (Stewart 1987). The *veladas*, mushroom ceremonies in which Mexican Indians communally consume mushrooms (**Teonanacatl**) with psychedelic effects, are similar (Wasson 1980). These rituals do not serve personal knowledge alone, but also the healing of the sick. Many healthy persons will take part in a *velada*, for the ritual will strengthen their health and further their progress on the path to the gods. The healthy people call the gods, for the sick may no longer have the strength. When the gods appear, they are asked to heal the sick, to protect the healthy from illness and loss, and to reveal the secrets of the past, present, and future.

Vision Quests

A vision quest is a personal ritual not linked to any cult (Drury 1989). As a result, this type of ritual is not concerned with the culturally supported gods, but rather with the recognition of one's own personal god. The intention is for a person to experience the personal aspect of his relationship to the universe and recognize and comprehend the vision he receives as a signpost for his life and his actions. A person on a vision quest may facilitate the desired vision by fasting or other ascetic practices, or by using magical plants (**Tobacco**).

Incantations

Incantations are rituals intended to conjure up a god, goddess, or demon (**Incense**). Not only is the person who conducts the ritual able to cause the god to appear, he is also able to ask questions of this god or to compel him to act in a certain manner. Rituals of this type bring us to the domain of magical divination. In the *Leyden Papyrus*, detailed instructions describe how to compel the gods to appear and the ways to command them (Griffith & Thompson 1974).

Oracles

The word 'oracle' was originally used to refer to a location at which a person manifested the gift of prophecy. Later, the term also came to be applied to the persons who served at such places. The rituals used at the sites of oracles are quite uniform throughout the world (Loewe & Blacker 1981). Through the aid of a magical plant, an oracle (person) enters a prophetic trance in which he or she is able to divine the future. Perhaps the most well-known example of a ritual of this type is the oracle of Delphi.

Here, the Pythia, the priestess of Apollo, inhaled **Henbane** smoke in order to induce the requisite state of consciousness (Rätsch 1987). Ancient Mexico and Peru had similar oracles. In these areas, plants of the gods (**Coca, Ololiuqui, Picietl, San Pedro Cactus, Tobacco, Villca**) were ingested by a diviner/priest. Many pre-Columbian prophecies, like their counterparts from Delphi, were renowned for their accuracy (Rätsch 1991a).

Sacrifices

Sacrifices and auto-sacrifices are rituals in which the searcher for knowledge finds the path to the gods by sacrificing his own self. Such sacrifices may in themselves elicit ecstatic states (Pattee 1989).

The ancient Maya developed a ritual of psychedelic auto-sacrifice in which a man withdrew into a cave or a dark temple chamber and induced an extraordinary state of consciousness by drinking a beverage containing a number of active ingredients (**Balche', Thornapple, Water Lily**; also certain species of toads). The auto-sacrifice was performed by thrusting a stingray spine through the penis. This act was intended to simulate the menstruation of the moon goddess. By performing this ritual, a man attained knowledge and was given an answer to a previously posed question.

Magical plants (**Thornapple**) were also used to prepare victims for human sacrifices conducted by the Aztecs and Mayans. An example of this type of ritual is described in the *Eddas*: the self-sacrifice of Odin, conducted in conjunction with the discovery of the runes.

Hunting Magic

Rituals of this type may be either public or private. Here, an individual utilizes a magical plant (e.g. **Ayahuasca, Borrachero, Epená, Guaraná, Maté, Ololiuqui**) to embark on a journey to the lord of the animals or the animal gods (Reichel-Dolmatoff 1975). Once there, he asks for information as to where prey may be found or the luck which his tribe can expect during the forthcoming hunt. He may also ask the lords of the animals for forgiveness if someone has killed more animals than necessary.

Eroticism

An erotic ritual is conducted in order to recognize the god or goddess in oneself or one's partner and thereby obtain information about the nature of the world. The cult of Tantrism is the best-known example.

In Tantrism, psychedelic aphrodisiacs (e.g. **Hemp, Nux Vomica, Opium, Thornapple**) are used to facilitate this spiritual process (Müller-Ebeling & Rätsch 1986). The Taoist alchemy and the occult sexual magic of Aleister

Crowley provide further examples of this type of ritual. The pederasty practiced by the ancient Greeks may have originally been associated with initiation into a mystery, and may thus also have been associated with a path to knowledge. The purpose of these erotic rituals is to break down the ego, an act which is not only healing, but is also associated with extreme pleasure. Freed of the ego, consciousness becomes much more open to messages from the gods.

In spite of their diverse nature, all of these rituals possess a common basic structure. The purpose of a psychedelic ritual is to integrate the knowledge obtained therein with everyday life and the process of personal growth. To do this, they follow certain well-defined steps, listed in the following chart. It may be that the psychotherapeutic rituals of LSD therapy, psycholytic therapy, and group therapy with empathogens such as MDMA (Adamson 1985; Grof 1981; Pinkson 1989) can also be understood within this frame. Nevertheless, it must be noted that Western therapists have a great deal of difficulty conducting efficacious traditional rituals. Here again, it becomes apparent how much we may still learn from the cultures of the non-Western world.

The key to understanding the role which rituals play in the traditional use of magical plants is to realize that they provide an external structure which is understood and accepted by the participants. Because of their knowledge of this structure and their trust that their fellows will also adhere to the ritual rules, a participant in a psychedelic ritual of knowledge is able to temporarily surrender his self-control, thereby facilitating an experience of non-ordinary states of reality and the insights which they entail. In the field of psychology, frequent mention is made of the ego-dissolution which occurs in such states. From an anthropological point of view, it is more appropriate to speak of the dissolution of an individual's *social personality*.

The shift away from the patterns of thought and behavior normal to a society which is the object of the preparatory period, and the succeeding experience of aspects of reality not normally available, serve to make quite distinct both those areas in which the individual is in harmony with the world around him and those areas in which harmony is lacking. The journey across the bridge of the gods is a journey towards knowledge which will serve the individual in daily life. The psychedelic journey is not concerned solely with the individual's own self, as it so often is in the Western context. Instead, it is a journey for the good of the group. The knowledge attained on such a journey suggests ways to attain greater harmony with the world, both the world of society, and the world of nature.

The Basic Structure of Psychedelic Rituals of Knowledge

Phase	*Internal Process*	*External Acts*
Preparation	Formulating the Question	Contemplation/ Reflection
	Purification	Meditation
		Fasting
		Ablutions/Vomiting/Enemas
		Changing Clothes/ Painting Oneself
Implementation	Creating the Sacred Space	Burning Incense
		Listening to Music/ Drumming
		Prayers/Invocations
		Offerings
		Ingesting the Plants
	Vision	Mantras/Magical Spells
	Knowledge	Concentrating upon Ritual Objects
Integration	Finding Answers	Communicating Visions
	Solving Problems	(Stories, Singing, Painting)

How Do We Know about Magical Plants?

Because information about magical plants may be private, belong to the esoteric domain of many cultures, or only be obtainable after initiation, the question naturally arises: what is the origin of all the information about so many magical plants that has been collected in this book?

Entire generations of researchers have helped to cast light upon this subject. Thanks to their often tedious work, their detailed anthropological and personal reports, and their publications, it is now possible to survey the subject of magical plants (here, especial mention should be made of Bibra 1855; Hartwich 1911; Lewin 1980; Schultes & Hofmann 1979). Moreover, the records of the Inquisition and the notes of the early missionaries and conquerors, although often fragmentary and very distorted as a consequence of their use of Christian terminology and ideology, also provide us with information. From time to time, we also recover handwritten texts in which magicians of the past recorded their knowledge. For example, archaeologists have uncovered papyri treating magical subjects, almanacs of prophecy, and libraries of magic, all of which were originally intended solely for the eyes of the initiated (cf. Betz 1986).

Since the turn of the present century, there has been a keen scientific interest in the study of magical plants. During the chemical and pharmacological analysis of such plants, a number of agents have been discovered which have revolutionized the world-view of scientific medicine. The discoveries of the opiates and of cocaine, mescaline, and the amphetamines have had profound effects upon the history of medicine (cf. Rätsch 1987f). All of these powerful substances were obtained from plants used by the magicians of different societies, often for thousands of years. Reflecting the scientific trend toward specialization, it is not surprising that some ethnopharmacologists have dedicated themselves primarily to the study of magical plants (e.g. Diaz, Dobkin de Rios, Emboden, Furst, Reichel-Dolmatoff). A complete bibliography of the publications which contain information on magical plants would certainly be a multi-volume work. The bibliography at the end of this book provides a list of selected primary and secondary works. Efforts have been made to include the standard references on the subject. At the same time, I have also attempted to take in works which can assist the lay reader interested in deepening his or her knowledge. Anyone desiring more detailed knowledge about a specific plant should consult the bibliography in a monograph on that plant.

For this English edition, the bibliography has been expanded to reflect both recent works and to include others not listed in the original German edition.

The Sacred and Magical Plants from A – Z

'Plant energies have been able to influence and shape entire epochs in the history of mankind. By gaining entry into the inner domains of man, they were able to penetrate into his spiritual world.'

Aleíjos

'Even the most courageous among us only seldom has the courage for that which he really knows.'

Friedrich Nietzsche
No. 2 of the Maxims and Arrows of
his *Twilight of the Idols*

Explanatory note
Where plants mentioned in the text appear in bold type, they can be cross-referenced for further information under entries of their own.

ACONITE (Aconitum spp.). Aconite species are found throughout the world, and are frequently utilized as poisons and as magical and medicinal plants. Aconite was sacred to Hecate, the goddess of nocturnal beings, magic, sorcery, and the manufacture of poisons. It was said to have grown from the slobber of Cerberus, the three-headed dog of the Underworld. Theophrastus and Dioscorides both discussed the magical effects of the scorpion-shaped aconite root, which can cast a paralyzing spell upon an approaching scorpion when held in its direction (the spell can be counteracted with **Hellebore**). The botanical classification of the Greek aconite is still unclear.

Friar's Cap or Monkshood (*Aconitum napellus*), which flourishes throughout Central Europe and is often cultivated for its beautiful blue flowers, has been feared as a poison since antiquity. The old Germanic tribes venerated the plant. They called it Thor's hat, for it was sacred to Thor (Donar), the god of thunder and fertility. Later, aconite was numbered among the witches' plants. The plant has earned itself a prominent place in the history of political assassinations, aconite poisoning often being attributed to sorcery. Aconite was also used in camouflage magic: 'The seed, wrapped in a lizard's skin and carried, allows you to become invisible at will' (Cunningham 1989:224). It was also one of the active agents of the **Witches' Ointments** as well as of love charms: 'Because of the difficulty in dosing the drug, however, the result was often not so much an increase in the ability to love as it was love frenzy or even death' (Haerkötter 1986:52).

Another, yellow-flowered aconite species (*Aconitum vulparia*) was once believed to fend off wolves. It was even utilized to poison the animals (hence its common name 'yellow wolfsbane'). In the Himalayas, several varieties of aconite are used as so-called 'great medicines'. The Tibetans use aconite to treat demonically induced illnesses of the heart. An Indian species, *Aconitum ferox*, is used to manufacture poisoned arrows. In Chinese plant lore, many species of aconite are utilized as internal medicines which provide warmth and dispel cold. They are often ingredients of lavishly prepared elixirs of love and youth. One remedy for impotence uses aconite mixed with cassia (*Cinnamomum cassia*). The aconite species *Fu-tzu* (*Aconitum carmichaeli*) was the main ingredient in *hanshi* powder (also known as 'five mineral powder'), which also contained ground stalactite, oyster shells (*Ostrea gigas*), and aromatic herbs. In Taoist sexual magic circles, it was taken in brandy as an aphrodisiac. He Yan, the discoverer of the powder, praised it highly: 'When a person takes the five mineral powder, not only are illnesses healed, but the mind is also aroused and opened to clarity'. The Ainu, the original inhabitants of Northern Japan, utilize aconite root in their shamanic bear ceremony. The festival of the bear is the magical and religious core of the Ainu culture, which has resemblances to Paleolithic cultures. As part of this festival, a poison is ritually prepared for the arrows used in the bear hunt. The shamans prepare the poison, known

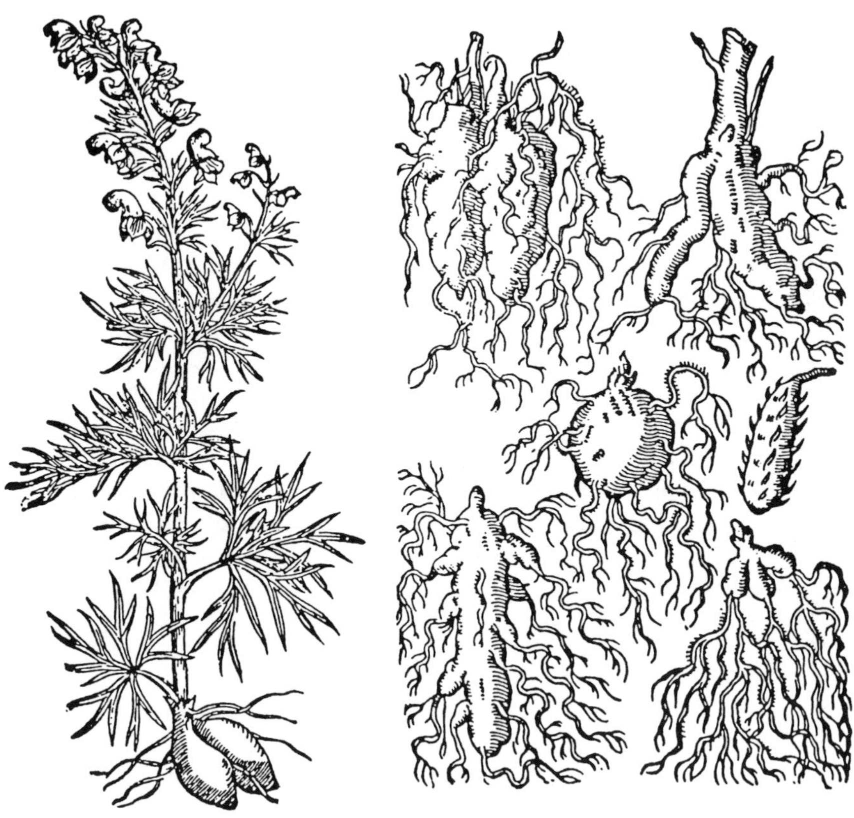

*Fig. 2: The roots of the poisonous aconite were formerly known in German as 'healing poison' (*Heilgift*). As this name suggests, aconites were utilized for both their toxic and their medicinal effects. In many areas (India, Assam, East Africa, Japan), aconite roots were used to manufacture extremely effective arrow poisons. The Ainu employed an arrow poison made from Aconitum japonicum in their ceremonial bear hunt (LEFT: the aconite plant; RIGHT: aconite roots. After Tabernaemontanus 1731).*

as *surku-kik*, with the assistance of secret spells. Only through the combined effects of the magical formulas and the extract of aconite roots is the poison powerful enough to kill the 'supernatural' bear.

Pharmacology: All aconite species contain highly toxic diterpine and norditerpine alkaloids. Monkshood (*A. napellus*) contains the extremely dangerous alkaloid aconitine (lethal dose for an adult: 3-6 mg). Some pharmacologists assume that aconitine has hallucinogenic effects in very small doses, and is capable of eliciting feelings of flying. The pharmacology of the *hanshi* powder is still largely unknown. *Fu-tzu* contains hypaconitine, aconitine, mesaconitine, talatisamine, and chuan-wu-base A and B.

Literature: Bensky & Gamble 1986; Clifford 1984; Cooper 1984; Mitsuhashi 1976; Wagner 1981.

ALOE (Aloe barbadensis syn. *Aloe vera).* The subtropical zones of both the Old and the New World are home to a number of varieties of aloe, most of which boast extremely colorful flowers. The thickened sap of the leaves is used most often. Generally, this is simply referred to as aloe. There is an aloe wood (*Aquilaria agalochum*) as well (also known as *Lignum aloes* or paradise wood) which is quite aromatic and was used in ancient times as a sacred incense (cf. **Incense**).

The Sumerians and Egyptians both used aloe and aloe wood as magical incenses and in ointments. Magical eye ointments, which contained aloe and were stored in shells, were successfully used to treat the 'Egyptian eye disease' (trachoma). In ancient times, varieties of aloe were ingredients of sacred incense burned at all religious and magical acts. Aloe incense was used in India and China (*Aloe arborescens*) as an apotropaic agent and to purify the soul.

In the Caribbean and in Latin America, a variety of aloe known today as *sabila* is still one of the most important medicinal and magical plants. It is used to fashion amulets and talismans. The ethnomedical uses of aloe are so numerous that one would be hard pressed to find a disease which the plant has not been used to treat. In Mexico and Columbia, it is known as *Sábila Sagrada* (the sacred initiate) and is invoked with magical spells. It is said that the plant is home to a goddess who can be put in a favorable mood through offerings and prayers. Among her gifts are health, wealth, and peace (cf. **Agave**). Aloe tea, when prepared with the correct magical formula, can make sterile women fertile and heal all manner of illness. Aloe is also used as a first-aid plant for treating burns, cuts, and sores.

Pharmacology: The thickened sap of the leaves yields a resinous, crystalline black substance which contains hydroxyanthracene derivatives (up to 40% aloin), chromone derivatives (aloesine), and the bitter constituent aloenine. The anthracenes function as a strong colonic laxative. The anthrones irritate the mucous membranes and increase their secretory activity. Aloe wood contains an essential oil which is liberated during fermentation.

Literature: Drury & Drury 1987; Manniche 1989; Rätsch 1987f; Vinci 1980.

Fig. 3: Stylized plant spirit on a magical paper made from the Mexican amate tree (drawing by Christian Rätsch).

AMATE (Ficus spp.). Some 50 different species of fig tree grow in Mexico which, following the Aztec name *amatl* (from *ama-quahuitl*, 'paper tree'), are known as amate. In pre-Columbian times, a paper was made from the inner bark of these trees which had the same name as the tree. This paper was used to manufacture clothing, books, and magical figures. Many Mexican codices were written on this paper. A veritable magical paper cult still survives among the Otomí Indians of Central Mexico. To make the paper, fresh bark is cut from the trunk, soaked in water, pressed, and then dried. Uttering incantations and magical formulas, figures are cut from the paper which may be used in both magic and sorcery. Figures depicting plant spirits, which are common motifs, are buried in the ground during planting to ensure good growth and a bountiful harvest (pastoral magic). They also protect the plants from animals, disease, winds (*aires*), and thieves. Anthropomorphic paper figures are worn as amulets and utilized to treat the sick. These figures depict the sick person as healthy. The magician offers incense and pulque (cf. **Maguey**) to the figures. Reciting magical incantations, the cause of the illness (a demon, an evil wind, or harmful magic) is expelled from the sick person and captured in the paper figure, which is then destroyed at a secret spot. These paper figures are also used for both love magic and death magic. For love magic, the spirit of the beloved is cut into the paper; for death magic, a portrait of the enemy is cut in. The figure is then pierced with a thorn or wooden point of a **Maguey**, soaked with blood, and buried.

Pharmacology: The fresh bark contains a slightly toxic latex with allergenic effects.

Literature: Christensen & Marti 1979; Dow 1986; Knecht 1966; Reko 1947; Spranz 1961; von Hagen 1944.

ANGEL'S TRUMPET (Brugmansia candida, Brugmansia spp.). These beautiful plants, also known as tree daturas, were already being cultivated by South American Indians as ornamentals and as magical plants in pre-Columbian times. They reproduce only through cuttings, planted seeds, and cultivation, and no wild forms are now known. The Angel's Trumpets are botanically closely related to **Borrachero** and **Thornapple**. They are also known as *Huacacachu, yerba de Huaca, huanco, chamico, floripondio, toa, tonga, campanilla, maicoa*, and even as **Borrachero**. All parts of the plant are utilized to prepare narcotic drinks which induce visions, send the magician or prophet into an ecstatic state, make it possible for him to speak to the spirits of the ancestors, establish contact with the gods, and cast light upon the treasures hidden in graves (*huacas*). Usually, however, only the leaves or the wonderfully scented trumpet-shaped flowers are used for these purposes. The plantations in the Sibundoy Valley of Columbia are quite renowned. A number of species are cultivated and prepared in this valley, and are sent from there to be traded throughout the entire Amazon region. Many Indians cultivate Angel's Trumpets for their beauty and their powerful pharmacological effects.They smoke the dried leaves, flowers, and seeds for asthma, bronchitis, and coughs, and as an aphrodisiac. Fresh leaves are placed upon the skin to treat open wounds, abrasions, tumors, osteomyelitis, burns, shingles, and painful joints and other afflicted areas. Freshly heated leaves are bound to the forehead to treat headaches and restlessness. The modern Tzeltal Indians of Mexico mix dried leaves of *Brugmansia suaveolens* with **Tobacco** (Nicotiana rustica) in order to 'see things', to recognize the cause of diseases, and to support their healing powers. To treat dislocations and sprains caused by 'wind in the body' (*aires*), they use a plant dressing made of 2-3 flowers and an equal amount of *Ricinus* leaves. In Mexico, it is said that fresh flowers which still carry a scent are capable of effecting deep sleep and beautiful erotic dreams when they are placed in the bed. The flowers also play a role in love magic.

Fig. 4: This early colonial representation shows a shaman or warrior with a power animal (bird) and a woman. The latter is holding a branch of Angel's Trumpet. This scene probably depicts an ancient Indian ritual (after a Keru lacquer painting, South America, late 16th century).

The seeds of the blood-red Angel's Trumpet (*Brugmansia sanguinea*), which are very potent, are added to chicha (cf. **Maize**). The resulting drink is said to be a powerful aphrodisiac. Angel's Trumpets are also added to schnapps and consumed as a tonic or added to **Ayahuasca**. Some species of Brugmansia are now used as ornamentals in all the tropic and subtropical zones. They are used in the same manner as **Thornapple** in folk medical traditions and in magic in Morocco, Nepal, China, the Philippines, and Indonesia.

Pharmacology: All parts of Angel's Trumpet contain tropane alkaloids which have simultaneously stimulating and inhibiting effects upon the central nervous system and inhibit the peripheral nervous system (primarily due to the presence of hyoscine, scopolamine, and some atropine). Even small concentrations are sufficient to cause so-called 'anticholinergic deliriums', characterized by hypnagogic and hallucinogenic states. The inebriating scent of the flowers has psychoactive and aphrodisiac effects.

Literature: Davis 1985; Lockwood 1979; McDowell 1989; Rätsch 1987f; Schultes & Hofmann 1980.

ARBOR VITAE (Thuja occidentalis). North American Indians use arbor vitae medicinally and ritually wherever it grows. Its branches are used to make teas to treat menstrual complaints, prostate problems, and fever. Decoctions of the branches are used to induce abortion. The aromatic twigs are used for ritual incenses, e.g. in sweat baths. The twigs are also said to protect against magic.

The 'tree of life' has also become established in Europe. An evergreen plant which can grow as tall as 20 meters, it is frequently planted near graves and in cemeteries, and serves the same purpose in Germany and England which the cypress plays in warmer countries. The arbor vitae has occupied a place in folk medical traditions since the eighteenth century. The tips of branches and small leaves are boiled and used as a sudorific, diuretic, and expectorant. In former times, more potent decoctions were also used to induce abortions. Because of these latter effects, arbor vitae was very likely also known as a 'tree of death'.

In European magical superstition, arbor vitae was often equated with **Juniper** and was used in the same manner.

Pharmacology: Arbor vitae contains the psychedelic and mildly toxic thujone, which is also present in **Artemisia** species and in yarrow. It also also contains thujine, thujugin, an essential oil, tannins, and resin.

Literature: Albert-Puleo 1978.

ARTEMISIA (Artemisia spp.). Artemisia species, which include mugwort (*Artemisia abronthanum*) and absinthium (*Artemisia absinthium*), are used medicinally and magically throughout the world. In India, artemisia is sacred to the gods Vishnu and Shiva. One Greek magical papyrus refers to it as an agent for kindling friendship and love. Artemisia received its name from Artemis (Diana), the goddess of the hunt, who was also responsible for plant growth and fertility and represented the boundary between the civilized world and the wilderness. She was venerated orgiastically in a manner similar to Dionysos. Later, in Catholic times, Artemis became the goddess of the witches and sorceresses (*araria*). Both varieties of artemisia (absinthium and mugwort) were sacred to her, and were used to brew psychoactive and aphrodisiac beverages (probably with a **Wine** basis) which were consumed in order to ecstatically join with the goddess as manifested in women. Artemisia was also sacred to Isis, the Egyptian goddess of magic. In cuneiform texts from Assyria, references have been found to the magical powers of two types of artemisia. Since ancient times, varieties of artemisia have been used as love magic and aphrodisiacs, abortifacients, additives to **Beer** and **Wine**, added to tonics, and utilized in fertility and healing agents. In China, the seeds of *Artemisia keiskiana* are used in a preparation for increasing vitality and youth.

The Eskimos, who possess only a handful of medicinal herbs, make use of *Artemisia tilesii*, a variety which grows in the northern tundra. They collect the stems and leaves and use these both fresh and dried to treat skin diseases (inflammations), arthralgia, and coughs. The herbage is boiled until a dark green liquid is obtained. This is used preventively for bathing the hands of small children and for washing inflamed areas of the skin. Astonishing antibiotic effects have been attributed to this decoction. Many North American Indians use fresh branches from a variety of types of artemisia or absinthium. Applied externally or taken internally as a tea, the twigs are regarded as an effective agent against rheumatism. Young girls suffering from menstrual pains, disturbances, or irregularities will enter a sweat lodge and throw branches of artemisia upon the fire. After a terrible fright, an Apache may inhale the smoke of *chin de i ze*, the 'Devil's medicine' (*Artemisia frigida*). The Cheyenne have a special ritual for collecting the plant which is said to improve its medicinal effectiveness: 'When the herbage and roots are collected, this sacred mugwort plant is carefully laid out with the tips to the north and the lower stalks to the south. The chief plant, which is always harvested first, is laid at the southern end of the stalk. After this, its common comrades are neatly laid out in order next to it, until they have reached the tips of the mugwort. They then continue in the other direction, and so on, looping back and forth. The plants are used in precisely the opposite order, until they finally come to the chief plant, which is used last of all' (Storl 1986:134-135).

During their *Evil Way Ceremony*, the Navaho drink a decoction made from the leaves and tips of the branches of the sage bush (*Artemisia scopulorum*) in order to cure 'spirit infections' which cause nightmares and make a person susceptible to evil. The sacred western mugwort (*Artemisia ludoviciana*) grows in the prairies. The shamans of North America considered this the most important magical plant of all. It is used to banish all evil, to gain entry into the realm of Wakan (the Great Spirit), to heal the sick, and to protect the healthy.

When the Spanish came to Mexico, they found a plant growing there which looked exactly like their native absinthium, but was much more aromatic. The Mexican Indians said that this plant (*Artemisia mexicana*) was good medicine. As Friar Bernardino de Sahagún wrote: 'It is a remedy for many things; it cures many things.... And if someone has fear in his heart or is burdened with a mood, then Iztauhyatl and Quauhyayaual should be ground, the inside of the stalk, without the outer rind; the inside is white and somewhat sweet in taste. One drinks it in order to become healthy again; when boiled, only the infusion is used. A person with a cough also drinks it.' The Aztecs even knew of a female diviner whose speciality was the use of this plant: 'Techichinani, "who sucks someone". When a child grows sick on the breast, she suckles it with artemisia, sucking out blood or pus. Some get healthy after this, others do not' (Sahagún). Today, Mexican absinthium varieties are smoked as a substitute for **Hemp**.

In the Peruvian Andes, absinthium (*Artemisia absinthium*) — known locally as *ajenjo* or *ajincuy* — is one of the healing plants customarily found in every herb garden. The leaves are used as a bath additive, especially to banish evil winds (*aires*). A tea made from this plant is a household remedy for colics resulting from excessive cold and too many winds. On the other hand, the Indians warn against letting a pregnant woman come into contact with the plant or ingest it, for it is considered an abortifacient. One variety of absinthium, known as *copa-copa*, is utilized as a mild inebriant and is imbibed to warm the body in cases of hypothermia. Absinthe, an extremely potent alcoholic beverage which contained absinthium oil, was a popular drink in the nineteenth century, especially in France, where it influenced many writers, artists, and other Bohemians.

Pharmacology: Most varieties of artemisia contain the essential oil thujone. Thujone has anthelmintic, toxic, psychedelic, abortifacient, narcotic, and antidotal effects — depending upon dosage and use.

Literature: Albert-Puelo 1978; Brondegaard 1972; Tierny 1974.

ASAFOETIDA (Ferula asafoetida). Asafoetida, Devil's Dung, and Food of the Gods are all names for the thickened resin of the gum asafoetida, a substance with a potent scent similar to garlic which is found in the subtropical zones of Western India. Asafoetida is one of the oldest magical tools of the shamans of the Himalayas, especially the Bönpo (magicians from the pre-Buddhist tradition of Tibet). It is primarily used to drive the demons out of possessed persons. It may also have been ingested or inhaled by shamans in order to induce trance. Today, asafoetida still occupies a central position in Tibetan medicine. It is mixed with valerian, **Calamus,** peacock feathers, snake skin, and cat dung to produce an incense for banishing spirits. Asafoetida is administered internally for all psychic ailments, particularly those caused by sexual imbalances. Asafoetida is said to inflame the fires of life, soothe the nerves, increase potency, and promote demon-free sleep.

One of the most frequently utilized medicinal and prophylactic substances in Mesopotamia in the third millennia BC, it was imported from India along with **Ginger**, **Calamus**, **Hemp**, cinnamon, sandalwood, and pomegranates. The use of asafoetida spread as far as Somalia. There, it was made into amulets to protect against evil spirits and demons.

Upon its introduction to Europe, asafoetida was immediately utilized in the same fashion. It was used to ward off witches and demons, to exorcise persons who were possessed, and to heal the insane. Since ancient times, asafoetida has served as a universal antidote and as an aphrodisiac, and has hence also been used in love magic. Even into the twentieth century, mothers hung small sacks of asafoetida around the necks of their children in order to keep away all children's ailments.

Pharmacology: Asafoetida is a cumarin drug composed primarily of umbelliferon. It has sedative, carminative, and antispasmodic properties. 'Taken internally, asafoetida produces a curious stimulation of the nervous system as well as an excitation of the urinary and sexual apparatus; as a result, it is said to lead to increased sexual desire among men and an irritation of the glans penis' (Haerkötter 1986:99).

Literature: Clifford 1984; Manniche 1989; Müller-Ebeling & Rätsch 1986; Schöpf 1986.

AYAHUASCA (Banisteriopsis caapi, Banisteriopsis spp.). In the Amazon, the name Ayahuasca is generally used to refer to an inebriating drink produced from a liana of the genus *Banisteriopsis* and other plants, most of which contain DMT (*Banisteriopsis rusbayana, Psychotria viridis* or chacruna, pucahuasca or *Diploterys caberana*; also **Angel's Trumpet,**

A Classification of Banisteriopsis Species Used in Ayahuasca (after Junquera 1989)

1.	Banisteriopsis	caapi	11.	Banisteriopsis	lucida
2.	"	ceduciflora	12.	"	martiniana
3.	"	cornifolia	13.	"	muricata
4.	"	cristata	14.	"	nigrenscens
5.	"	heterostyla	15.	"	nutans
6.	"	inebrians	16.	"	oxyclada
7.	"	laevifolia	17.	"	padifolia
8.	"	leiocarpa	18.	"	peruviana
9.	"	leptocarpa	19.	"	pubipetata
10.	"	longialata	20.	"	quitensis

Jurema, Manaca root, Tobacco).

The Indians revere the beverage, which they call the 'drink of true reality'. Only shamans, magicians, and healers are allowed to make ayahuasca and utilize it for curing and in religious ceremonies. Ayahuasca, which is very widely used, is associated with a rich store of myths. The beverage is also known as *yagé, natema, caapí, nape*, and *bejuco de oro* ('vine of gold'). The liana most frequently used to make ayahuasca is Banisteriopsis caapi. 'The natives fearfully keep secret the location of these plants, around which myths have formed which are as eerie as those surrounding the gigantic octopods of the sea. It is said that in the night, they entwine their branches around wanderers and crush and strangle them.

Strangely, they make no secret of the inebriating beverage which is made from them.... Numerous Indian tribes utilize it to put themselves into a state in which they believe they attain prophetic talents. In various ceremonies, they prepare a beverage from the plant which must be administered in the still of the night and in the dark, supposedly because its effects are stronger then and the dreams are more abundant ...' (Reko 1986:96-97).

One missionary, Father Tastevin, wrote to his bishop that 'the Indians believe in a veritable telepathic effect of yagé, as they call the drink which they obtain from the ayahuasca or caapi plant. They take it in order to find out whether a sick person will become well, to look into the future, to divine, to find out how, for example, one of their own is doing who is on a journey, etc. They also believe that it enables them to promptly recognize approaching dangers' (cited in Reko 1986:98).

All the Indians of the Amazon use ayahuasca in a similar fashion. The following account is typical: 'When a Zaparo magician visits someone who

*Fig. 5: Inflorescence of the ayahuasca liana (*Banisteriopsis caapi*) and the characteristic butterfly-shaped fruit (drawing by Sebastian Rätsch).*

is ill, an act which takes place only during the night, he never neglects to take repeated small sips of this beverage beforehand. The magician believes this will enlighten and enable him to correctly diagnose the illness before he has even seen the patient. He claims that the nature spirits whisper the method of treatment to him and also reveal the name of the appropriate medicine' (Reko 1986:97). Among the Muinane, most illnesses are attributed to sorcery. In order to heal an illness, the magician must identify the evil sorcerer while in a clear-sighted condition. This condition is produced by ayahuasca. The healer first leaves the 'real world' and travels to a place far above the earth. From heaven, he sees the earth as a large ball. Now, he can see and recognize every person on earth. Everyone stands erect—everyone, that is, but the sorcerer. The healer sees the sorcerer crouching and blowing into the hollows of his hands. Shamans use the drink to travel into the blue zone, which is located somewhere beyond the Milky Way. There, they meet the rulers of the animals and fishes.

Ayahuasca is the most culturally prevalent preparation made with magical plants: 'It enters into almost all aspects of the life of the people who use it, to an extent equalled by hardly any other hallucinogen. Partakers, shamans or not, see all the gods, the first human beings, and animals, and come to understand the establishment of their social order (Schultes & Hofmann 1980:122).

The following table illustrates the precision of the knowledge concerning the effects and the contents of the visions:

Native Classification of Ayahuasca Types By Effects and Symbolism (after Junquera 1989:1236).

Classification of the *Harakmbet* Indians	Meaning - Effect - Symbolism
1. *Boyanhe*	Green (unripe): produces visions of hunting, fishing, searching for property, migrations, visits, etc.
2. *Sisi*	Flesh of ancestors: visions of heaven, here understood as the universe of the past to the present.
3. *Kemeti*	Flesh of the tapir: signs which aim at recreating the mythical universe.
4. *Mbakoi*	Bird: pictures with vivid colors. Birds are considered the ideal beings for undertaking shamanic journeys.

5. *Wakeregn*	White: white images which show the journey to Seronhai, a place where the dead stay. In this place, it is possible to speak with the Tonemei-Kindah (the first *harakmbet*).
6. *Benkuja*	Blue: impressive images. This agent is only utilized by shamans after the fourth or fifth session, as its effects are permanent.
7. *Yari Huangana*	(animal or place): vivid and colorful images. A strong agent producing delusions which should be used with caution, as it can lead to complete unconsciousness from which it is not permitted to return.
8. *Nembuyu*	Little forest: quickly points out those animals which the shaman requires to journey to the various zones of the universe.
9. *Bihihi*	Laziness: Produces images of the mythical universe.
10.*Keren*	Thunder.
11.*Pet-pet*	Jaguar: This agent leads to the land of the jaguar, where the medicine men receive magical clothes which enable them to transform themselves.
12.*Benkuje*	Woodpecker: The leaves of this agent contain a spirit who chops apart the illness and inaugurates the healing process.
13.*Anidoyak*	Drawing: forms an image in the body of the sick person if there is a possibility of a cure. The image remains in the body of the person after the cure so that he or she does not become ill again.
14.*Wenekey*	Yellow bird: This agent elicits yellowish colors and speeds up or slows down movement.
15.*Takature*	Exotic spirit: enables the witch's assistant to creep into him, so that he may see what the witch does in order to remain in trance.
16.*Soeti*	Monkey: This agent is a beverage of flour and herbs which make it possible for the shaman to spring from tree to tree during the night without getting injured.
17.*Waksik*	Fish (*Myletes*): Allows the shaman to dive under water and thereby acquire knowledge about this area which can aid him in his activities.

18. *Wadnpi*	Tigrillo: Is used during hunting ceremonies or for similar purposes during the medicine man ritual.
19. *Yahenko*	To knock on the earth: The spirits disappear under the earth and arrive in the realm of the Toto in order to render them ineffective.
20. *Ebahote*	See far: The shaman uses this to see from the heavens where magical medicines which can heal illness can be purchased.
21. *Etuhehen*	Roll together: The assistants takes extracts of this plant in order to disguise themselves in a little forest where they wait for evil spirits, so that they can inform the shaman how to render these evils harmless.
22. *Ehehurik*	Smell: The smells of this agent are vital for victory.

Ayahuasca has also entered into the practices of suburban magicians (*brujos*) in Brazil, Columbia, Ecuador, and Peru. Here, the ayahuasca liana is revered as a 'teacher'. Practitioners who call themselves vegetalistas (from which the term *vegetalismo* is formed) believe that certain plants, which they call *doctores* (plant-teachers), have spirits from which knowledge about this and other worlds may be gained — if these plants are ingested under certain conditions involving sexual segregation and they adhere to a diet that may extend from six months to several years. Several of these plants have psychoactive properties, or contain important biodynamic compounds. Two of these plants, *Banisteriopsis caapi* and *Psychotria viridis*, are used in the preparation of ayahuasca, which the *vegetalistas* use to contact the spirit world in order to diagnose and cure illnesses. Other 'plant-teachers' may also be added to the basic ayahuasca preparation (cf. Luna 1986).

A great deal of anthropological and ethnobotanical research remains to be carried out on the ayahuasca complex:

> It may be that the South American yage-ayahuasca complex is the largest psychedelic cult in the world. From Panama to Bolivia, from the Pacific coast to deep into Brazil these visions are regularly sought out, individual practitioners making their reputations on the quality of their brews, chants and cures. Like all shamanic practices, the ayahuasca cult is the creation of highly individual personalities. For this reason simple laboratory analysis of drug samples will not dispel the air of real mystery surrounding ayahuasca.
>
> Ayahuasca is as good as the person who makes it is meticulous and

demanding. The culture of rural Peru faces a shattered past and a turbulent future. The fate of the ayahuasca mystery hangs tremulously in the balance while at the collective level the culture gropes towards a decision to repress or re-enforce the institution of hallucinogenic shamanism.

To truly understand ayahuasca would take years, for there are as many ayahuasca as there are *Banisteriopsis* varieties plus admixtures. Local variations in ingredients and procedure should be systematically studied' (McKenna 1989a:190).

Pharmacology: All *Banisteriopsis* varieties contain the carbolines harmine, harmaline, and harmol, which have also been found in **Syrian Rue**. The carbolines act as MAO inhibitors, i.e. they prevent the degradation of certain neurotransmitters and exogenous amines. Substances containing DMT are usually added to ayahuasca preparations. DMT (N, N-dimethyltryptamine, methoxy-N, N-dimethyltryptamine) is not effective orally (cf. **Snuff**). It is broken down by the enzyme monoamine oxidase (MAO) before it can pass the blood-brain barrier. When DMT is combined with carbolines, however, it becomes orally effective. Thus, the psychedelic effects ascribed to ayahuasca are the result of the synergistic combination of harmine, harmaline, and DMT. Other magical plants also contain MAO inhibitors: **Iboga, Niando, Rue, Syrian Rue, Yohimbe.**

Literature: Ayala Flores & Lewis 1978; Deltgen 1979; Dobkin de Rios 1970a, 1970b, 1972, 1978, 1981; Langdon 1979; Lewin 1986; Luna 1986; McKenna 1989a, 1989c; McKenna, Luna & Towers 1986; Münzel 1977; Naranjo 1983; Reichel-Dolmatoff 1971, 1975, 1978; Rosenbohm 1991; Rouhier 1986; Taussig 1987; Walton 1969.

Table of Ayahuasca Admixture Plants
(after McKenna, Luna & Towers 1986; modified and enlarged)

Vernacular Name	Species	Active Constituents (?=none reported)
abaca	*Ocimum micrantum*	(**Pichana**)
abuta	*Abuta grandifolia*	tropolone isoquinolines, palmatine, oxo-aporphins
ajo sacha	*Mansoa alliaceae*	?
amaron borrachero	*Pontedaria cordata*	?
amasisa	*Erythrina peoppigina*	erythrina alkaloids, (**Colorines**)

ayahuasca	*Banisteriopsis rusbyana*	harmala alkaloids, DMT, ß-carbolines
ayahuasca	*Juanulloa ochracea*	?
ayahuma	*Couroupita guianensis*	indole alkaloids
bellaco-caspi	*Himatanthus succuba*	fulvoplumieron, flavonoids
bobinsana	*Calliandra angustifolia*	amino acids
borrachero	*Iochroma fuchsioides*	alkaloids (**Guatillo**)
caimitillo	*Abuta grandifolia*	tropolone isoquinolines, palmatine, oxo-aporphins
capirona negro	*Calycophyllum spruceanum*	?
catahua	*Hura crepitans*	tiglione diterpenes, lectins, piscicidal compounds
chacruna	*Psychotria viridis*	DMT
chicorro	*Cyperus cf. prolixis*	?
chiricsanango	*Brunfelsia chiricsanango*	scopeletine (**Manaca**)
chuchuhuasí	*Maytenus ebenifolia*	sesquiterpenes, nicotinyl alkaloids, triterpenes, maytensine, etc.
clavohuasca	*Tynnanthus panurensis*	?
caupuri	*Virola surinamensis*	neolingans
cuchura-caspi	*Malovetia tamaquarina*	steroid alkaloids, conopharyngine
cumala	*Virola sp.*	tryptamines, ß-carbolines, neolingans, 2-Me-Ketones
garabata	a) *Guettarda ferox*	canthemine, heteroyohimbe alkaloids (**Yohimbe**)
	b) *Uncaria guianensis*	spiro-oxindoles, bisindoles, heteroyohimbe alkaloids
hiporuru	*Alchornea castenifolia*	alchornine, imadazole alkaloids, corynanthine (**Niando**)
huacapu	*Vouacapoua americana*	?
huairacaspi	*Cedrelinga catenaeformis*	?
lupuna	*Ceiba pentandra*	?
miya	*Phrygilanthus eugenoides*	?
mucura	*Petiveri alliaceae*	oligo sulfides, triterpenes, trithiolans
mureru	*Cabomba aquatica*	?
nuchu pichana	*Scoparia dulcis*	triterpenes, 6-MeO-benzo-xazolilinone
oje	*Ficus insipida*	furocoumarins, triterpenes, biphenyl hexahydroindolizines, phenanthroxin dolizines
palisange	*Sclerobium setiferum*	?
pali santo	*Sclerobium setiferum*	?
pichana	*Ocimum micrantum*	sesquiterpenes
picurullana-quina	*Alternanthera lehmani*	?

piri-piri	*Cyperus sp.*	quinones, essential oils, saponines, sesquiterpenes
pokere	*Epiphyllum sp.*	?
pucahuasca	*Diploterys caberana*	DMT
pulma	*Calathea veitchiana*	tryptophan
raya balsa	*Montrichardia arborescens*	?
remo caspi	*Pithecellobium laetum*	phytomitogenes, lupeol, spinasterol
renaco	*Coussapoa tessmannii*	?
renaco	*Ficus ruiziana*	furocoumarins, triterpenes, biphenylhexahydroindolizines, phenanthroxindolizines
sanang	*Abuta grandifolia*	tropolone isoquinolines, palmatine, oxoaporphins
shinguarana	*Cornutia odorata*	?
shoka	*Lomariopsis japurensis*	?
suelda con suelda	*Phtirusa pyrifolia*	?
tachaí del monte	*Lygodium venustum*	antifertility agents
tahuarí	*Anthodiscus pilosus*	?
tahuarí	*Tabebuia heterpoda*	dibenzoxanthines, lapachol, napthoquinones
tahuarí	*Vitex triflora*	diterpene lactones, iridoid glycosides, flavonoid glycosides
tamshi	*Carludovica divergens*	?
tangarana	*Triplaris surinamensis*	?
tchaí	*Opuntia sp.*	N-methyl-tyramine, mescaline
toe	*Brugmansia suaveolens*	tropane alkaloids (**Angel's Trumpet**)
toe negro	*Teliostachya lanceolata*	?
uchu-sanango	*Tabernaemontana sp.*	bisindol alkaloids, terpenoids, cornaridine
?	*Erythrina glauca*	alkaloids
?	*Iresine sp.*	cinnamic acid amides

BALCHE' (Lonchocarpus violaceus). Many Mesoamerican peoples (Maya, Lacandon, Pokomchi) attribute strong magical powers to the cultivated balche' tree and have long held it sacred. An inebriating beverage of the same name is brewed using the bark and roots of this tree. While incantations are being chanted, the pieces are added to honey water, which immediately begins to ferment (a type of **Mead**). A number of other magical plants (**Thornapple, Tobacco, Water Lily**), spices (cocoa, vanilla, frangipani), toads (*Bufo marinus*), and tree frogs (*Dendrobates spp.*) are also added to this brew. The resulting drink is consumed only during ceremonial occasions.

The ancient Maya practiced a magical ritual in which balche' was administered rectally (cf. **Maguey**). Modern Mayan healers utilize balche' concoctions for divinatory purposes. By placing a quartz crystal in the drink over night, the next day they are able to attain insights into normally invisible domains (usually after consuming **Ololiuqui** or **Thornapple** as well). Among the Lacandon of Naha' in Chiapas, the classical Mayan ritual has been preserved to the present day.

The balche' ritual, which is a ritual circle, is conducted in response to 'environmental' catastrophes and serious illnesses. It is said that the gods themselves gave this ritual to the first ancestors of the Lacandon, the 'great old men who still found the paths to heaven'. This ritual, which entails the communal consumption of the inebriating balche' drink, was originally devised by the god of creation himself. First, the gods became inebriated by the beverage. Then, from that time forth, the first ancestors of the Lacandon and their descendants were enjoined to imitate the inebriation of the gods in their ritual circles and reexperience this exhilarating state of consciousness which maintains harmony between heaven and earth.

Balche' is prepared in a ceremonial canoe manufactured especially for the occasion. This canoe is first filled with 'virgin' water. Then, honey from wild or domesticated bees is dissolved in the water. Used pieces of bark (which harbor yeast colonies) are then added to this solution along with several strips of fresh, living bark. The mixture is ready when the fermentation process has been completed. The finished drink contains between 1 and 5% alcohol, which aids in dissolving various other active ingredients present in the bark. The methods for brewing balche' are part of a precisely defined magical act involving the recitation of magical incantations and prayers. The person brewing the drink is identified with Bol, the god of inebriation. Uttering a long magical incantation, he summons the invisible souls of all the poisonous animals and plants of the forest and asks them to place the essences of their poisons into the drink so that it may be especially strong. After one to two days, the beverage is ready. Now, the 'soul' of the balche' drink must first be offered to the gods. Praying continuously, the brewer (lord of the balche') uses a palm leaf to offer each of the gods a draught of the beverage. The soul of the balche' then rises into the heavens, where it is manifested as a drink which the gods use to become inebriated. The gods love the effects of balche', and they sing, dance, and have a wonderful time when these rituals are conducted below. Finally, after the gods have received their share, the humans are allowed to partake.

The communal drinking bouts, which usually begin shortly before dawn, are attended by 'the entire circle of humans'. After the initial offering, the brewer sounds a conch calling the people to the ritual. The people come. No one is required to participate, but any initiate may come. The men go into the house of the gods, and the women meet in the ceremonial kitchen. The brewer assigns each participant a place in a circle surrounding a clay vessel filled with balche'. Using a measure, the brewer pours each of the participants in the circle an identical amount of the drink. The participants drink simultaneously, and they all drink the same amount. In just a few short hours, each of the participants consumes some 17 liters of the beverage. The shared inebriation, and the concomitant shift in consciousness, rather quickly become noticeable. The Lacandon say that balche' causes the mind to 'go astray' or 'turn around', and 'exposes' it to the adventure of inebriation and drunkenness. The effects of balche' are unlike those of beer, wine, or any other inebriant known to us. A person becomes euphoric, while perception is sharpened, the muscles are relaxed, the stomach and intestines emptied, and the heart is brought to laughter. Very large doses (20 liters) have narcotic and analgesic effects. Affective changes are especially pronounced. An inebriated Lacandon may burst into laughter or become sentimental and affable. Aggressiveness gives way to laughter, joy, and affection. Balche' also has mild psychedelic effects, especially when a large amount of fresh bark has been used in its preparation.

Ritual circles are often held to cure an ill person or promote well-being in the consciousness of heaven (*yoli kaan*). When the Lacandon join into a circle and imitate the inebriation of the gods, the drunken gods in heaven are put in such a good mood that they allow their magical healing abilities to work on the sick person or to avert an environmental catastrophe by causing the rain to fall and the maize to grow.

Balche' rituals also play an important role in promoting cohesion within the Lacandon community. The communal shift in consciousness is simultaneously a form of social therapy which appears to be encouraged by the specific effects of the drink. When two men who have been at odds with one another take part in a ritual, one may say to the other: 'Come, let us drink, for there is something between us'. Together, they will very quickly consume a large amount of balche'. In fact, they consume so much that their stomachs are unable to contain the liquid. Thus, the two quickly alter their consciousness and (because of the large amounts of liquid) are soon vomiting and emptying their intestines and bladders together. In this way, the beverage purges their bodies, exposes their minds to intense inebriation, and cleanses them of their mutual problem.

The ritual ends only after all of the beverage that has been prepared has been consumed. The inebriated Lacandon usually fall into a dreamless sleep. When they awaken some hours later, their minds are clear and their bodies purified. There are few unpleasant side-effects or after-effects.

Table of Known and Suspected* Balche' Additives

Mayan name	*Botanical/zoological identification*	*Active principle(s)*
bab	*Bufo marinus*	bufotenine, tryptamines
bac nicte	*Polianthes tuberosa*, P. sp.	volatile oil
bukluch	*Vanilla planifolia*	vanillin
hach kakaw	*Theobroma cacao*	theobromine, phenethylamine
k'uts	*Nicotiana* sp.	nicotine
kuxum lu'um	*Panaeolus venenosus**	psilocybin
lol lu'um	*Psilocybe* sp., *Stropharia cubensis**	psilocybin, psilocin
macuil xuchit	?	?
nab	*Nymphaea ampla*	aporphine, nuciferine
nicte	*Plumeria alba, P. rubra*	volatile oil
ninichh cacao	*Theobroma bicolor*	theobromine, phenethylamine
wi' (= 'root')	*Lophophora williamsii**	mescaline, phenethylamines
wo'	*Bufo* sp.	tryptamine derivatives
xtabentum	*Turbina corymbosa**	lysergic acids
xtohk'uh	*Datura inoxia*	tropane alkaloids
xut'	*Dendrobates sp.**	steroidal alkaloids

Pharmacology: The bark contains rotenone and various longystilines, which are chemically analogous to kawain (cf. **Kava-Kava**). Rotenone has toxic and purgative as well as inebriating effects. In all likelihood, hitherto unknown synergistic effects probably lie at the heart of the sweeping effects of the balche' beverage.

Literature: Emboden 1979; Ma'ax & Rätsch 1984; Müller-Ebeling & Rätsch 1986; Rätsch 1985, 1986a, 1986b, 1988b, 1989a; Smet 1985.

BAY LAUREL (Laurus nobilis). Bay laurel was already an important cultic and magical **Incense** in the ancient cultures of Mesopotamia. In Greece, the plant was sacred to Apollo, the god of oracles. The leaves and seeds were chewed or burned in order to aid clairvoyancy and help in divining the future. The Pythia, the oracle priestess of Delphi, chewed laurel leaves and inhaled smoke (cf. **Henbane**) before she fell into a trance and Apollo manifested himself in her body. Bay laurel leaves and seeds were also added to **Wine**. Bay laurel had a similar significance in ancient Rome. Sacrificial offerings were always burned together with bay laurel and **Juniper**. According to Proclus, laurel branches were needed to detain or ward off spirits which suddenly appeared. In the Middle Ages and in the early modern period, bay laurel was considered a magical agent which gave one the ability to see what was hidden. Some Indian tribes used the American (bay) laurel (*Magnolia virginiana*) as a ritual incense and medicine.

Pharmacology: The leaves contain an essential oil, a bitter substance, fatty oil, starch, sugar, various glycerides, and myricil alcohol. The sap promotes the circulation and has stimulating and antiseptic properties. The smoke may be psychoactive, but has not yet been studied.

Literature: Rätsch 1987e; Sigerist 1963.

BEANS (Leguminosae). Beans, the seeds of various leguminous plants, play an important role in magical belief systems everywhere. In antiquity, beans (*Phasaeolus vulgaris*) were considered the guardians of the life energy, as a food of the gods, as sacred creepers, and as magical weapons and amulets. Today, beans and bean-like seeds are still used for divinatory purposes still used for divinatory purposes (cf. **Colorines, Jequirity**) and for pastoral magic. Anthropomorphic bean creatures played an important yet unfortunately unclear role in the shamanism of the Peruvian coastal

Fig. 6: Anthropomorphic representation of a Mochican magical bean (Peru, pre-Spanish; after Kutscher).

dwellers. Today, Peruvian fields of *Canavalia maritima* beans are protected against all bad influences. *Canavalia* beans have also been recovered from Mexican graves. On the Gulf Coast, the dried seeds and leaves are smoked as a substitute for **Hemp**.

Red mescal beans (*Sophora secundiflora*) have been used for magical purposes for at least 7,000 years. In the North American Southwest, dried beans were placed in graves as food for the dead. Little is known of the mescal bean cult, which was supplanted by the **Peyote** cult at an early date. Nevertheless, the magical significance of the mescal bean was long preserved among the Wichita Indians, and in a more rudimentary form among the Apache, Comanche, Delaware, and Omaha Indians as well. They ground the beans and ingested them in order to ritually purify themselves and to receive visions during initiation ceremonies. The beans were also used in the manufacture of fetishes and questioned as oracles. Today, in the peyote cult, the leader of the nocturnal ceremonies still wears necklaces of mescal beans.

Pharmacology: Canavalia beans contain the alkaloid *l*-betonicine, which may have psychoactive effects. The principal alkaloid in mescal beans is cytisine (**Genista**); N-mythalcytisine, lupinine, Δ^s-dehydrolupanine, anagyrine, and termopsin (cf. **Lupinus**) are also present. These alkaloids are extremely toxic and produce nausea, vomiting, and death through respiratory paralysis.

Literature: Adovasio & Fry 1976; Diaz 1979; Mercatante 1976; Sauer & Kaplan 1969; Schultes & Hofmann 1980.

BEER. Today, the word beer is normally used to denote a mildly alcoholic beverage made from malted barley (*Maltum*), hops (*Humulus lupulus*), and water through the action of Brewer's yeast (*Saccharomyces cerevsiae*). Wheat (*Triticum sativum*), rye (*Secale cereale*), millet (*Panicum, Sorghum, Penisetum*; cf. **Maize**), and rice (*Oryza sativa*) may be used in the place of barley (*Hordeum vulgare*). In contrast, many of the beers of antiquity also contained a number of other pharmacologically highly active ingredients.

Beer was originally a ritual drink used as an offering to the gods or as a magical agent for altering everyday consciousness. The key ingredients in these ritual beers were the additives, known as 'beer worts'. In the course of time, a number of magical plants have made their way into beer: **Henbane**, **Mandrake**, **Wild Rosemary**; more recent additives are **Hemp** ('Hi-Brew Beer') and **Thornapple**. Myrtle (*Myrtus communis*), ash leaves (*Fraxinus excelsior*), and oak bark (*Quercus sp.*) have also been utilized as additives. The German Regulations on Purity ('Reinheitsgebot') of 1516 made it illegal to brew beer using such potent additives, in particular henbane. The 'Reinheitsgebot' thus represents the first drug law of modern times.

The Germanic tribes venerated beer and placed it under the protection of Aegir, the god of the sea, the brewing art, and the kettle. Aegir was renowned for the carousals held in his honor (cf. **Wine**). During the Germanic carousals, beer and **Mead** were consumed so that the gods would leave the heavens, come to earth, and sojourn among the humans. Even today, special beers brewed for many traditional festivals held throughout the year recall the ancient beer cult: the Christmas beer, the May bockbeer, and Octoberfest beer. There are signs that the formidable bockbeer, also known as original bock, was sacred to Thor (Donar), the Germanic phallic god of thunder, and consumed in his honor. Ironically, this beer is still brewed today — in Catholic cloisters.

The millet beer of Tibet (*chang*) is used for both ritual (cf. **Soma**) and hedonistic purposes. The West Africans also brew a beer from millet (*dolo*) which, depending upon the ritual occasion, may also contain a number of additional plant additives: *Grewia flavescens, Hibiscus esculentus, Acacia campylacantha*, balanos (*Balanites aegytica*), or **Thornapple** seeds (*Datura stramonium*). 'All important religious ceremonies are accompanied by an animal sacrifice, followed by a ritual libation of *dolo* upon the altar of the god. The priest pours some *dolo* from a calabash onto the altar, and the remainder is distributed among the elders, who attend the ceremony as representatives of families of the village' (Voltz 1981).

Pharmacology: Depending upon the method used in brewing, beer contains between 5-27% original wort. Between approximately 3% and maximally 10% of this is alcohol. The effects of beer are primarily the result of the alcohol content and the additives, or beer worts. For example, hops have sedative and hormonal effects, while henbane has psychedelic and inebriating effects. Brewer's yeast is extremely healthy, with detoxifying effects upon the liver and skin.

Literature: Laing & Hendra 1977; Lohberg 1984; Moore 1989; Robertson 1978; Voltz 1981.

BELLADONNA (Atropa belladonna). The Sumerians used belladonna as a remedy to treat many ailments attributed to the actions of demons. While the ancient Egyptians were unaware of the plant, the Greeks were familiar with it. They considered it a sibling of **Mandrake**. They added belladonna to wine and used it as an aphrodisiac. It was also an important ingredient in many of the love drinks prepared by the Thessalian witches. Many East

Fig. 7: Since antiquity, belladonna has been feared for its toxic effects and esteemed for its magical properties. Its genus name, Atropa, is derived from Atropos (the 'inflexible' one), the Greek goddess of death. Of the three Greek Moirai, or Fates (similar to the Germanic Norn), it was Atropos who cut the thread of life (woodcut from Gerard).

European folk traditions utilize belladonna root in love magic. When a man wishes to gain the favor of a maiden, he must first find a belladonna plant. He will then dig up its root, making sure to leave several offerings to the spirit of the plant in the resulting hole. Other regions have similar digging rituals. Like the **Mandrake**, belladonna roots may be used as amulets and magical roots. It can grant good fortune in games and in love (cf. **Scopolia**).

Because of belladonna's propensity to evoke aphrodisiac as well as delirious effects, it was numbered among the witches' plants and was consequently used as an ingredient in **Witches' Ointments**. The plant was identified with a beautiful and seductive female spirit (belladonna = beautiful woman) who would aid a person who knew the proper rituals and magical formulæ. Care was necessary when dealing with the plant, however, for it could also bring madness, frenzy, and death.

The old Germans called the plant *walkerbeere*, berry of the Valkyries. The plant was thus associated with Wotan (the god of ecstasy), Walhalla (the heavenly castle), and the warriors' (berserkers') cult of death and afterlife.

In Central Europe, hunters taking part in extended expeditions often ate several belladonna berries to sharpen their powers of perception.

Pharmacology: The entire plant contains atropine and other tropane alkaloids (cf. **Angel's Trumpet, Henbane, Manaca, Pituri, Thornapple**). Atropine has stimulating effects which can lead to delirious states and eventually to death through respiratory paralysis. Plant extracts have strong hallucinogenic properties and may produce behavioral changes (desire to dance, frenzy, exaggerated laughter, chimerical images, breaks with reality, etc.).

Literature: Hansen 1981; Harner 1973; Hauschild 1981; Mehra 1979; Münch 1785.

BENZOIN (Styrax tonkinense). The resin of the Indian and Indonesian Styrax trees, which has an agreeable vanilla-like odor, is known as benzoin. Although both are obtained from the same plant, two types of benzoin (Siamese benzoin and Sumatran benzoin) are marketed. In Asia, benzoin is sold under the name *an-hsi-hsiang*. Benzoin is an ancient remedy, natural cosmetic, and one of the most important ingredients of medicinal and ritual incenses. It is inhaled for sore throats, dry coughs, asthma, and bronchitis. Everywhere it is used, benzoin is also said to ward off spirits.

In the hands of the magicians of Mali, benzoin also exhibits magical powers. A b'lian (magician) from Ulu Aring described a magical ritual in which he used benzoin to transform himself into a tiger: 'You go deep into the jungle. There, when you are quite alone, you squat down and ignite some incense (benzoin). After this, you form your right hand into a tube and, at the height of your face, blow captured smoke through this in three directions. You then repeat the process while you hold your hand completely on the ground. Now you simply say *ye chöp* ("I go forth") and your skin immediately transforms, stripes appear, a tail grows, and you become a tiger. When you later say *ye wet* ("I go home"), then you immediately take on your normal form' (after Martin 1905). There is also evidence that Taoist alchemists used benzoin in the production of life-extending elixirs. In alchemy, benzoin is assigned to the element air and the 'planet' sun (cf. **Incense**).

Pharmacology: The drug consists primarily of coniferyl benzoate; cinnamyl benzoate, free benzoic acids, and vanillin are also present. These substances have expectorant and slightly disinfectant effects. Psychoactive effects have been reported, but the agents responsible have not been identified. The scent is said to amuse and improve one's mood.

Literature: Drury & Drury 1987; Henglein 1985; Martin 1905; Skeat 1967; Wagner 1985:90.

BETEL (Areca catechu and Piper betle). The name betel is generally used to refer to two unrelated plants indigenous to Asia: a climbing shrub from the pepper family (*Piper betle*) and a palm, also known as the areca palm (*Areca catechu*). The pepper variety is used for its fresh leaves, while the palm provides the betel nut, the 'morsel of desire'. Since ancient times, the medical systems of India and Southeast Asia have utilized betel nuts for their stimulating and digestive effects.

Betel also has a reputation as a panacea. It is used internally for headaches, stomach pains, venereal disease, and digestive disturbances. Betel is prescribed for external use to treat fever, rheumatism and arthralgia, fatigue, itching, insect bites, tooth disease, fresh wounds as well as those which heal with difficulty, etc. Betel is an ingredient in many of the combination preparations used n Ayurvedic medicine. According to an ancient Indian-Brahmanic tradition, betel is one of the eight types of pleasure: scents, women, clothes, song, betel, food, bed, and jewelry.

Usually, ground or crushed betel nuts are combined with a variety of spices (cloves, pepper, cardamon, **Kava-Kava, Nutmeg**) and baked lime. The resulting mixture is then rolled into a betel leaf. Known as *sirih*, these morsels or plugs of betel are popular throughout Asia, where they are usually chewed after meals.

Both the medicinal use of betel nuts and the hedonistic use of betel plugs are very ancient. Theophrastus made reference to the betel nut, which also appears in early Sanskrit texts under the name *guváka* or *pinlang*. The ancient Persians ingested betel, and the Arabs had become acquainted with the practice of chewing betel packets by the eighth century. Chewing betel was said to still hunger and thirst and kindle sensuality.

In India, betel use is integrated within a social and religious system: 'As in the social domain, betel also serves to facilitate communication during rituals, to stimulate and consolidate interpersonal relationships or the relationship between humans and the supernatural. In contrast to everyday behavior, however, such ritual use is standardized, formalized, and symbolic. The simplest ritual use of betel is as an offering to the gods. It is said that the gods lack betel in heaven and that humans should offer them betel to keep them in a beneficent mood' (Moser-Schmitt 1981a).

In India, betel packets are associated with a fertility symbolism of a distinctly sexual nature: 'The leaf, whose basic form is that of a triangle, is identified with the vulva (or *yoni*), the female sexual organ, and thus represents female fertility.... The areca nut is also known as *phal* (= fruit). The betel leaf, which is folded to serve as a container, hides parts of the areca nut, i.e., the fruit which is ripening from the male seed. The filled packet of betel symbolizes the fertilized womb, which opens up, brings forth life, and leaves behind the red color of blood' (Moser-Schmitt 1981a).

Betel packets also serve as aphrodisiac love charms. Women or courtesans often 'enchant' betel packets in such a way that anyone who partakes of them is overcome by ardent sexual desire and immediately leaves his own wife. According to Erika Moser-Schmitt, these 'enchanted' effects result when two additional ingredients are also added to the packets: hashish (cf. **Hemp**) and opium (cf. **Poppy**). On the Maldive Islands, enchanted packets of betel may also contain several **Coca** leaves. The betel nut is also used alone as a magical charm and amulet. In Morocco, betel nuts are worn to protect against the evil eye. Burned in charcoal grills, the resulting smoke is said to ward off demons.

Pharmacology: Areca nuts contain several alkaloids: arecoline, arecaidine, guavacine, and guavacoline. Arecoline has parasympathomimetic effects and has been shown to be at least a partial MAO (monoamine oxidase) inhibitor (cf. **Ayahuasca**). This accounts for its exhilarating effects. When chewed with lime, arecoline is broken down to arecaidine, a stimulant whose effects are not as profound. The betel leaf contains an essential oil which has slight local anesthetic effects and promotes digestion.

Literature: Boulos 1983; Meier 1913; Moser-Schmitt 1981a; Penzer 1952.

BLACK DRINK (Ilex cassine, Ilex vomitoria). These shrubs, which are related to **Guayasa** and **Maté**, grow in the forested areas of southeastern

North America. They are also known as the yaupon plant or the cassina holly. Many Indian tribes of the region (Choctaw, Creek, Seminole, Alabama, Cherokee, Natchez) and the Karankawa Indians (who live in Texas but whose culture is closely related to those of the peoples of the southeastern forests) use the leaves of these plants to prepare a ritual drink. Among the Alabama, the plant is venerated as a ceremonial medicine and taken to clear out the system and produce ceremonial purity. Sometimes, they also add **Tobacco** to the drink to alter its effects. The leaves are first roasted and then added to water. The finished black drink is consumed from conch shell cups (made from *Strombus gigas* or *Busycon contrarium*). The Indians consume the black drink as a purifying and stimulating agent to help them prepare for rituals, burials, councils, seasonal ceremonies, and when they are going on the warpath. The black drink plays an especially significant role during the Busk Ritual or Green Corn Festival, a Seminole ritual of renewal. Black drink is usually consumed in great quantities. When it produces vomiting, the fluid which is expelled is as clear as that which was consumed. Black drink is still used today to train Seminole medicine men.

Pharmacology: The leaves contain a high concentration of caffeine as well as various bitter constituents. The effects are strongly stimulating and emetic.

Literature: Hudson 1979; Moerman 1986.

BORRACHERO (Methysticodendron amesianum). The Sibundoy Indians of the Columbian Andes cultivate a tree known as borrachero, the 'one who makes drunk', or *culebra borrachero*, the 'snake who makes drunk'. It is closely related to **Angel's Trumpet** and is used in shamanic practice in essentially the same manner. The shamans prepare a tea from fresh leaves which they ingest for healing, divinatory, and prophetic purposes. There is some evidence which suggests that the beverage is also used in harmful magic.

A Sibundoy Indian provided the following description of the plant and its effects: 'The snake borrachera is not used for curing, but rather to add a sickness to someone. If you take it, you will just see a bunch of snakes, you will find yourself in the middle of snakes. They say that if someone has done you harm, you can take borrachera and do harm to that person so that they cannot be cured. That person will have to die. Or they will have to find someone who can take it stronger than the other. Those who can take borrachera are greatly respected by everyone else. People don't want problems with them. They might say: "If I have a problem with him he will send me an evil, and I won't be able to find a cure, and I will die" ' (cited in McDowell 1989:138).

In Columbia, a number of other magical plants are also referred to as borrachero: **Angel's Trumpet, Guatillo, Manaca, Thornapple, Morning Glory**, *Desfontainia spinosa, Gaultheria anastomosans, Pernettya spp., Vaccinium floribundum*. All are used for similar purposes.

Pharmacology: The entire plant contains the tropane alkaloids scopolamine and atropine as well as lesser amounts of alkaloids of an undetermined structure. The effects of borrachero tea may be excitant, hallucinogenic, or hypnotic.

Literature: McDowell 1989; Schultes & Hofmann 1980.

CALABAR BEAN (Physostigma venenosum). The calabar bean is a liana which is found in the tropical forests of West Africa. The ancient Egyptians knew of the bean, which they called 'priest's poison'. The peoples of West Africa, who refer to the seeds as 'ordeal beans', have long used them as an arrow poison and as a magical tool for use in ordeals. In these, a person accused of a crime is forced to drink a cup of ground calabar beans soaked in water, or chew and swallow raw seeds. If he dies, then the gods have found him guilty. If he survives, the gods have shown that he is innocent. Those who survived returned to their people with high esteem. West African magicians and fetish priests utilize calabar beans (*itunda, esere*) both for toxic death magic (to poison their victims) as well as for healing purposes. In the *benge* poison oracle of the Zande, beans are fed to chickens, and their behavior is then interpreted.

Pharmacology: Calabar beans contain a variety of indole alkaloids, the major portion of which is physostigmine. Physostigmine is an indirectly active parasympathomimetic agent with very toxic properties. The lethal dose varies considerably, and reactions to identical doses can be quite different. For these reasons, it is well suited for use in ordeals. Death results from respiratory paralysis.

Literature: Andoh 1986; Engel 1982; Evans-Pritchard 1976; Lewin 1929.

CALAMUS (Acorus calamus). Calamus grows in marshy areas around the world. The aromatically scented root has been used medicinally and ritually since ancient times. The plant was an important ingredient of the magical incenses (cf. **Incense**) of the ancient Sumerians and Egyptians (*kyphi*). The ancient Egyptians also used calamus as an aphrodisiac. Everywhere it grows, the plant is used for medicinal baths, massages, stomach-strengthening teas, and magical powders. Slavic peoples spread calamus in front of the entrances to their homes to bring luck.

Calamus also grows in the New World. The Cree Indians call it *wee-kees*, 'muskrat root', and use the root as a stimulant and aphrodisiac. They use it to make a potent tea which they drink when they are exhausted. Old people in particular chew a piece of root daily in order to remain young and healthy. Among the Ojibwa, a dose is equal to the length of the patient's index finger. They either chew the fresh root, brew the dried root into a tea, or grind it and smoke it or sniff it. The Blackfoot chewed or swallowed the fresh root as a cure-all. There are indications that a strong decoction was used as an abortifacient. The root was also chewed for toothache and drunk as a tea to treat fever, digestive weaknesses, colic, and stomach ache. The Saulteau mixed the ground root with **Tobacco** and smoked this to relieve headaches. They also made a plant plaster from the fresh root which they applied to wounds and abrasions and used to treat toothaches and cramps. The Potawatomi used the powdered root as a snuff to treat catarrh. Almost all the tribes of North America used calamus tea as a remedy for stomach aches and all types of digestive disturbances. Because of this variety of uses, calamus root came to be venerated as a magical plant.

Pharmacology: The essential oil present in the root has been found to contain the mescaline-like ß-asarone (7-8%) as well as αpinene, camphor, eugenol, asarylaldehyde, calameon, calamenol, and furfural. In higher concentrations, asarone has been found to have both carcinogenic and inebriating effects upon humans. Apparently, asarone is metabolized into a psychedelic phenethylamine (TMA-2), small quantities of which stimulate the circulation and strengthen the nervous system. The effects of TMA-2 are similar to those of mescaline (cf. **Peyote**).

Literature: Henglein 1985; Manniche 1989; Smet 1985; Thorwald 1962.

CAMPHOR (Cinnamomum camphora). Camphor is the name given to the resin which exudes from the bark of a tree of the same name. Indigenous to Southeast Asia, camphor has long been used as an incense to ward off evil spirits and demons (cf. **Incense**). It is also an important remedy in Tibetan medicine.

Pharmacology: Camphor contains an essential oil (various ketones) which in high doses (1.2 g) can elicit powerful states of ecstatic inebriation. Pure camphor is precipitated from this essential oil. Camphor is an ingredient in a number of cough remedies and balsams.

Literature: Drury & Drury 1987; Lewin 1980; Müller-Ebeling & Rätsch 1989b.

CANELLA (Canella alba, C. winteriana). The shamans of the Araucano, a group living in the southern Andes and the adjoining coastal areas, view the cinnamon-scented canella tree (*C. alba*) as one of their most important plants. The small tree is an object of cultic veneration, is considered sacred, and represents the world tree which links the earth with the heavens. It is used for divination and for medicinal purposes; planted during the festival which celebrates the naming of a child, it will serve as an ally against the dark forces throughout that person's life. Its branches are a symbol of peace and are exchanged when alliances are formed. Branches of the canella tree are also burned during all shamanic acts. The scent which they exude liberates the soul of the tree and carries the thinking soul of the shaman into the world beyond. In order to make their spells and prayers effective, shamans blow **Tobacco** smoke over the limbs of the tree. The smoke activates its magical effects, which then penetrate into the person who is sick. In order to draw the illness and the evil magic out of a patient, the shaman also rubs his client's body with fresh leaves. Araucano diviners used canella to enter clairvoyant states. When they wished to divine, they entered a darkened hut, smoothed the floor, and inserted a leafless branch into the ground. On the end of this branch, they hung a fluff of llama wool. This little tree connected the diviner with the world beyond, a world where past, present, and future merged. With the scent of the tree, he entered into this world, bringing back messages for the other members of his tribe.
Canella winteriana is one of the 21 plants of the *omeiro*, the sacred elixir given during initiation into the South America Santería cult. The aromatic tree is protected by the Yoruba god Oshún. It has many medicinal uses.

Pharmacology: Canella bark contains up to 1.25% essential oil with l-α-pinene, eugenol, cineol, caryophyllene, 8% resin, and 8% mannitol. The essential oil has stimulating effects upon the entire body. No psychedelic effects have yet been detected.

Literature: Andoh 1986; Rätsch 1987f; Ruben 1952.

CANNA (Mesembryanthemum sp.). Canna, Kanna, and Channa are variations of the name for a magical plant used by the African Hottentots: 'They chewed it and kept it in their mouths for a long time. It made them inebriated and excited. Their "animal spirits came to life", their eyes sparkled, their faces showed laughter and happiness. A thousand charming ideas arose within them, a soft joy which was amused by the simplest pranks' (Lewin 1980:296). Today, a number of African *Mesembryanthemum* species are known by the name Canna. Their roots, leaves, and stalks may be chewed or dried and smoked. This does not, however, produce the effects described in earlier reports. Canna may thus be one of the lost magical plants. Or it may be that the magicians may keep its true identity concealed from Western scientists. On the other hand, 'canna' may actually refer to another plant, kankan (*Elaeophorbia drupifera*). Kankan grows in West Africa and is used as a medicine, fish poison, and hallucinogenic additive to **Iboga** drinks (Emboden 1972:29). Canna may also be identical to **Hemp** or to two other inebriating plants, *Sclerocarya caffra* and *Sclerocarya schweinfurthi*.

Pharmacology: *Mesembryanthemum tortuosum* contains two alkaloids with narcotic effects (mesembrine, mesembrenine). The effects of chewing *Mesembryanthemum* are similar to those of chewing **Coca**.

Literature: Emboden 1972; Lewin 1980; Schultes & Hofmann 1980.

CEDAR (Cedra libani, Pinus cedrus, Juniperus spp., Cedrella mexicana). Many people have and still do esteem cedar woods and oils for their scent as well as their medicinal and magical properties. Unfortunately, there is some confusion about the taxonomic status of cedar. The ancient Egyptians used enormous quantities of cedar oil (from *Cedra libani, Juniperus phoenicea*, and *J. drupacea*; cf. *Juniper*) to produce magical cosmetics, sacred perfumes, sumptuous incenses, and to embalm their mummies. The cedar (which the Romans called *cedris*) played a central role in the Egyptian tree cult; since it arose from the god Osiris, it became a symbol of eternal return. For this reason, its wood, but especially its oil, was thought to contain magical powers which the proper magical formulae could call forth. One such formula has been preserved in a pyramid text: 'Oh Balsam, oh Balsam, rise up, hurry! [You who are] upon the brow of Horus, come forth! *First class cedar oil*. Hurry! [You who are] on Horus, you are spread upon the brow of this Una, so that he may experience the sweetness under you, that you make him to a spirit under you. You grant him power over his body, you make it so that his terror is in the eyes of all the spirits when they look upon him and in the eyes of all who hear his name. Una of Osiris, I bring you the eye of Horus, which he takes, which is upon your brow. *Shining Libyan oil*' (after Nrier 1984:86). Cedar also acquired a similar importance in Mesopotamia. Dioscorides wrote: 'It has the power to cause living bodies to rot, and dead bodies to be preserved. For this reason, some have called it the life of death.'

In the New World, several cedar species have been numbered among the sacred trees and magical plants. The Guaraní Indians consider the Paraná cedar (*Cedrella sp.*) a sacred tree, and they use its wood and oil for magical purposes: 'A maiden wanted to enter paradise [= the land without evil] without dying. This was only possible through chastity and ritual dances invented by a shaman. On the evening of completion, a young Guaraní warrior wooed her love, and she succumbed to the temptation. Thereupon, Nanderuvuzu (the Guaraní god of creation) transformed her into this cedar. Its wood is so hard that it will not rot even under water. The Guaraní call it Ywyra Ne-ery, "she who makes the word flow". The sap of the cedar is a part of eternity, and with it the shaman can awaken a dead man to life. If a deceased person is laid in a cedar coffin, his resurrection is ensured. The original cedar stands in paradise. It was the very first tree which Nanderuvuzu created' (Melzer 1985:41).

In former times, the Lacandon Indians carved statues from cedar wood (*Simaba cedron* or *Cedrella mexicana*) which were venerated as magical in the villages along the Usumacinta river. They were used to ward off the diseases carried by the winds (such as head aches, vomiting, stomach aches). In the North American peyote church, cedar chips (from *Juniperus oxycedrus*; cf. **Juniper**) are burned during all the ritual acts which have to do with **Peyote**. This smoke is said to ward off all that is evil and tainted and to aid the peyotists in their search for themselves.

Pharmacology: Cedar oil is similar in composition to the essential oil of *Juniper*. Its effects are mildly irritating, insecticidal, and antiseptic. *Simaba cedron* contains quassinoids, including cedronine and cedronyline, which have antimalarial and anti-inflammatory properties (for *Juniperus* oil, see **Juniper**).

Literature: Brier 1984; Lurker 1987; Manniche 1989; Ma'ax & Rätsch 1984; Melzer 1985.

COCA (Erythroxylon coca). In pre-Columbian South America, the coca shrub was one of the sacred plants of the gods. Because of its invigorating effects, it was said to be of divine origin. Leaves and seeds have been found with grave goods and in other ritual contexts among pre-Incan cultures. Coca was considered a seductive goddess who could bless humans with her power. The leaves (the use of which was strictly regulated among the Inca) were primarily used in ceremonial contexts. Specialists used them to divine, offered them to the god-like Incas and to the gods, and passed them out at religious and state holidays. We know of no purely hedonistic use. Even the use of coca leaves as an aphrodisiac occurred within a religious ritual context. Prior to the coca harvest, the harvester was required to have slept with a woman so that Mama Coca would be in a favorable mood. A decoction of coca or saliva containing coca was rubbed onto the penis. This procedure prolonged the erotic adventure which took place under the auspices of the highly benevolent goddess. The physicians and magical priests of the Inca used coca as a remedy and an anesthesia. Coca extracts were also used during operations, especially trephinations (operations in which holes were bored into the cranium). They continued to be used during religious festivals and for prophecy (cf. **Ergot**), as well as for the difficult work in the mines and in daily life. The coca oracle entailed tossing fresh or dried coca leaves. In this geomantic method, one who knew could then interpret the toss to discern hidden aspects of reality.

Coca also played a ritual and magical role among the Mochica-Chimu, a pre-Incan culture of ancient Peru. The Mochica widely practised anal sexual magic. For this purpose, the persons participating were administered an enema which apparently contained concoctions of coca and other magical plants (**Angel's Trumpet, San Pedro, Villca**, cf. also **Maguey**). These unusual practices aimed at facilitating contact with beings not normally visible.

Today, coca is used by many Amazon Indians. As the example of the Pirá Indians illustrates, its use typically takes place within a magical context: 'Every adult male spends approximately three hours daily making coca powder from the roasted leaves of the coca shrub. During the day, the men consume this powder almost without interruption. It increases their physical efficiency, prevents exhaustion, and dampens sensations of hunger. But the Yebámasa [= shamans] do not consume it for these reasons alone. With the coca, they simultaneously ingest the magical power inherent in it, which vitalizes them and thus protects their body and spirit. In addition, coca powder has an important social function: offering one another coca powder is a gesture of contact and friendship' (Deltgen 1979:23). The shamans of various tribes often smoke so many coca leaves that they are able to traverse across a 'bridge of smoke' and enter the magical world of the spirits. Once there, they are able to activate their magical powers.

Pharmacology: Coca leaves contain up to 2.5% alkaloids, especially cocaine (up to 1%); also cinnamylcocaine, benzoylecgonine, hygrine, cuscohygrine, α- and ß-truxilline; and an essential oil, wax, tannins, and minerals. The main active ingredient is cocaine, which stimulates the central nervous system and has euphoric and sensually stimulating effects. Applied locally, it also has anesthetic effects.

Literature : Andrews & Solomon 1975; Antonil 1978; Dobkin de Rios 1980; Martin 1969; Mortimer 1974; Naranjo 1974; Quijada Jara 1982; Rätsch 1987f; Thamm 1986; Weil 1975, 1980.

COFFEE (Coffea arabica). The first use of coffee to produce a stimulating drink occurred in Yemen when people there boiled the berries and leaves of the coffee bush. According to a Yemeni legend, the stimulating powers of this bush were first discovered by Ethiopian goatherds who noticed that their goats became unusually excited after eating some of the beans. The goatherds gathered the reddish beans and took them to the dervishes of a neighboring cloister. The dervishes immediately recognized the great power and potential of coffee. It is also said that they discovered the technique of roasting the beans. They used coffee to prepare a drink which enabled them to listen to long prayers without falling asleep.

The name coffee is derived from the Arabic word *gahwe*, 'wine'. Many early coffee preparations had inebriating effects which were due to various additives: cardamom, cinnamon, **Betel, Ginger**. The inhabitants of the Swahili Desert believe that coffee beans are the home of spirits who have magical healing powers. For this reason, coffee may only be brewed using genuine coffee beans. African sufis greatly esteem coffee, for it enables them to participate in their night-long mystical rituals without falling asleep and to more readily enter ecstatic states. In the pagan/Islamic rituals of the Bantu-speaking peoples, spiced coffee is used as a ritual drink. It is served at all festivals and ceremonies. In Central Africa, coffee is often consumed together with **Hemp**.

When coffee came to Europe, it immediately acquired a reputation as a panacea, cure-all, and aphrodisiac. The black beans were attributed with magical powers that were just as dark. Vestiges of this reputation have been retained in the act of reading coffee grounds.

Pharmacology: Coffee beans contain caffeine, a central nervous system stimulant (cf. **Guaraná, Guayusa, Maté, Tea**).

Literature: Ferré 1991; Mercatante 1976; Sheikh-Dilthey, in Schröder 1985:253-256.

COLA (Cola nitida, Cola acuminata, Cola spp.). West Africa is home to a number of varieties of cola nut trees. The 'nuts' are not nuts at all, but the dried embryos of the fruits. Cola nuts are the most important stimulant in West Africa, and beverages made from them are consumed throughout the day. The use of cola is very important to the inhabitants of the region. Without cola, most acts are inconceivable. Apart from its stimulating effects, the nut also protects its possessor from all sins.

The cola nut was originally a food of the gods: 'One day, when the Creator (Nzambi) was visiting the earth to see his people and was busy near them, he set aside a piece of cola nut he had been eating and forgot to pick it up when he left. The man had observed this and picked up the enticing morsel. The woman came to him and warned him against using the food of the god. But the man placed it in his mouth and found that it tasted good. As he was chewing, Nzambi returned looking for the missing nut and noticed that the man was attempting to quickly swallow it. He swiftly reached for his throat and forced him to give back his prize. Since that time, men have a projecting larynx, a sign of the firm pressure of the divine finger' (after Hartwich 1911:382).

Cola nuts are esteemed in West Africa as charms and remedies, as amulets and as aphrodisiacs. White or light-colored nuts effect love magic, while red have the opposite effect. Usually, pieces of the fresh nut are chewed. Dried cola nuts have also been used as currency and in divination (geomancy). They are also given as tokens of friendship.

Pharmacology: Cola nuts contain up to 2.16% caffeine and 0.05% theobromine; the caffeine is bound to tannins. For this reason, the nuts are more potent fresh than dried. Small doses of cola are stimulating, while higher doses can be mildly inebriating. The effects of cola are generally greater than those of **Coffee** or **Tea**.

Literature: Hartwich 1911; Müller-Ebeling & Rätsch 1986.

COLEUS (Coleus blumei, Coleus pumilus). The some 150 species of coleus are members of the *Labiatae* family. All come from the tropical regions of the Old World. Brought to America at an early date, they quickly acquired a place in native systems of magic. The Mazatekens utilize coleus leaves as a substitute for **Salvia Divinorum**, and their magicians claim that the effects are similar to those of the latter plant. They regard the species *C. pumilus* as 'masculine' (*el macho*) and consider *C. blumei* as a 'child' (*el nene*) or 'godchild' (*el ahijado*).

In Brazil, coleus is known as *maconha*. It is used as a marijuana (**Hemp**) substitute (another Brazilian plant used for the same purpose is *Cestrum laevigatum*). Coleus is protected by the Macumba god Ossae, the god of sacred and medicinal plants (**Jurema**). To venerate Ossae, *maconha* (coleus or **Hemp**) is smoked at Macumba ceremonies. Since the aim of these Macumba rituals is to enter a state of trance in which the god takes possession of a dancer in order to express himself, the use of *maconha* is especially helpful for opening a person up to the divine.

Pharmacology: No psychoactive components of coleus have yet been identified. Reports of self-experimentation have also been negative. Further study may help cast light upon the use of this plant.

Literature: Schultes & Hofmann 1980.

COLORINES (Erythrina americana). The brilliant red seeds of this *Leguminosae* (cf. **Beans**) tree are used for divinatory purposes by the magicians and prophets (so-called 'daykeepers') of a number of Guatemalan Indian groups (Ixil, Mam). They also use the beans to count off the important days in the divinatory calendar. The tropical tree was invoked as a magical remedy in the medicinal spells of the post-classic/early colonial Maya Indians of Yucatán (*Ritual of the Bacabs*). The modern Lacandon Maya string the seeds into chains which are traditionally worn only by the women. The Aztecs referred to the plant as the *tzompantli* tree and associated it with sacrificial death. They carved figures of their gods from its wood. In modern Mexico, the wood is fashioned into small ithyphallic figures intended as amulets for protecting the hearth, home, and food. The red beans are used as an aphrodisiac and as a drug for producing dreams. It appears that they were also used to produce nymphomaniacal inebriations in women. The use of other species of Erythrina for divination is not as common.

Pharmacology: The seeds contain cytisine and indole alkaloids with psychotropic effects (cf. **Beans, Genista, Jequirity**). While the alkaloids appear to have inebriating effects, they are also capable of eliciting ecstatic madness and death. Unfortunately, no reports of actual experiences are available at the moment.

Literature: Heffern 1974; Rätsch 1986a; Reko 1986.

COPAL (Pinus spp., Protium copal, Protium guaianensis, Protium heptaphyllum, Protium shipii). The word copal, derived from the Aztec word copalli, is a generic term for tree resins which are used for incense (cf. **Incense**). The resin was and is obtained from pine trees and various resinous trees (*Liquidambar styraciflua, Protium sp., Icaca sp.*) by slicing the bark. The Indians of Mesoamerica used copal (*pom* in Mayan) as an incense for all religious and magical rituals. Occasionally, **Thornapple** seeds were also added to the mixture. Copal smoke was believed to form a bridge to the gods and to link together heaven and earth, gods and humans. The smoke was said to carry the souls of sacrificed humans to the gods. Among the Maya, copal was also known as the 'brain of heaven' or the 'placenta of heaven'. During healing ceremonies, the smoke was intended to make the gods take notice of the afflicted. In this way, the gods were shown where they should direct their healing powers. Copal was also used medicinally to treat diseases of the respiratory tract and the skin. The resins of several other trees were also used ritually in Mesoamerica: Peruvian balsam (*Balsamum peruvianum*, obtained from *Myroxylom balsamum* var. *prereirae*), American elemi

(*Bursera gummifera*), *Hedwigia balsamifera*, guayac wood (*Guaiacum sanctum*). In Europe, copal was also known as *olibanum americanum*.

Pharmacology: The resins contain essential oils and triterpenes. It is possible that burning them produces empyromatic substances with inebriating effects (cf. **Incense**).

Literature: Martinetz, Lohs & Janzen 1989; Rätsch 1985, 1986a.

DATE PALM (Phoenix dactylifera). The date palm is indigenous to Mesopotamia, where it has been the object of cultic veneration for at least 8,000 years. The peoples of the area, like the Arabs and Egyptians, revered the date palm as a sacred tree of divine origin and used all parts of the plant. The dates were eaten or pressed. The seeds were ground and made into 'date coffee'. Date seeds were one of the magical instruments of ancient Egyptian magicians. The Egyptians washed the bodies of the dead with date wine during mummification, but we know little of any other possibly magical use.

Sumerian physicians utilized the roots, bark, leaves, and seeds of the date palm. The panicles were used as amulets and magical weapons. The magician priests used date panicles as magical weapons as well, increasing the efficacy of these weapons by uttering a spell: '... my spell is the spell of Ea, my charm is the charm of Marduk, the magic of Ea is in my hand, I hold the **Tamarisk**, the mighty weapon of Anu, in my hand; I hold the spathe of the date, powerful in decision, in my hand. They may not come close to my body, they may not do anything evil before me, or follow after me ... You are banished through heaven! You are banished through the earth!' (excerpt, after Sigerist 1963:85f.).

A juice is tapped from the trunks of older date palms which immediately begins to ferment. The resulting drink was known as palm wine. Although used as a ritual inebriant, it was particularly esteemed for its aphrodisiac properties. For such purpose, it was used in conjunction with a variety of other magical plants, presumably **Henbane, Thornapple, Mandrake**, or **Hemp**. A cuneiform text describing the inebriating effects of this wine has been preserved:

> 'When a man has drank inebriant beverage and his head is "packed with it", he forgets his words, while it "wipes out" his speech, his reason does not hold tight,... and his eyes are motionless, for his recovery you should rub licorice juice [a traditional antidote for Thornapple poisoning]..., beans, and oleander together, and he should drink this with oil and inebriating beverage before the arrival of Gula [= in the evening before the stars arise], in the morning, before the sun has risen and anyone has kissed him, then he will recover'

The symptoms described in this passage are typical effects of the nightshades.

Pharmacology: Apart from riboflavin (vitamin B_2) the date palm contains no active ingredients. Both the inebriating effects of palm wine and its aphrodisiac properties are the result of its alcohol content.

Literature: Manniche 1989; Sigerist 1963; Thorwald 1962.

DITA (Alstonia scholaris, A. venenata). Dita is a 30 to 40 meter tall tree which grows in the tropical forests of India and Southeast Asia. The bark was formerly used to produce parchment for making amulets for Tantric magic and in Ayurvedic and traditional folk medicine. The bark was also made into teas which were prescribed for epilepsy and mental deficiency. The seeds were considered an aphrodisiac and were consumed during Tantric sexual magic practices. They were used to sustain the prolonged erections necessary for the long rituals and prevent the men from ejaculating. The Tantric magicians drew their strength from the transforming energy produced by these impeded ejaculations. The African variety, *Alstonia boonei*, is used to build altars to the Ashanti god of heaven.

Pharmacology: Dita seeds contain a number of indole alkaloids with hallucinogenic effects (alstovenine, venenatine, chlorogenine, reserpine). The bark contains the alkaloids ditamine, echitamine, and echitenine.

Literature: Andoh 1986; Miller 1985; Rätsch 1990a; Schultes & Hofmann 1980.

EPHEDRA (Ephedra americana, Ephedra spp.). Ephedra, also known as ma-huang (*Ephedra sinica*), Indian tea, Mormon tea (*Ephedra nevadensis*), or popotillo, is probably one of humanity's oldest magical plants. Remains of ephedra (*Ephedra sp.*) have been recovered from a Neanderthal grave in the caves of Shanidar (Iraq) dated to 60,000 years B.P. Ephedra (*Ephedra vulgaris*) also played a role in the ancient Iranian **Haoma** cult; in the post-Vedic period, it was used as a substitute for **Soma**. The plant was incorporated into Tantric moon rituals. People in the ancient land of Margush (in the southeast of the desert of Karaleum) also made ephedra into a ritual drink (second millennium BC).

The ancient Egyptians, Greeks, and Romans knew of the plant (*Ephedra fragilis, E. distachya*). Prophets referred to it as a 'food of Saturn', thereby grouping it with other Saturnian plants (including **Belladonna** and **Henbane**) and linking it to the orgiastic Saturnalia, where ephedra was consumed in **Wine**.

North American Indians use ephedra tea (*Ephedra californica*) as a stimulant and to prepare for vision quests. The Indian use of ephedra is very ancient, and spread across both American continents. The ancient Aztecs used ephedra (*Ephedra americana*) both medicinally and magically. Today, Mexican Indians smoke a mixture of *Ephedra americana* and **Tobacco** as a headache treatment. In modern sexual magical practices, a decoction of ephedra is used in conjunction with **Hemp** as an aphrodisiac.

Pharmacology: All *Ephedra* species contain the amphetamine-like alkaloids ephedrine, pseudoephedrine, norephedrine, and other alkaloids, tannins, saponins, flavones, and an essential oil. The herbage has vasoconstricting and diuretic effects and relieves bronchial spasms. It also stimulates the circulation, increases blood pressure, stimulates the central nervous system, suppresses the appetite, and suppresses hay fever reactions (cf. **Qat**). High aphrodisiac effects are reported by many women.

Literature: Miller 1983; Rätsch 1987f, 1990b; Sarianidi 1988; Wasson 1972.

ERGOT (Claviceps purpurea). Ergot is the winter stage of a parasitic fungus which grows on grasses and grains. Grains infected with ergot were probably used to produce the drink (*kykeon*) given as part of the initiation into the Eleusinian mysteries. The beer-like drink also contained stream mint (*Mentha aquatica*) and perhaps opium (cf. **Poppy**). Ergot may have also played a role at the oracle of Delphi (Rätsch 1987e). Since the Middle Ages, midwives and witches have used ergot to induce uterine contractions. Because it is also the cause of St Anthony's fire, a disease (ergotism) whose symptoms are gangrene and terrible hallucinations, it was thought to be a magical plant descended from the devil (cf. **Saffron**). Ergot grains were also used in more modern magical drinks intended to induce clairvoyance and the gift of prophecy. In modern Peru, diviners sometimes use ergot as a part of the geomantic **Coca** oracle.

Pharmacology: Ergot contains a number of different ergot alkaloids, varying with location, host, and climate. Most of these are derivatives of lysergic acid (LSD-like substances; cf. **Ololiuqui**). Some of these alkaloids have psychedelic effects, while others have toxic properties.

Literature: Findlay 1982; Hansen 1981; Hofmann 1964, 1979, 1983; Kolta 1987; Spilmont 1984; Wasson *et al.* 1978.

Fig. 8: Saint Anthony was the patron saint of persons afflicted with St Anthony's fire (Ignis sacer), now known as ergotism. This disease results from ingesting grains infested with the toxic ergot fungus. Towards the end of the Middle Ages, a number of epidemic-like outbreaks of ergotism occurred throughout Europe. Those afflicted were exposed to hellish torments. Their arms and legs became gangrenous, and they had terrible hallucinations, probably not unlike those envisioned by many of the painters who have produced works based upon the motif of the Temptation of St Anthony (e.g., Bosch, Grünewald, Peter Huys, Lucas de Leyde, Nikolaus Manuel Deutsch, Schongauer, Cranach, Bernardo Parenzano). Because St Anthony was viewed as someone who had vanquished the devil, victims of ergotism were placed under his protection. This illustration shows one such victim on the lower left. Today, some 'acid heads' consider St Anthony their patron saint.

FALSE MANDRAKE (Allium victorialis). The root of the false mandrake, which is covered with a net-like tissue, was the most important European substitute for genuine **Mandrake**. Genuine mandrake was both very expensive and difficult to find, and only the most wealthy were able to afford to use it as a magical charm. As a result, the poor turned to 'false mandrake', a less expensive alternative. Known also as 'wild mandrake', false mandrake was used as a magical charm to protect against injury, black magic, and evil spirits and ghosts. Knights wore it as an amulet, hoping to make themselves invulnerable. Miners used it to protect themselves against the treacherous 'little man of the mountains' ('Bergmännlein'), falling

*Fig. 9: Because it had the power to bring victory, one of the Germanic names for the root of the false mandrake was 'root of victory' (*Siegwurz*). As its English name implies, the false mandrake was often used as a substitute for true mandrake (after Tabernaemontanus 1731).*

rocks, and avalanches. In Switzerland, false mandrake roots were still being sold in pharmacies as 'alraun' (mandrake) or 'alrunmennle' (little mandrake man) in the 1960s.

Pharmacology: The root contains steroidal saponin and chelidon acid (cf. **Garlic**).

Literature: Gessmann n.d.; Rätsch 1990a.

FANG-KUEI (Peucedanum japonica). The root of this East Asian *Umbelliferae* is used for medicinal purposes. According to ancient sources, however, its magical qualities should not be underestimated. In the *Tao Hung-ching*, it is said that 'feverish persons should not take this, for it has narcotic effects and allows spirits to appear.'

Since ancient times *Peucedanum decursivum*, a related species from China, has been considered an aphrodisiac and a potentiator of the life energy. The root also has nervine properties.

Pharmacology: unknown, possibly toxic constituents.

Literature: Li 1978; Stark 1980.

Fig. 10: The fang-k'uei plant (from the Chêng-lei pên-ts'ao, *1249 AD).*

FLY AGARIC (Amanita muscaria). The fly agaric mushroom is found throughout the world. Everywhere, shamans, magicians, and healers revere it as a magical plant, while normal people fear it as a poison. Dried fly agaric caps or pieces added to the squeezed juice of **Vaccinium** or Epilobium *augustifolium* are ingested by Siberian shamans in order to enter shamanic trance. The Taoist alchemists utilized extracts of fly agaric as additives to a variety of elixirs of immortality. In the Hindu Kush, an ancient ritual is still preserved in which fly agaric pieces are boiled with *Impatiens montana* and the overacidified brine from goat's cheese. Seed-bearing calyxes of **Henbane** are sometimes added to this brew. In this region, the fly agaric is known as *tschasch baskon*, 'eye opener'. The mushroom has often been associated with the classical plants **Haoma** and **Soma**.

Fly agaric has been known since antiquity. The Egyptians called it 'raven's bread', a name which it has retained in Central and Eastern Europe to the present day. It was said that Saint Anthony ate of this raven's bread before the ancient pagan gods appeared to him as demons. According to Graves (1961), the followers of Dionysos consumed fly agaric during the Dionysian festivals and mysteries, for it 'bestows enormous physical power, erotic potency, delusional visions, and the gift of prophecy'. One author has even argued that Christianity began as a fly agaric cult (Allegro 1970). There is also some evidence that the pre-historic 'Beaker People' of Stonehenge, and later the British Celts, used fly agaric in a cultic context.

Among the ancient Germans, the fly agaric was associated with Wotan/Odin, the god of ecstasy and the discoverer of the magical runes. According to legend, fly agarics appeared where the foam from Wotan's horse fell onto the earth. The name raven's bread refers to Wotan's two all-knowing, all-seeing ravens. The name fly agaric is probably derived from the fly's reputation as a magical animal and/or the mushroom's ability to enable a person 'to fly'. There are no grounds for attributing its name to any use as a 'fly poison'. Similarly, there is no truth to the myth that the mushroom is capable of transforming humans into berserkers (cf. **Wild Rosemary**).

Fly agarics also grow in North and Central America (*Amanita muscaria* var. *americana*). The Lacandon know it as *hkib lu'um*, 'the light of the earth', and know that eating it leads to changes in consciousness. The shamans of the neighboring Chuj Indians collect fly agaric in the pine forests and dry the caps. When a patient comes to consult with them, they smoke a mixture of fly agaric pieces and several **Tobacco** leaves (*Nicotiana rustica*). The smoke places them in a clairvoyant trance, in which they are able to detect the causes of diseases and unleash special healing powers. They associate the consumption of fly agaric with the god of lightning and thunder.

Several Alaskan tribes also use the mushroom. Fly agaric is eaten as part of the initiation of Dogrib shamans, during which the initiate must adhere to certain culturally prescribed patterns of visions. First, he should experience death, then the curative ecstasy. In Alaska, the mushroom is often eaten or smoked for divinatory purposes. A similar use has been discovered among the Ojibwa.

Recently, it became known that the Igorot, the aboriginal Malayan inhabitants of the Philippine island of Luzon, have maintained a traditional fly agaric cult. They call the mushroom *ampacao*. They brew six fresh mushrooms into an hallucinogenic drink which is consumed during rites of passage. In modern circles practising sexual magic, dried fly agaric is mixed with cannabis and henbane or thornapple, and the resulting mixture is smoked to increase sexual arousal and erotic ecstasy.

Pharmacology: Fresh fly agaric mushrooms contain choline, acetylcholine, muscarine, muscaridine, muscazone, butyltrimethyl-ammonium, and the trace elements selenium and vanadium. Fresh mushrooms also contain ibotenic acid, the content of which decreases through decarboxylation when drying. Through this process, the mildly active ibotenic acid is transformed into muscimol, a highly active psychedelic substance. Reports on experiences with fly agaric paint a somewhat contradictory picture of its effects.

Literature: Alegre 1980; Allegro 1970; in Efron 1967; Bianchi & Festi 1990; Lowy 1974, 1977; Ott 1976b; Pollock 1975; Rätsch 1986b, 1987f, 1990b; Rosenbohm 1991; Sandford 1973; in Schröder 1985; Schulte n.d.; Wasson 1972, 1979.

FO-TI (Hydrocotyle asiatica minor). This small marsh plant may be found throughout Asia. The fresh leaves are eaten in Sri Lanka, where they are believed to give health and long life. The plant is also an important part of the Ayurvedic system of traditional healing. The Chinese name, *fo-ti-tieng*, means 'elixir of long life'. The Taoists make magical use of the plant, often combined with **Ginseng**, in order to come closer to immortality. In Taoist sexual magic, fo-ti is also utilized as an aphrodisiac (cf. **Woodrose**).

The name fo-ti-tieng is also used to refer to other plants which are used in similar manners: *Centella asiatica* (also known as *Gotu Kola* and, in Hawaiian, *Pohe Kula*; Indian Pennywort), *Polygonum multiflorium* (also known as Ho Shou Wu). Cf. also **Solomon's Seal**.

Pharmacology: The leaves and seeds of *Hydrocotyle asiatica minor* have been found to contain an alkaloid which has been given the provisional name 'vitamin X'. It appears to have stimulating and rejuvenating effects upon the nerves, brain, and endocrinal glands. Gotu Kola (*Centella asiatica*) contains the antibiotic substance asiaticoside. The pharmacology of the tonic Ho Shou Wu is still unknown.

Literature: Bensky & Gamble 1986; Cooper 1984; Emboden 1985; Miller 1985; Stark 1980.

GAISE NORU NORU (Ferraria glutinosa). During the ecstatic healing dances of the Kalahari Bushmen, magical plants are sometimes employed to help facilitate healing trances (*kia*). The Iko Bushmen use **Hemp** or a decoction of gaise noru noru for this purpose: 'During the dance, all men drank of this, apart from those who were not to dance. All that danced have drunk of it. Those who have not yet attained kia have drunk more than those who have already reached kia. We, the eldest, since we already attained kia long ago, only drank a little of it.... You feel how something begins to move in the stomach, in the chest, and in the back. It pulses in the back, and you feel something like a stabbing there.... You feel how the backbone begins in front to pulse with the beating of the heart and how it begins to shake. I say that this gaise noru noru is strong because a person does not simply drink it. A man must have been cleansed, and must have been given certain foods. Certain foods were forbidden, and a man was rubbed with freshly killed meat and the blood of the animal. After this, the man was washed once more with something else. All of this is tied to this gaise noru noru. And thus I say, that it was strong' (after Katz 1982). This drink is prepared using the roots of the plant.

This plant is also known as *!kaishe*. It is likely that the Bushmen used a number of other psychoactive plants as well to induce healing trances or ecstasy: *Albizia anthelmintica [kydi], Cassia spp. [daman/um], Cissampelos mucronata [naieg!kan], Loranthus oleaefolius [chichi], Plumbago zeylanica [khaba].* All of these plants require further research.

Pharmacology: The hallucinogenic or psychoactive substances contained in the roots, said to be capable of inducing trance, have not yet been found.

Literature: Katz 1982; Winkelman & Dobkin de Rios 1989.

GALANGAN (Kaempheria galanga). This relative of **Ginger** grows in the moist tropical zones of Southeast Asia. The aromatic root is utilized as a spice, a medicine, and a magical plant. It is also known under the names maraba root and camphor root. In New Guinea, the root is made into an hallucinogenic drink which is said to have euphoric and aphrodisiac effects. In the Jamu medicine of Indonesia, the root is added to all stimulating, life-extending, and love-inciting powders. Further research is needed into this rare magical plant.

Pharmacology: The rootstock contains essential oils with psychoactive effects. Their precise chemical composition and pharmacology are unknown.

Literature: Rätsch 1990a; Schultes & Hofmann 1980.

GARLIC (Allium sativum). Originally from Siberia, garlic spread throughout Asia and into the Near East at a very early date. It was known to the ancient Egyptians and Babylonians. Its primary use was as a food for the simple farmers, as a medicinal plant of the physicians, and as a magical plant of the priests and farmers. Egyptian farmers venerated garlic as a god and used it as an aphrodisiac. The belief that its aroma is capable of warding off spirits is quite common, and has enabled garlic to become famous throughout the world as a magical means to protect against spirits (such as nereids and lemurs), demons, devils, vampires, bloodsuckers, diseases, pestilence, and the evil eye. Garlic was sacred to the ancient Hebrews, who used it as a talisman. The magicians and witches of ancient Greece are said to have offered garlic to evoke the favor of Hecate, the goddess of the underworld and the protectress of women magicians. For a 'night meal of Hecate', one was required to place several bulbs of garlic on top of a pile of rocks at a crossroads in the middle of the night. Garlic bulbs were used throughout the entire Mediterranean region to protect against the evil eye and against man-eating erotic demons.

In ancient times, garlic had already become associated with the hermetic magical plant **Moly**. Its use as an aphrodisiac was also quite widespread. During the festival of Ceres, the goddess of fertility, the Romans prepared a love drink from garlic and coriander. Garlic was also considered the *Theriaca Rusticoriam*, the 'theriac of the simple folk'. Theriac is a collective term used to designate magical mixtures held to be universal antidotes and rejuvenating elixirs. Theriac usually contained opium (cf. **Poppy**) and snake flesh. The Scots use garlic cloves in a magical rite intended to aid the person carrying out the rite to attain a wish. In New Mexico, a custom introduced by the Spanish is still extant today. When a girl wants to get rid of an unwanted lover, she rubs garlic onto two nails and then hides these at a crossroads. As soon as her suitor passes over these, he loses his desire for that girl.

Pharmacology: Garlic contains an essential and characteristic oil consisting of alliin, allicin, and allinase. These substances have antibiotic effects and stimulate cell division (mitosis). Garlic has also been found to contain so-called mitogenetic rays. These rays also stimulate mitosis and are said to have rejuvenating effects upon living organisms.

Literature: Harris 1980; Kronfeld 1981.

GENISTA (Cytisus canariensis). Genista is indigenous to the Canary Islands. The Guanches, the original inhabitants of the Canary Islands, may have used the plant in their native rituals of worship. In the European folk medical tradition, the yellow flowers are decocted into aphrodisiac love drinks. Later, genista was introduced into Mexico, where it has become widely known. Yaqui magicians use the seed capsules to prepare a drink which enables them to divine, to travel into the past and future, and to increase their healing powers. In sexual magical circles, genista flowers and **Hemp** are smoked together as an aphrodisiac.

Pharmacology: All parts of the plant contain the toxic alkaloid cytisine (cf. **Beans, Colorines**). Other psychoactive substances may also be present.

Literature: Fadiman 1965; Schultes & Hofmann 1980.

GINGER (Zingiber officinarum). Originally from Southeast Asia, ginger is now endemic in all tropical zones. In India and China, it has been used as a spice, medicine, and aphrodisiac since very ancient times. In Japan, rooters (known as rhizotomes) are used to uncover especially thick ginger roots, which are highly valued as aphrodisiacs. According to Ayurvedic teachings, ginger is said to ignite *agni*, the creative and divine inner fire — in this sense, ginger is reminiscent of **Soma**. In Islamic medicine, ginger is venerated as a sacred plant, for it is mentioned in the Koran. It is also considered an aphrodisiac in the Islamic world. In all folk medical traditions which differentiate between *cold* and *hot* remedies, ginger is attributed with *hot* qualities.

In the South Pacific, ginger is esteemed as a food and medicine, and the root is also an important tool of magicians. On the Gazelle Peninsula in New Pomerania, ginger roots and leaves are utilized in almost every magical practice. This use is of such importance that anthropologists have come to refer to ginger as the 'mandrake root of the aborigines' (cf. **Mandrake**). In these practices, ginger exhibits its magical powers only when activated by an experienced magician. This occurs by weaving the leaves into certain patterns or uttering spells over the roots. Pieces of the plant which have been charged with magical powers are wrapped in **Betel** packets for use as love magic and attached to or hung around the necks of the persons they are intended to affect, placed in magical places, and stored in the magic bag of

Fig. 11: An early illustration of a ginger plant (after Garcia da Orta, 1913).

the possessor. Magicians also utilize woven ginger leaves as a medium for the destructive forces involved in death or harmful magic:

> 'In doing so, the magician colors his hair half red, half black in the Iniet manner and then dons the black and red strands of a flowing plume of feathers. Around his neck, he ties a garland of ginger leaves or simply sticks a bundle of these leaves under the cord around his neck. In this garb, he recites his magical formula: "The ginger leaf decoration flies, the sea eagle flies, the e magit beings [allies of the magician] fly. I move invisibly. I will tear out the entrails [of the people]. I will make their bellies shrink. I will look from side to side in flight. I will smash them. I will twist off their intestines. I will make their stomachs shrink. The ginger leave decoration flies, the sea eagle flies..." ' (Meier 1913:290f.).

Pharmacology: Ginger root contains an essential oil with zingibers, zingiberol, borneol, cineol, and several pungent substances (gingerol, shoagol, zingeron). These substances promote digestion, stimulate the appetite, strengthen the stomach, and stimulate the circulation. No psychotropic effects are known.

Literature: Engel 1978; Meier 1913.

GINSENG (Panax ginseng, Panax quinquefolium). The ginseng plant, indigenous to East Asia but now cultivated widely, has an adventurous and legendary history in the magic, alchemy, and medicine of the East. Because of its anthropomorphic root, the plant has often been called the **Mandrake** of the East. In India, it is considered a brother of **Soma** and an elixir of life. The name ginseng comes from *gin*, 'man', and *seng*, 'essence'. The root is considered the crystallization of the essences of heaven and earth in the form of a person. Within it dwell the life forces of heaven and earth, or of yin and yang. It is the material manifestation of the spiritual part of nature. Anyone who eats the root will become healthy and young and may even attain eternal life. Taoist magicians often used the root when preparing elixirs of immortality and combined it with other magical plants (**Date, Hemp, Ginger, Poppy, Tea, Wine**). In the *Tao Hung-ching*, it s said that 'necromancers use them (**Hemp** seeds) together with ginseng in order to traverse time and see future events.' The dried, carved, and occasionally clothed root is a powerful amulet. Its possessor becomes young and stays healthy, is fertile, and wins wealth and respect. The root is also a potent spring medicine (aphrodisiac) and is able to effect love magic. Since anthropomorphic roots are rare, they are correspondingly expensive and often counterfeited (e.g. by using less valuable *Panax* species). Ginseng is the most important medicinal plant in the Chinese Materia Medica. It is considered a universal tonic which harmonizes the yin and yang energies.

There is also a wild North American species of ginseng (*Panax quinquefolium*). Amazingly, the cultural and magical importance of this plant for the North American Indians was similar to that of its Asian cousin. Its name in many native (Indian) languages may be rendered as 'man-root' or 'little people'. It is used as a magical agent, aphrodisiac, and medicinal plant, and is frequently combined with other magical plants. It is smoked together with **Tobacco** (*Nicotiana glauca*) and mixed into **Lobelia** for love magic.

Pharmacology: Ginseng roots contain a biogenic complex of active substances consisting of panaquilon, panaxin, panacen, photosterol, panax acid, ginsenin, hormones, vitamins, sugar, and enzymes. The overall effects are antidiabetic, calming, stimulating, antidepressive, aphrodisiac, and harmonizing. It strengthens the circulatory system, has generally tonic effects, and stimulates the metabolism. To date, none of the alleged psychoactive properties or agents have been found.

Literature: Fulder 1984; Heffern 1976; Hu 1976; Kappstein 1980; Kimmins 1975; Kreuter 1982; Müller-Ebeling & Rätsch 1986; Rätsch 1990a.

GUARANA (Paullinia cupana, P. spp.). The guaraná liana grows in the central Amazon basin. The Indians there, especially the Maué and the Mundurucu, cultivate the plant and use it as a stimulant, medicine, and magical plant. In the mythology of the Tupi, the guaraná is said to have had a shamanic origin. Omniamasabé, a female shaman whose 'knowledge of the real world that is hidden from humans' was very extensive, was impregnated in sylvan solitude by Mboy, the snake god. Shortly thereafter, she bore a son. Thereupon, her jealous brother charged a shaman to kill the child. This shaman drank **Ayahuasca** and assumed the form of an arara parrot. In this shape, he searched for and killed the boy. As the tears of the mother flowed over his corpse, he was transformed into the guaraná bush. Since that time, shamans eat guaraná fruits so that they may be initiated into the secrets of the knowledgeable shaman Omniamasabé (Melzer 1987:39-44).

After drying, guaraná seeds are ground, mixed with water, and kneaded into a dough. This dough, which sometimes contains manioc flour and cacao powder as well, is made into fist-sized, cylindrical guaraná breads, which become extremely hard when dry. To use, this bread is grated and the shavings are added to cold water or brewed as tea. When used as a simple stimulant, only a small amount of guaraná is taken; for shamanic purposes, larger doses are used. In the Amazon, guaraná is considered a hunter's drug. It is used quite effectively in hunting, for it keeps a person awake and attentive and simultaneously suppresses the appetite.

Pharmacology: Guaraná contains up to 5% caffeine, tannin, saponin, resin, starch, a red dye, and guaranin, a little studied essential oil. Its high caffeine content makes guaraná the most potent of all purine drugs; it is three times as strong as **Coffee**. The oil has mild psychoactive and aphrodisiac effects. Interestingly, guaraná decreases the pulse frequency and heightens perception. Drinks made from guaraná make a person awake and are consumed for migraine, neuralgia, menstrual headaches, and bladder ailments, and to combat fever and diarrhoea and as an aphrodisiac and antidepressive agent.

Literature: Melzer 1987; Miller 1985; Rätsch 1987f.

GUATILLO (Iochroma fuchsioides). This plant, also known as *arbol de campanilla, nacadero, paguanda,* and **Borrachero**, grows in the Columbian Andes. Kamsá Indian shamans use the fresh leaves and bark to make a decoction which they drink in order to attain a clairvoyant state, become more effective curers, and for divinatory and prophetic purposes. They take this drink, whose unpleasant after-effects last for days, only in difficult cases.

Pharmacology: The plant contains alkaloids which presumably belong to the tropane group (cf. **Angel's Trumpet, Thornapple**) and have hallucinogenic properties.

Literature: Schultes 1977.

GUAYUSA (Ilex guayusa). In the rain forests of Ecuador, a variety of holly grows which is closely related to **Maté** and is known by the name guayusa. The effects of the leaves are similar to those of Maté, so that both varieties were long considered to belong to the same species.

In 1785, the German missionary Franz Xavier Viegl wrote: 'When the barbarian must leave home for several days, then he carries his little pot, together with a bundle of guayassa leaves, hanging around his neck.' The Jíbaro and the Canelos Indians drink a tea or decoction of the leaves in the morning. They say that the plant gives strength and suppleness and provides the hunter with auspicious dreams. Strong decoctions serve as emetics and as enemas to clean the stomachs and the intestines of children. Shamans drink very strong guayusa preparations prior to consuming **Ayahuasca** in order to completely cleanse themselves internally. Guayusa leaves have been found in Indian graves dating from the period around 500 BC. They were found in a medicine bag together with snuff pipes (cf. **Villca**) and devices for administering enemas. This indicates that the ritual and magical use of guayusa is quite ancient.

Pharmacology: Guayusa leaves contain bound caffeine, theobromine, theophylline, chlorogenic acid, aromatic substances (including traces of vanillin), fatty oil, tannins, and resin. Guayusa is a potent stimulant, purgative, diuretic, and appetite suppressant. In higher doses, it induces vomiting and is inebriating.

Literature: de Smet 1985; Rätsch 1987f; Trupp 1984.

HAOMA (not yet identified). The Avesta, the sacred text of ancient Iran and the basis of Zoroastrianism, mentions a sacred magical beverage called haoma, which corresponds to the Vedic **Soma**. Haoma was a plant which grew in the mountains and was cultically consumed in a mixture with milk. The Parsees consumed haoma drinks in order to obtain visions of a more real reality, to approach the Gods, to gain insight into the spirit world, and to recognize the causes of disease and misfortune:

> 'We honor the golden, high-growing haoma, the haoma which supports living beings ... we honor haoma who protects against death, I call your zest for inebriation upon me, oh gold colored ... who defeats the Drug [emissary of the world of lies = demons] ... the gold colored ... haoma ... we honor the protector against death (haoma), we honor all haomas...' (Yast 20.1-2). The haoma drink was also the most important offering to the Gods: 'You offer him, the asa, believing Zarathustra in the Aryan Vaejah, the good Daitya with [milk] containing haoma ... with ... spells. And he asked them for this success...' (Yast 9.25).

Haoma was also the most important apotropaic incense. Parts of the plant were also used in both public and private magic. One Avesta text describes its use as a magical plant:

> 'I carry with me [as a magician] a haoma [stalk] which saves from doom, I carry a victorious haoma [stalk] with me, I carry the protector of property with me, I carry the protector [of my] person with me — when a person wears a haoma [stalk] [as an amulet], he escapes the shackles in battle...' (Yast 14.57).

Even today, vestiges of haoma cults can still be found in Iran in Zoroastrian communities. They prepare a haoma drink either from pomegranate juice (*Punica granatum*) and **Ephedra** or from **Rue** and milk. The apotropaic effects are achieved with **Syrian Rue**. It is possible that haoma was a drink prepared from Syrian rue, ephedra, and (fermented?) milk. Other vestiges of the haoma ritual have been preserved in the **Fly Agaric** cult in the Hindu Kush (cf. also **Moly**).

Pharmacology: According to descriptions contained in the Avesta, the haoma drink must have contained a potent psychedelic drug. Its effects can hardly be explained by the presence of the relatively weak **Syrian Rue**. Experimental work is needed to clarify whether the addition of **Ephedra** can augment the effects so greatly. Because it has almost no psychoactive properties, **Rue** can be disregarded as a candidate. The **Fly Agaric** mushroom has strong effects which may be supported or synergistically changed by the Syrian rue and the ephedra. Pomegranates contain MAO inhibitors. Perhaps a previously unknown plant containing tryptamine (such as DMT) was also added to the drink (**Reed**).

Literature: Flattery 1984; Flattery & Schwartz 1989; Hermanns 1980; Wolff 1910.

HELLEBORE (Helleborus officinalis, Veratrum album). Since ancient times, black hellebore (*Helleborus officinalis*) and white hellebore (*Veratrum album*; also known as European hellebore) have been important medicinal, poisonous, and magical plants. Their primary use was in treating cases of madness caused by demons.

Prophets and diviners referred to white hellebore as the 'seed of Hercules', and called the black variety *melampodion*; both were said to possess divine powers. Melampus, the seer, gave women possessed by Dionysos hellebore in goat's milk in order to sober them up and expel the raging god. The root was often added to **Mead, Wine,** and **Cedar** oil and used as an emetic. Black hellebore was used as an amulet. Digging the root was a ritual activity:

> 'You also strew it around dwellings, for it is held to be cleansing. For this reason, those who dig it stand up and pray to Apollo and Asclepius by watching the flight of the eagle. For it is said that this does not fly without danger, for the bird would bring death if it observed the digging of hellebore. But it must be dug up quickly, for the scent makes the head heavy. For this reason, diggers eat **Garlic** and drink **Wine** so that they will be spared from harm' (Dioscorides IV,149).

There have been suggestions that hellebore was the mysterious **Moly**.

In the early modern period, it appeared in recipes for **Witches' Ointments**. Dried leaves of black hellebore were mixed with sugar and ingested to preserve youth. White hellebore became an important magical narcotic incense. At the turn of this century, mixtures of white hellebore and **Fly Agaric** were fashionable in occult and parapsychologically oriented circles in Prague, used as inebriants and as magical agents and were said to open doors to a magical world.

White hellebore is also used in Siberian and Chinese folk medicine and magic. Unfortunately, we have little information about this use.

Pharmacology: Helleborus officinalis contains the toxic glycosides helleborine and helleborein. The powder incites sneezing, a fact which accounts for the German name *Nieswurz* ('sneezing spice'). *Veratrum album* contains steroidal alkaloids (protoveratrine, jerpine), veratramine, germerine, chelidon, and veratrum acid. Hellebore extracts have effects upon the brain and the vasomotor nerves.

Literature: Gessmann n.d.; Rowell 1978.

Fig. 12: The name hellebore is applied to a variety of botanically distinct plants which, when dried, powdered, and sniffed, provoke sneezing. During the beginnings of the modern era, such sneezing powders were in common use as medicines (woodcut from Gerard).

HEMLOCK (Conium maculatum). The poisonous hemlock has been feared since antiquity. It has been used to carry out many assassinations and murders (the most famous incident involved the 'cup of hemlock' that was given to Socrates). Hemlock was sacred to Hecate, the dark goddess. The Greek name *conium* means 'stimulating dizziness' and is indicative of the pseudo-psychedelic effects of the plant. Since ancient times, however, it has also been used as a medicine, an anaphrodisiac, and as an incense. The plant was an ingredient in many **Witches' Ointments** as well. According to German folk tradition, the hemlock was home to a toad, which lived beneath it and sucked up its poisons. The hemlock was probably one of the magical plants used by the Old Germanic female soothsayers (*seid*). Unfortunately, however, little is known of this.

Pharmacology: The entire plant contains a very toxic alkaloid mixture consisting of coniine (90% of the total alkaloid content), γ-coniceine, conhydrine, pseudoconhydrine, methylconiine. Death results from respiratory paralysis (lethal dose = 500-1000 mg coniine). In lower doses, coniine is said to have psychotropic effects and produce sensations of flying. For poisonings, hemlock was often added to **Wine** and opium (cf. **Poppy**).

Literature: Engel 1982; de Waal 1984; Hansen 1981; Müller-Ebeling & Rätsch 1986; Rätsch 1990b.

*HEMP (Cannabis sativa, C. indica).** Hemp is one of humanity's oldest cultivated plants. Many groups in Asia and Europe discovered the manifold uses of the plant. At the present time, it is impossible to know how long hemp products have been used as inebriants and as magical and medicinal agents. It is certain, however, that the medicinal use of hemp is at least 5,000 years old.

Hemp was apparently first cultivated in China. The ancient Chinese considered it divine, for it contained not only medicinal and magical power,

* The taxonomic categories of *Cannabis* are still unclarified. Some biologists maintain that *Cannabis sativa* represents a non-psychoactive variety of hemp and that *Cannabis indica* is the psychedelically active variety. Other botanists, including Richard Schultes, have argued that the genus *Cannabis* consists of three species: *C. sativa, C. indica, and C. ruderalis*. Chemical investigation of a mixed planting of the three varieties demonstrated that 70% of all plants contained the active agent THC, while the rest contained no narcotic constituents. This finding may have great importance in clarifying the legal or illegal status of the plant (cf. Emboden 1981b).

but was also a valuable provider of food and raw materials. The ancient Taoists ate hemp to increase their concentration when reading sacred texts. The stalk of the hemp plant was used as a magic wand. It was tapped against the bed of a sick person in order to break the bad magic.

> 'In the 15th century, the *rhya* first mentioned the ritual or shamanistic use of *Cannabis*. This book of medicines of Shen-Nung, composed during the Han dynasty, mentions *ta-ma* as one of the basic ingredients of an elixir of immortality. This elixir transformed a mortal into a divinely transcendent person. The teachings of the Tao emphasize that to attain the goal of the Tao, one must forget his own consciousness. This is precisely the condition that can be achieved with *Cannabis*' (Emboden 1981c:328).

In the *Pen Ts'ao Ching*, the traditional standard work of Chinese herbal lore, it is stated that 'when *ma-fên* is taken in excess, it lets one see a devil. If it is consumed regularly for an extended period of time, then it enables one to associate with the spirits and the body to hover in the air.' Meng Shen, the author of the medicinal book *Shi-liao pen-ts'ao* (7th century AD), gives details of a recipe: 'Those who wish to see the spirits use equal parts of raw *ma* fruits, ch'ang-p'u (*Acorus graminae*), and k'uei'chiu (*Podophyllum peltantum*; **Mandrake**), roll these into pills the size of a marble and take them daily in the face of the sun. After one hundred days, one can see the spirits.' The Taoist alchemists made an incense from hemp flowers which provided them with visions and brought them closer to immortality. Interestingly, hemp has also been combined with **Thornapple** and with **Ginseng** and used as an antidote for **Aconite** poisoning.

The ancient Assyrian name for the plant was *quunabu*, 'Indian hemp'. Presumably, the Sumerians imported the plant into Mesopotamia from India ca.3,000 BC. Hemp was used as a remedy for pain, bronchitis, bladder ailments, rheumatism, and sleeplessness. Thorwald has suggested that hemp was also used to produce the inebriated state needed for the diviners and magical priests to do their work . In India, hemp has been listed as a medicinal and a magical plant in the religious and medical literature since Vedic times (1,400 BC). In addition to the many medicinal uses of cannabis products, evidence also indicates that it has been used as a delightful aphrodisiac since ancient times. Agehananda Bharati stated 'that *vijaya* [= cannabis] is the only real aphrodisiac'.

In Tantric rituals, cannabis drinks are consumed to promote erotic ecstasy (Aldrich 1977). In the yogic system, hemp is used to support the *siddhis*, spiritual powers which are commonly referred to as magic. Patanjali, the founder of classical yoga, stated:

> 'The siddhis are either inborn or awaken through the use of certain herbs [hemp, **Soma, Thornapple**] or through absorption in the innermost self or through asceticism.' The hemp plant itself was the object of religious veneration: 'To a Hindu, hemp is sacred. A guardian lives in the *bhang* leaves. When a person sees the leaves, the plant, or a *bhang* tea in a dream, then they will have good fortune. A longing for hemp forebodes good cheer. It heals diarrhoea and sunstroke, loosens mucous, accelerates digestion, stimulates the appetite, smoothens the lisping tongue, refreshes the intellect, gives vigor to the body, and fills the mind with happiness. These are the good things for which the Almighty [Shiva; cf. **Thornapple**] made hemp... The spirit of hemp is the spirit of peace and knowledge. In hemp ecstasy, the flash of eternity transforms the haziness of matter into pure light. Hemp is the "giver of joy", the "flyer of heaven", the "divine leader", the "poor man's heaven", the "calmer of sorrow". No god, no man, is as good as the religious hemp-drinker.' (*Hemp Drug Commission Report*, 1884, cited in Andrews & Vinkenoog 1968:145).

The Ayurvedic system of medicine has long prescribed hemp preparations for many ailments, especially lack of appetite and impotency. The most popular Ayurvedic medicine with hemp is *jatiphaladi churna*, a recipe of the *Sarngadhara Samhita*. The mixture consists of *ganja* and a number of exotic spices. Other hemp-based aphrodisiacs are *madana modaka* and *kamesvara modaka*.

Hemp is the first of the 10,000 healing plants mentioned in the ancient Iranian Zend-Avesta (cf. **Haoma**). It is likely that the Celtic druids knew of the psychoactive effects of hemp and revered it as a magical plant. The ancient Germans used the plant as a tranquilizer and consecrated it to Freya, their goddess of love. Dioscorides prescribed hemp for earaches. Democritus stated that visions could be produced by consuming hemp mixed with **Wine** and myrrh (Touw 1981:24). Since the ninth century, Sufis have used cannabis to promote religious ecstasy. Medieval Arabian physicians praised hemp as a sacred medicine and aphrodisiac (Nahas 1982, Sami-Ali 1971). It has even been suggested that the Prophet himself secretly enjoyed hashish. Hildegard of Bingen (twelfth century AD) stated that hemp had curative properties. It promotes digestion and, while it may increase headaches in sick persons, is quite good for healthy ones.

The Moslem and Arabian physicians of the Middle Ages used hashish as a remedy for asthma, gonorrhea, and constipation, and as an appetite stimulant, aphrodisiac, and universal antidote for all types of poisoning. It was said that hashish was 'marvellous music for the sense of hearing' and 'opens the doors of [sexual] desire' (Nahas 1982:823). In seventeenth-century Persia, pills were prepared using hemp leaves and seeds with honey for use as an aphrodisiac (Most 1973:571). Serbian gypsies consider hemp flowers, powdered and mixed with menstrual blood, to be a magical aphrodisiac (Aigremont 1986:24). In Central Asia (Tashkent), there are many recipes for *nasha* (hemp) which are used in conjunction with erotic procedures or as aphrodisiacs. The strongest aphrodisiac is the 'mush of joy', which consists of nasha, almond butter, dried rose leaves, pellitory root (*Anacyclus pyrethrum*), clove pink petals, **Saffron, Nutmeg**, cardamom, honey, and sugar. Hemp is considered a remedy, aphrodisiac, and magical plant in almost every region of the world in which it is cultivated.

A variety of hemp preparations are used in such recipes:

- the blooming, dried female inflorescences
  (ganja, marijuana, Flores cannabica)
- the resin exuded by the inflorescences
  (kif, hashish, caras, polen, Rhesina cannabica)
- the fresh or dried leaves
  (bhang, grass, Folia cannabica)

In Asia and Africa, hemp is usually combined with such other psychoactive substances as opium (**Poppy**), **Thornapple, Tobacco, Wine**, or **Nux Vomica** for psychedelic use (Touw 1981:26). Hemp is also used as an antidote to counter opium overdoses.

Pharmacology: The principle active agent extracted from the resinous portions of the drugs (cannabinols, cannabinoids) is $\Delta^{1(9)}$-tetrahydrocannabinol (THC). Other THC derivatives play only a secondary role in producing the psychotropic effects. THC appears to have no direct effect upon consciousness. Instead, it evokes an enzymatic process within the body which in turn effects the desired alteration in consciousness. This complicated process must be 'learned' by the body.

Literature: Aldrich 1977; Andrews & Vinkenoog 1968; Behr 1982; Brunner 1977; Crowley 1979; Emboden 1981b; Kimmins 1977; Li 1974, 1978; Markale 1989; Morningstar 1986; Nahas 1982; Rätsch 1990a, 1990b; Rubin & Comitas 1976; Touw 1981.

HENBANE (Hyoscyamus niger, Hyoscyamus spp.). Since antiquity, henbane species have been known and feared as medicinal and magical plants. These plants flourish especially well in subtropical zones ranging from the Mediterranean and Asia Minor to beyond India.

The ancient Egyptians and Sumerians knew of henbane's magical and medicinal properties. The plant is mentioned in papyri and cuneiform inscriptions. The Greeks consecrated the plant to the sun god Apollo (hence the name *Apollinaris*) and used it as a narcotic and an aid to divination. Apparently, henbane (*Hyoscyamus albus*) was the active ingredient in the incense which the Pythia, the prophetess of Delphi, used to induce her clairvoyant ecstasy. The Romans associated henbane with Juniper, their principle god, and used parts of the plant in manufacturing love philtres. The old Germanic tribes used henbane in their rain magic and to increase the efficacy of their **Beer** and **Mead**. In the Middle Ages, the potent herb was numbered among the witches' plants, but was still used for divinatory purposes. At the same time, henbane seeds and the oil they yielded were among the most important medicines available to the doctors of the late Middle Ages and the beginnings of the modern era. Henbane (German = *Bilsenkraut* or *pilsener krut*) was added to 'pilsner' **Beer** and mixed into the **Witches' Ointments**. In the infamous lascivious bath houses, henbane seeds were poured onto heating plates and used as a fumigant to incite love and increase pleasure.

The ancient Chinese knew henbane (*Hyoscyamus niger* var. *chinensis*) as *lang-tang*. The seeds and leaves were added to wine and prescribed for a variety of illnesses. This medicine was a general tonic which also enabled the patient to directly contact the spirits and devils. In Kashmir, dried henbane is mixed with **Hemp** or **Tobacco** and smoked as an hallucinogen. In the old Arab countries, it is known as *bang* and is utilized as an incense for warding off demons and as a narcotic and aphrodisiac. The seeds of *Hyoscyamus faleslez* are also added to the ritually important spiced **Coffee**. The Tungus of southern Siberia drink a coffee substitute made from roasted henbane seeds (*Hyoscyamus physaloides*).

Apparently introduced into the Americas by the Spanish, henbane quickly spread and established itself as a magical and medicinal plant among the shamans and medicine men of a number of Indian tribes. The Serí Indians, who live on the Gulf of California and on Shark Island (Mexico), utilize henbane in the same manner as **Thornapple**. They add leaves or seeds to water or to an alcoholic drink such as chicha (cf. **Maize**) or pulque (cf. **Maguey**) and drink the mixture as an analgesic or sleeping agent. The dried leaves are smoked alone or mixed with **Tobacco**. Modern North American Indian healers or medicine men advise asthmatics and sufferers of whooping cough to use a smoking mixture made from henbane leaves, **Thornapple**, different varieties of **Artemisia**, and sage (*Salvia spp.*).

Pharmacology: All henbane species contain the tropane alkaloids hyoscyamine, scopolamine, and atropine, which have anticholinergic, inebriating, and psychedelic effects. Caution must be exercised, as high doses can be toxic.

*Fig. 13: The lang-tang plant (*Hyoscyamus niger *var.* chinensis Makino*) from the* Chêng-lei pên-ts'ao*, 1249 AD).*

Literature: Hansen 1981; Heiser 1969; Li 1978:19; Perez de Barradas 1957:310; Rätsch 1987e, 1987f, 1990c; Rowell 1978.

IBOGA (Tabernanthe iboga, T. manii). The iboga plant, a member of the dogbane family, grows in the tropical forests of West and Central Africa. For centuries, the people living in these regions have used the plant for medicinal, magical, and ritual purposes. The plant has many names, including *iboga, eboka, libuga, bocca, mbasaoka, moabi, gifuma*, and *eboga* (= 'miraculous plant'). According to legend, the first plant grew from the remains of a pygmy who had been dismembered by a god.

The aphrodisiac effects of iboga are widely known and much esteemed. In the Congo, pieces of iboga root are infused in palm wine for several hours to produce a powerful aphrodisiac (Bouquet 1969:67). But the root does not only exhibit aphrodisiac powers, it also prolongs all erotic joys and is even capable of healing impotency and frigidity and promoting fertility. We have countless reports about the secret powers of the root. These suggest that anyone who chews it long enough is able to carry twice as much of a load as usual, walk twice as far, etc., without any great exertion. Hunters often chew pieces of the root throughout the night so that they will have sufficient endurance. It is also said that the root makes it possible to remain motionless for up to two days in order to bag the coveted lion trophies.

Magicians and fetish priests use iboga root extensively. They chew the root or decoct it and drink the resulting extract. Afterwards, they are able to divine, locate hidden objects (such as buried treasures hidden by the ancestors), recognize diseases and their causes, recite epic texts, and discover the secret nature of the world. Iboga also helps the magicians and fetish priests to communicate with their fetishes. They ingest iboga to detect fetishes, discover places of power, and to establish contact with the spirits of the trees, springs, and rocks. They frequently prepare a magical drink using iboga, **Yohimbe, Niando**, and other plants which have not yet been identified botanically (cf. **Voacanga**).

Iboga root plays a major role in the Bwiti cult. Bwiti is the name of a mystical God venerated by a number of secret societies. Only persons who have seen Bwiti are allowed to become members of these societies. A person can only see Bwiti when they have ingested very great quantities of iboga root. The initiates receive a long and exact preparation from the magicians. They are then given enough iboga root to kill a normal person. This apparently produces a near-death experience whose purpose is to enable the initiates to contact their ancestors and learn the proper way to live under the influence of the magic root. If they obtain mystical insight into the works of Bwiti and the knowledge of the ancestors, then they are admitted into the secret society. Such groups have established themselves throughout Gabon, the Congo, and in Zaire, and they are steadily growing. These mystical cults are a response to the oppression of Christianity, Islam, and Western culture. In this sense, the Bwiti cult has much in common with the Native American Church, which utilizes **Peyote** as a sacrament.

To the Fang, Bwiti is a 'religion of the trees'. For this reason, initiates are rubbed with a powder made from the ground bark of '12 sacred trees from the forest of Bwiti' during their initiation into the secret society. Through the influence of the iboga root, this powder makes it possible for an initiate to travel to Bwiti, to his God, and to his ancestors.

The Twelve Sacred Trees from the 'Forest of Bwiti'

asam	*Kapaca guineensi*
asas	*Bridelia grandis*
aseng	*Musanga acropioides*
azap	*Mimusops djyve*
azem	*Psilanthemus manii*
elegalenga	*Ocimum americanum*
eteng	*Pycnanthus angolensis*
eyen	*Distmananthus benthamianus*
mbel	*Pterocarpus soyanxii*
mfôl	*Enantia chlorantha*
ôtunga	*Polyalthia suaveolens*
ôvung	*Guibourtia tessmannii*

(after Fernandez 1982)

While none of these plants is known to have psychoactive effects, some of these sacred trees are used medicinally: *Bridelia, Guibourtia, Mimusops, Ocimum, Pterocarpus* (cf. Chesi 1989).

Pharmacology: The entire plant contains the principle alkaloid ibogaine and at least eleven other indole alkaloids (thabernanthine, ibogamine, ibolutein, etc.). Ibogaine is present in very high concentrations, especially in the roots. Ibogaine stimulates the central nervous system and acts as an MAO inhibitor. Higher doses produce lively fantasies, visions, and occasionally even hallucinations when the eyes are closed. Many subjects who have ingested ibogaine have reported prolonged erections, hour-long copulation, and tremendous sexual desire, while others have described typical toxic symptoms. Lower doses have stimulating and mood-improving effects. Very high doses are fatal. Combining ibogaine with yohimbine can produce very dangerous states of inebriation, as yohimbe is also a powerful MAO inhibitor (cf. **Yohimbe**). We do not yet know why the Bwiti initiates survive otherwise lethal doses, although this may be a result of their internal expectations. For some years, ibogaine has also been used successfully in psychotherapy.

Literature: Bouquet 1969; Fernandez 1972, 1982; Müller-Ebeling & Rätsch 1986; Naranjo 1969; Pope 1969; Rätsch 1990b; Swiderski 1965.

IKEMA (Cynanchum caudatum). This small tuberous plant from the *Asclepiadaceae* (milkweed) family is the sacred plant of the Ainu, the original inhabitants of Northern Japan (Hokkaido) and the Sakhalin Peninsula. Their religion is based upon shamanism and features a bear ritual reminiscent of the Paleolithic. Ikema roots, which are considered divine, were used as magical devices to protect against evil spirits and demonic powers. Because of their poisonous properties, only shamans were allowed to prepare the root. Because the culture of the Ainu was largely destroyed by the Japanese invaders, the original knowledge of the ikema root is unknown.

Pharmacology: The root tuber contains a complex mixture of glycosides, including some twenty new steroidal aglykones. The glycoside mixture has toxic properties.

Literature: Mitsuhashi 1976.

INCENSE. Incense is a generic term used to refer to tree or plant resins which are ritually burned to produce smoke. The smoke produced by burning resins is used to venerate the gods, makes it possible for spirits or demons to appear (and can banish them), and aids in establishing contact with worlds that are normally invisible (cf. **Aloe, Asafoetida, Bay Laurel, Benzoin, Cedar, Copal, Juniper, Pichi-Pichi**). The ancient custom of burning incense was most likely discovered in the Stone Age when resinous woods were thrown onto fires. The religions and cults of the ancient Orient attached especially great significance to incense; no public or private rituals could take place without it. Burning incense was particularly important during animal and human sacrifices. It has been suggested that on such occasions, incense also functioned as a disinfectant. The most important incenses of antiquity were:

Aloe wood	*Aquilaria agalochum*
Balm of Gilead	*Balsamodendron gileadense*
Bdellium	*Commiphora mukul*
Benzoin	*Styrax benzoin*
Camphor	*Cinnamomum camphora*
Cassia	*Cinnamomum cassia*
Cinnamon	*Cinnamomum ceylanicum*
Galbanum	*Ferula galbaniflua*
Ladanum	*Cistus ladaniferus*
Mastic	*Pistacia lentiscus*
Myrrh	*Commophora spp., Balsamodendron myrrha*

Myrtle	*Myrtus communis*
Olibanum	*Boswellia spp.*
Onycha	**Onycha**
Storax	*Storax officinalis*

A number of other plants were also used to obtain the aromatic resins coveted for burning. In fact, the trade with incense became so important that one of the principle trade routes of antiquity became known as the Incense Road. Even amber (bernstein), which is fossilized tree resin, was used as incense. In ancient times, certain incenses, whether from resins, animal scents, or other magical plants, were assigned to the days and the planetary gods:

Sunday	Sun	**Aloe Wood**, ambergris, balsam wood, **Bay Laurel**, **Benzoin**, ladanum, mastic, myrrh, olibanum, rosemary, red sandalwood, **Saffron**
Monday	Moon	**Camphor**, caraway, clover, myrtle (cf. **Beer**), **Poppy**, sage (cf. **Artemisia**)
Tuesday	Mars	balsam wood, bdellium, cypress, forest thistle, foxglove, **Genista, Hellebore**, red rose
Wednesday	Mercury	**Bay Laurel**, cinnamon, cinquefoil (*Potentilla reptans*), clove, fennel, juniper, mastic, olibanum, sulphur, thyme
Thursday	Jupiter	**Aloe**, ambergris, ash (cf. **Beer**), **Benzoin**, heather (cf. **Vaccinium**), lavender, mint oil tree, storax
Friday	Venus	**Aloe** wood, ambergris, musk, red rose, **Saffron**, tulip, **Vervain**, white sandalwood
Saturday	Saturn	costus (*Saussurea lappa*), field cypress, **Hellebore**, **Henbane, Mandrake**, myrrh, **Nutmeg, Poppy**

Pharmacology: All of the various types of incense contain resins (terpenes), essential oils, and other substances. These form empyromatic compounds when burned. Burning olibanum produces THC (cf. **Hemp**), which can have very mild psychedelic effects. These empyromatic compounds have been little studied.

Literature: de Waal 1984; Laarss 1988; Martinetz, Lohs & Janzen 1989; Rätsch & Guhr 1989; Vinci 1980.

JAMBUR (Copelandia cyanescens). This mushroom grows in Java and Bali during the rainy season on the dung of cows, buffalo, and horses. The center of Javanese mushroom consumption is located in the region around

Yogyakarta, the ancient city of the sultans near the Buddhist shrine of Borobodur. It is not certain whether magicians and healers use this mushroom, but the local batik artists do consume this magic mushroom so that they will see visions and receive inspiration for their art. Statue manufacturers make a wide variety of mushroom figures. Similar statues are also produced on the island of Bali. Occasionally, these are used to decorate the sacrificial balls of the temples. Although all the Balinese are aware of the magical powers of the mushroom, no indigenous mushroom cult has yet been discovered. We do not know whether the mushroom cult which Aldous Huxley described in his novel *Island* is or was carried out on Bali, but it is likely.

Pharmacology: These mushrooms contain the same active ingredients as the magic mushrooms of Mexico (**Teonanacatl**), albeit in a stronger concentration and in a different composition. Laboratory studies have shown they contain 1.2% psilocin and 0.6% psilocybin. The mushroom's effects are said to be quite strong. Everyone who has ingested them speaks enthusiastically of extraordinary visions. The batik paintings of the Javanese artists in the city of Yogyakarta provide an artistic expression of these colorful visions and their strong mythological orientation.

Literature: Schultes & Hofmann 1980.

JANGIDA (Withania somnifera). After **Soma**, jangida is the second most important magical plant of the Vedas; it is mentioned frequently in the Atharva Veda. The plant was venerated as a powerful instrument of magic, a divine remedy, a panacea, an elixir of life (*rasayana*), an agent to ward off witches and evil sorcerers, and as an aphrodisiac (*vajikarana*). Jangida was compared to **Moly** and **Ginseng** and often identified as **Mandrake**. Recently, however, the Indian ethnobotanist R. Kumaraswamy has been able to botanically identify this mystical plant: *Withania somnifera*, known since Vedic times by the name *ashwagandhara*, 'horse-root'. The anthropomorphic roots which this plant sometimes develops are especially coveted, and are said to have much greater magical powers than all the other parts of the plant.

Today, jangida roots are still used in South India as amulets. Fresh root pieces are strung together and placed around children's throats to protect them from diseases of the lower abdomen. In the Ayurvedic system, *ashwangandhara* is considered an aphrodisiac without equal. The root is used to make magical love drinks for inducing compliancy in the object of one's desire. In Kerala, the roots are used in conjunction with magical formulae to ward off all evil spirits. In Tantric magic, the roots are known as *pilli ventron*, 'vanquisher of evil'.

Pharmacology: The root contains various steroidal chemicals known as withanolides. The stimulating, antibacterial, anti-inflammatory, and biogenic effects of these are pharmacologically similar to those of **Ginseng**.

Literature: Kumaraswamy, in Schröder 1985:109-120; Majupuria & Joshi 1988.

JEQUIRITY (Abrus praecatorius). The red-black seeds of the jequirity, a vine belonging to the *Leguminosae* (cf. **Beans**), are known as jequirity beans or rosary peas. The plant thrives in all tropical regions of the world. The seeds are often used to make jewelry and rosaries. The ancient Aztecs called them *atecuxtli*, 'crab's eyes'. Magicians used the seeds for lethal magic; jealous women stirred powdered seeds into their husbands' food to exact revenge for their unfaithfulness. Whole or powdered seeds were among the poisons most frequently used by Central African magicians. In some parts of Africa, jequirity seeds were used as currency. They were instruments of death magic on the Seychelles, where they were ground and brushed across the threshold of the house. When the intended victim crossed the threshold barefoot, he would die shortly thereafter.

In India, the plant is used both as a medicine and as an aphrodisiac. It is also used for weather prophecy.

Pharmacology: The seeds contain the contact poison abrin and the glycoside abric acid. The toxins present in just one seed are sufficient to kill a man. Glycyrrhizin is present in the leaves and roots.

Literature: Andoh 1986; Diaz 1979; Müller-Ebeling & Rätsch 1989a; Krause 1909; Resch 1987.

JUNIPER (Juniperus spp.). Juniper bushes grow in almost every temperate zone in the world. Most people who live in areas in which junipers are found have discovered their medicinal and magical potential. In ancient times, juniper wood was used for cultic and medicinal incenses (cf. **Incense, Cedar**). The ancient Germans considered juniper sacred; it was the 'tree of life'. They attached juniper branches to their houses to protect them from demonic powers, and gave them to the dead to aid them on their path to Valhalla. The old Germans and Finnish tribes used juniper berries as an additive to their ritual **Beers**. Juniper branches were burned continuously during the Middle Ages to dispel the many demons, devils, witches, goblins, vermin, and 'satanic' snakes from human settlements. Decoctions of juniper berries were said to give the gift of prophecy, while the inflorescence was claimed to effect love magic and was used in necromantic exorcisms.

The shamans of many Siberian groups inhale juniper smoke to induce trance. The shamans of most of the peoples of the Himalayas (Sherpa, Tibetan nomads, Tamang, Nepali) inhale juniper smoke prior to carrying out rituals, oracles, exorcisms, or healings. They generally use needles of the mountain juniper (*Juniperus recurva*). Often, these are mixed with incense resin. The juniper is sacred to the shamans of the Dards (a group living in northwest Pakistan) and to the trance priests of their neighbors, the Kafirs. They inhale its smoke before all of their magical activities. The Hunza say the following about their shamans, known as *Bitaiyo*:

> 'In Hunza, the *Bitaiyo* are viewed as humans with supernatural powers whose services are used for prophecy, magic, and healing. They manifested their abilities only after inhaling the smoke of burning juniper branches and drinking warm goat blood. Afterwards, they danced to rhythmic drumbeats until they attained a state of trance. When asked about the future, they would pass on the fairies' messages in the form of songs' (Felmy 1986:19).

Sometimes, the Hunza combine juniper branches with seeds of **Syrian Rue**. Many American Indian groups used juniper branches in a similar manner. The Tarahumara in particular used juniper as a ritual incense.

Pharmacology: All species of juniper contain an essential oil which is primarily composed of monoterpenes (α-pinene, camphene, terpineol, borneol, isoborneol, juniper camphor). This oil has tonic, antiseptic, diuretic, depurative, and digestive effects. No psychotropic properties have yet been detected.

Literature: Drury & Drury 1987; Felmy 1986; Knoll-Greiling 1959; Knecht 1971.

JUREMA (Mimosa hostilis, Mimosa nigra and Pithecolobium diversifolium). Jurema is a Brazilian name for a drink resembling **Ayahuasca**. Many Amazon Indians (Pankarurú, Karirí, Tusha, Fulnio, and others) produced jurema drinks from the roots of a number of mimosa species and consumed these in communal ritual circles. Among the Indians, however, the use of jurema has all but disappeared. It is only occasionally mentioned even in the older ethnographic literature. It is said that this 'mysterious drink' provided the medicine men with fantastic dreams pregnant with meaning, it 'enchanted the natives and carried them to heaven'. In the jurema ceremony, 'the old master of the ceremony, shaking a rattle decorated with feather mosaics, handed the participants a bowl of tea made from jurema root. They then obtained wondrous visions of the spirit world, of flowers and birds. They might obtain a glimpse of the roaring rocks which crushed the souls of the dead on their journey or see the thunderbird as he shoots lightning from the gigantic bundle of feathers on his head and lets the thunder rumble' (after Lowie, in Schultes & Hofmann 1980:154). Crushed mimosa roots were also smeared upon the soles of the feet, which effected aphrodisiac love magic. This practice was said to have been especially popular among females.

By the turn of the century, the ritual and magical use of a vinho de jurema had already been integrated into several Afro-Brazilian cults (Candomblé, Macumba). A *vinho de jurema*, made from the roots of the jurema branca plant *Pithecolobium diversifolium*, appears to have established itself among adherents of a number of West Africa cults. Using natural consciousness-expanding drugs was a way to honor the Candomblé god Ossain, the great magician, protector of the sacred plants, and discoverer of medicinal plants (cf. **Coleus**).

Pharmacology: The roots of *Mimosa hostilis* and *M. nigra* contain 0.57% N,N-dimethyltryptamine (DMT). Since orally ingested DMT is only psychedelically effective in the presence of an MAO inhibitor, one of the ingredients of the jurema drink must be an as yet unknown plant containing harmaline or a similar substance (cf. **Ayahuasca, Snuff**). Whether this plant is **Ayahuasca** has not been determined, although more recent reports suggest that this is a possibility. The composition and pharmacology of *Pithecolobium* are unknown. Jurema offers a fertile area for future work.

Literature: Schultes & Hofmann 1980.

KAVA-KAVA (Piper methysticum). In the South Pacific, kava-kava is the name of a plant from the pepper family as well as the name of a stimulating or inebriating drink made from this plant. Kava-kava is cultivated in plantations on most of the Pacific islands (Fiji, Tonga, Marquesas, Wallis et Fortuna, and others). The physician-sorcerers of the South Seas use the plant, and especially its root, as a powerful weapon against demons and as a healing plant to soothe all manner of ailments. Chewing kava-kava is also said to incite the power of love.

The social and ceremonial use of kava-kava is extremely important. Every outsider or visitor is offered kava-kava in greeting. To prepare it, the grated root is macerated in cold water. The resulting drink stimulates and refreshes. Kava-kava roots and drinks are also offered to the Gods:

> 'Here is Awa [= kava-kava] for you Gods, gaze with friendship upon

this family, let it thrive and grow and let us all remain healthy; let our plantings, our fruits be good; give us an abundance of food. Here is Awa for you Gods of War! Let a strong lineage grow in this land for you. Here is Awa for you Gods of Wind! Do not come to this land, but go across the ocean to another' (after Lewin 1886:23).

In communal rituals, especially on Ponape, young men or women chew vast amounts of fresh kava-kava roots and then spit the resulting root and saliva mixture into a ceremonial pot filled with water. After several hours, the kava-kava drink is 'ripe', i.e., has been fermented by the saliva. Cups of the drink are then distributed to all the participants in the ceremony. Everyone drinks together, and they all drink the same amount. Before they begin, they sprinkle several drops onto the earth in order to ward off evil spirits and demons. After several rounds, the drink begins to take effect. It is said that the participants leave their bodies and glide bodiless over the tropical island world and into the heavens, where the kava-kava plant originated. They experience sensations of fraternization and unity with their environment. Erotic visions are also common.

Hawaiian Huna magicians (*kahuna*) also used kava-kava (awa) to prepare a poisonous drink. They boiled kava-kava along with the leaves of *Tephrosia piscatoria, Daphne indica*, and *Lagenaria sp.* It was said that collecting the awa roots on days of abundant rain would increase their efficacy. Occasionally, pieces of kava-kava are also added to **Betel** packets.

Pharmacology: Kava-kava roots contain the pyrones kawain, dihydrokawain, dihydromethysticin, and methysticin, which are chemically related to longystiline (cf. **Balche'**). These substances have stimulating effects. When fermented with human saliva, they are transformed into substances with opiate-like effects (**Poppy**). Kava-kava is an effective antidote for strychnine poisoning (cf. **Nux Vomica**).

Literature: Efron 1967; Kepler 1983; Lewin 1886; Lindstrom 1987; McBride 1988.

KORIBO (Tanaecium nocturnum). This climbing plant, a member of the begonia family, is found in the tropical regions of Central and South America and in the West Indies. Its long, white flowers open at the onset of night and exude a powerful scent similar to that of almond oil. The Lacandon Indians of southern Mexico, who ritually manufacture rubber figures to offer to the gods or for magical purposes, use the milky sap contained in the stalk as a vulcanizer. The Karitiana Indians of Brazil use the plant for healing. A tea made from the leaves of the koribó liana and an as yet unidentified bean vine is ingested to treat heavy diarrhoea. In South Columbia, the Choco Indians esteem the plant for its aphrodisiac properties.

The Paumarí Indians, who live in the center of the Amazon region, use koribó leaves to prepare a ritual **Snuff**. They roast and then pulverize fresh leaves of the liana. The fine powder which results is mixed with ground **Tobacco** (*Nicotiana tabacum*). The Paumarí appear to be the only group to make and use this snuff, which is known as *koribó-nafuni*. Only men (primarily shamans) may use the snuff. It is sniffed at all ritual occasions, including rites of passage (initiations), with the aid of a bone tube. The shamans sniff it prior to every treatment of a patient. This aids them in recognizing diseases and removing their causes (evil magic). Through the aid of *koribó-nafuni*, the shamans enter a clairvoyant trance which normal people cannot attain. A Paumarí man who was not a shaman provided the following description of the powder's effects: 'It makes you dizzy, gives headaches, and makes a person want to throw themselves into the sea'. Although women are not allowed to use the snuff, they do use the koribó vine. They make a tea from the root cortex which is said to cause drowsiness, weakened concentration, and distorted perceptions. It is not known why the women drink this tea. It may be that it also has erotic effects and is used as an aphrodisiac.

Pharmacology: The fresh leaves contain a high concentration of hydrogencyanides which have toxic and perhaps psychoactive effects (dizziness, feebleness, vomiting). Saponines are present in the entire plant. True hallucinogenic substances have not been detected.

Literature: Prance et al. 1977; Schultes & Hofmann 1980.

KRATOM (Mitragyna speciosa). This tree, a relative of **Yohimbe**, is found in Southeast Asia. Its leaves are especially used in Siam. In Thailand and Malaysia, the leaves are chewed, smoked, or made into tea. Many Malays were observed using the leaves chronically (several leaves 3-10 times a day) for over five years, and no side-effects or addictive behaviors were detected. It is chewed as an opium substitute (cf. **Poppy**), and serves as a narcotic additive to **Betel** packets. The dried leaves are also smoked as a substitute for **Hemp**. Chewing kratom is said to calm the mind. An oily liquid known as *mambog* is distilled from the fresh leaves. This is also used as an opium substitute.

Pharmacology: The leaves contain at least 22 alkaloids from the indole and oxindole family. The LSD-like indole alkaloid mitragynine is the main active ingredient. This substance has euphoriant and mild psychoactive effects. Medicinally, it acts as an antipyretic and analgesic agent. Stimulant effects not unlike those of cocaine have also been observed. The stimulating effects of the leaves begin after 5-10 minutes. In Thailand, experiments are being conducted to determine whether mitragynine is suitable as a substitute for methadone and as a general treatment for opiate addiction.

Literature: Emboden 1972; Jansen & Prast 1988a, 1988b; Scholz & Eigner 1983.

LAKSHMANA (Calonyction muricatum). The lakshmana liana is a member of the **Morning Glory** family. It grows in India, where it creeps over bushes and trees like a snake. In the Ayurvedic system, lakshmana is *the* classical aphrodisiac (*vajikarana*). It is said that the root induces fertility, increases potency, and multiplies all erotic pleasures. The liana is a yoga medicine which is used to practise kundalini yoga. The kundalini is a non-material serpent which snakes through a person's energy centers (chakras) in order to raise consciousness to a higher level, thereby granting the yogi insights into a higher domain; like **Hemp**, the vine is considered food for the kundalini serpent. In Tantric magical practices, the lakshmana plant is used together with a bezoar stone (cf. Rätsch & Guhr 1989) to make a magical ointment. The Tantrics massage this ointment onto their foreheads at the precise point where the third eye is hidden. The ointment causes an irresistible love magic and provides mystical insights. In Ayurvedic alchemy, lakshmana oil was used to thicken mercury. The entire plant is mentioned as an elixir of life for rejuvenation. When an old man takes the plant for 90 days, his skin once more becomes smooth, his hair dark, his muscles taut, and he becomes filled with tremendous life energy. A paste of crushed leaves and urine is smeared into the nasal apertures as an antidote for snakebites. South Indian snake charmers carry the root with them to magically protect themselves against snakebites. The root is also considered to be a universal antidote for every type of poisoning.

Pharmacology: The entire plant contains up to 3.7% behenic acid, a central nervous system stimulant which also has psychoactive and aphrodisiac effects.

Literature: Kumaraswamy, in Schröder 1985:109-120; Rätsch 1990a.

LAUGHING MUSHROOM (Paneolus papilianaceus). The first mention of this mushroom — referred to as *hsiao-ch'ün* — occurs in the Chinese natural history of Chang Hua (290 AD): 'In the mountains south of the Yangtze, mushrooms grow on tall trees from spring until summer which taste delicious but can be deadly. It is said that these mushrooms are usually poisonous. They grow by the Fêng trees (*Liquidambar*); if they are eaten, they cause a man to laugh without reason.' It was thought that the poison was produced by the snakes which slithered past. The antidote was **Tea** with alum and fresh spring water.

In Japan, the mushroom is known as *waraitake*, 'laughing mushroom'. The Taoists probably used it when preparing their life-extending magical drinks. The laughing mushroom has a wide geographic distribution. Portuguese witches consume it ritually (Graves 1961). This mushroom may be identical with the mysterious 'fool's fungus' (*Narrenschwämmen*) mentioned in many old books of herbal lore.

Pharmacology: The laughing mushroom may possibly contain the psychedelically active indole alkaloids psilocybin and psilocin (cf. **Teonanacatl**). According to Ranke-Graves, eating the mushroom evoked effects similar to those of mescaline (cf. **Peyote**).

Literature: Li 1978; Graves 1961; Sandford 1972.

LETTUCE (Lactuca virosa). In ancient Egypt, lettuce (*L. sativa* and *L. virosa*) was one of the most important attributes of Min, the god of fertility. A lettuce patch was carried in procession during the festival of the god. The plant was considered an aphrodisiac and was a popular sacrificial offering. Both lettuce species were used medicinally. The Copts had a recipe consisting of *virosa* latex, **Opium**, and honey. Strangely, the Greeks, and most likely especially the puritan Pythagoreans, thought that lettuce (*L. sativa*) was an anaphrodisiac. Since the Middle Ages, lettuce (*L. virosa*) has been an ingredient in **Witches' Ointments** and the source of lactucarium or 'lettuce opium'. This 'opium' is obtained by drying the white sap contained in the stalk. North American Indians mixed this 'lettuce opium' into their ritual and magical smoking blends. Lettuce leaves and roots are smoked as an aphrodisiac in modern secret sexual magical circles. Additional research into the use of lettuce is required.

Pharmacology: The milky sap contains lactucin (a morphine analog), lactucerol, lactuan acid, gum, essential oil, and mannitol. The sap has mild narcotic and sedative properties. The aphrodisiac and anaphrodisiac effects are still controversial.

Literature: Andoh 1986; Lurker 1987; Manniche 1989; Miller 1985.

LING-CHIH (Ganoderma lucidum). The name of this naturally very rare, woody, and non-perishable mushroom means 'divine mushroom of immortality' (cf. **Fly Agaric, Mushrooms, Soma**). It is a symbol of eternal life, perfect wisdom, and a happy fate. Anyone who finds and partakes of it becomes immortal. The Taoist alchemists sang the praises of this mushroom and its divine magical powers. It was numbered first among the 120 'plants of the gods'. It gives eternal youth, makes a person immortal, confers perfect health, and is a good omen. Chinese folklore contains numerous legends describing the adventurous search for the ling-chih, the 'plant of the legendary magician'. Even today, very expensive specimens can be purchased at the Canton herbal market. They are still considered wondrous magical plants. Mixed with **Ginseng**, they are drunk as elixirs of life.

In Japan, the mushroom is known as *reishi*. Because of its great rarity, it is also referred to as the 'phantom mushroom'. Its hardness and durability are reflected in another name, *mannentake*, the 'ten thousand year mushroom'. In Japan, it grows almost exclusively on plum trees. When it emerges in very dark surroundings, it does not form a cap, but rather takes on the appearance of antlers (*rokkakushi*). These unique *reishi* mushrooms possess especially great magical powers and command great prices as aphrodisiacs and amulets. When used as an amulet or talisman, they are hung over doors and house entrances or carried by a person. It wards off all that is evil and attracts all that is good. When hung over the bed, it also safeguards a person's fertility. It is especially famed as a medicine for treating all unknown and incurable diseases. An ancient Japanese text states that 'when you eat it regularly, it will refresh your body and arrest aging. It will extend your age and you will become one of the legendary magicians.'

Pharmacology: The woody fruiting body contains organic acids and a sterol alkaloid. Extracts of the mushroom strengthen the heart, protect the liver, stimulate sexuality, have tonic effects, and shield the nerves. They are used to treat chronic bronchitis, diseases of the coronary arteries, stomach ulcers, hepatitis, arthritis, and high blood pressure. In Japan, the once priceless mushroom is now cultivated and is in clinical use as a highly effective cancer treatment.

Literature: Matsumoto 1977; Rätsch 1990a; Wasson 1972.

LOBELIA (Lobelia cardinalis, Lobelia spp.). In the New World, many lobelia species are used as remedies and as inebriants and magical plants. The Penescot Indians of the northeastern forests of North America used the herbage of *Lobelia inflata* internally to expel evil spirits and for sweating and vomiting cures. The Iroquois considered *Lobelia cardinalis* a cure-all, and mixed it into a number of different medicines. It was said that the plant contained magical powers which strengthened the effects of and had a positive influence upon the other ingredients. The plant also protects from witchcraft, makes its possessor attractive to the opposite sex, and heals all complaints caused by sorrow. Dried leaves of many varieties of lobelia are smoked alone or mixed with **Tobacco**. As a result, lobelia also became known as 'Indian tobacco'. The Mapuche in Chile smoke the herbage of *Lobelia tupa* because of its mild narcotic effects. They call the plant *tupa*, and in Spanish *tabaco del diablo*, 'tobacco of the devil'. The Mapuche and the Araucano obtain a milky sap from the roots which they use externally to treat toothaches and headaches. Further study of the magical use of tupa is needed.

Pharmacology: All varieties of lobelia contain a number of alkaloids (lobeline, lobelanidine, norlobelanidine). These alkaloids effect a short-term stimulation of the body which lasts for only a quarter of an hour. Higher doses may also have narcotic effects.

Literature: Emboden 1976; Herrick 1983; Rätsch 1987f; Schultes & Hofmann 1980.

LOCOWEEDS (Oxytropis lambertii, O. sericea, and Astralagus spp.). When the first white settlers penetrated into the plains and prairies of North America, they soon noticed that their cattle and horses began to behave erratically after eating certain prairie plants. As a result, these small flowering herbs became known by the Spanish/English name locoweeds (*loco* = crazy). In the course of ethnobotanical research, it was found that the Sioux Indians called the *Oxytropis* species *sunkta' pejút'a*, 'horse's medicine', for they had clear psychotropic effects upon their horses (the Lacandon Maya refer to **Thornapple** and **Angel's Trumpet** using a similar term: *ts'ak tsimin*, 'medicine of the horse/tapir'). We know of no ethnomedical use of the locoweeds. In South Dakota, however, it is rumored that the Prairie Indians ingested locoweeds in order to induce visions and that they may have played a role in vision quests.

Pharmacology: The locoweeds contain various toxins which have not been precisely studied. It is not known whether these have psychotropic effects upon humans.

Literature: Reko 1986; Van Bruggen 1983.

LOTUS (Nelumbo nucifera). The lotus is venerated in all Asian and Oriental cultures as a divine plant and viewed as a symbol of perfection, immortality, and enlightenment. The manner in which the plant grows is symbolic of the straight path out of the primeval mud, of the original act of procreation from cloudy water into radiant light. The lotus grows like a **Water Lily**, but its magnificent and pleasantly scented blossom rises far above the surface of the water. In India, the lotus flower symbolizes the origin of the feminine aspect of the universe, especially of the goddess of love. For this reason, the flowers are also capable of effecting love magic. In China, lotus roots and seeds are eaten as a tonic and used as amulets. The ancient Egyptians knew of a related plant (*Nymphaea lotus*) which they cultivated in Pharaonic gardens and venerated as 'the first flower of creation, in which the sun lay hidden'. The lotus flower signified love and was copied in clay or other materials for amulets. Today, we cannot say for sure whether the magical

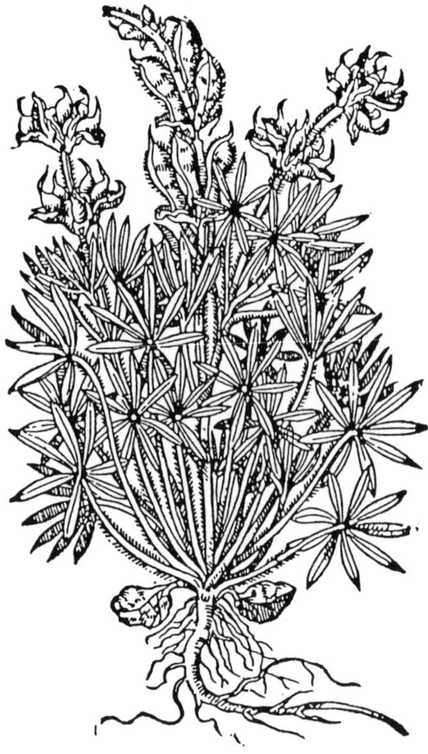

Fig. 14: In ancient times, lupines were used as oracular and magical plants. Members of the Leguminosae, *all lupine species contain tryptamine derivatives and alkaloids (woodcut from Tabernaemontanus).*

powers which were attributed to the lotus were indeed its own or whether they were those of the blue **Water Lily**.

Pharmacology: The edible parts of the plant contain starch, minerals, and vitamins, The flowers contain an essential oil. Psychotropic substances have not been detected.

Literature: Emboden 1978; Engel 1978; Majupuria & Joshi 1988.

LUPINE (Lupinus hirsutus, Lupinus angustifolius). In ancient Greece, lupines were used as food and for their healing and magical powers. The pilgrims who came to the death oracle of Acheron were required to consume large quantities of lupine seeds so that they could establish contact with the dead. Unfortunately, since the oracle guarded its secrets quite well, we know nothing precise about the oracular use of the lupine.

Pharmacology: The seeds contain the alkaloid lupinine, which is chemically related to cytisine (cf. **Beans, Colorines, Genista**). Lupinine has toxic properties which produce restlessness and cramps. Nothing is known about any possible psychotropic effects.

Literature: Baumann 1982; Rätsch 1987e.

MAGUEY (Agave americana). Since ancient times, the Indians of Mesoamerica have cultivated maguey for raw materials (fibers), medicines, food (sugar), and magical charms. The spine-like leaves were used in blood-letting rituals. In Mexico, maguey is used to make an inebriating beverage known as *octli, metl*, or *pulque*. This drink is brewed from the juice which collects in the flower stalk of the maguey over a period of years. To harvest it, an incision is made in the flower stalk as soon as it has begun to sprout. The honey-sweet juice then collects in the resulting cavity. The juice is drawn off periodically and allowed to ferment for three weeks. When the pulque is ripe, it has a grey color and a slightly sour aroma. The maguey plant is home to the Aztec goddess Mayahuel, who was abducted from heaven at the beginning of time and taken into the Sonoran desert, where demons killed her and chopped up her beautiful body. The plumed serpent Quetzalcoatl, the beneficent creator, used her bones to make the first maguey plant.

Formerly, the Aztecs and their neighboring tribes viewed the consumption of pulque as a religious act. A person was not allowed to drink more than four bowls. The Aztecs also used pulque for medicinal purposes. The beverage was known to other Mexican Indian groups as well. The Huaxtec, who lived on the Gulf of Mexico, used pulque in all of their rituals. In contrast to the Aztecs, they glorified the inebriation produced by the drink. There are also signs that pulque was utilized in sexual magic. The evidence suggests the Huaxtec venerated erotic statues. Lying before these statues, men conjoined with women and were administered pulque enemas by the magicians or priests. Ritual anal intercourse appears to have predominated in these rites (**Coca**).

Today, many Mexican Indians still utilize maguey as a medicinal plant. Besides the pulque, all of the other parts of the plant may also be used for medicinal purposes. Pulque is often used as a basis for other medicinal and magical plants, including **Ololiuqui, Peyote, Thornapple,** and **Morning Glory** seeds. It is also considered an aphrodisiac. Maguey leaves, and especially the thorn-like tips, are used as amulets. Attached to the house, they ward off evil, bless the home, and protect from the evil eye (*ojo*) and disease-bearing winds (*aires*).

Pharmacology: The sap contains about 8% sugar (agavose), a pungent essential oil, 3-4% hecogenin, saponin, some papain, and oxalic acid. The leaf tissue produces substances of an 'unclear nature' which act as biogenic stimulants.

Literature: Barrios 1984; Gentry 1982; Guerrero 1985; Pinkava & Gentry 1985; Rätsch 1987f; Smet 1985).

List of Agave species with Ethnobotanical Significance

Species	*Common name(s)*	*Uses*
A. americana	maguey, mescale, metl, pita, tacamba, uadá	pulque, food, medicine, fuel (pencas, 'spikes')
A. augustifolia	babki, mescal de maguey	mezcal (liquor; 'mezcal bacanora') fiber
A. atrovirens	maguey, metl, tlacametl	pulque, medicine (poultice)
A. ferox	maguey	pulque
A. fourcroydes	henequén blanco, saqui	fiber (ropes, hammocks)
A. ixtli	ch'elemci, chucumci, citamci, henequen, xixci, xtuhki	fiber (coarse fabrics, cleaning pads), ritual uses
A. lechuguilla	lechuguilla	fiber ('istle')
A. longifolia	kahumki	fiber
A. lurida	maguey	pulque (syn. mexicana)
A. mapisaga	maguey mapisaga	pulque
A. minima	chukumki, kitamki	fiber
A. potatorum	tlacametl	pulque
A. rigida	zozci	fiber

A. salmiana	maguey de pulque, tlacametl	pulque
A. silvestris	babki, ch'elem, ch'elemki	fiber; magical instruments
A. sisalana	ci, henequen, kih, sisal yaxki, henequen verde	fiber (ropes, hammocks, etc.); medicine (sap); stings for auto-sacrifice
A. tequilana	maguey tequilero, mezcal azul, tequila maguey	Tequila, Mezcal (liquor)
A. undulata	boxhunpets'k'inki	fiber

MAIZE (Zea mays). This corn or grain was cultivated by paleo-Indians in Mexico some 4,500 years ago. The Indians of Central America venerate maize, for it keeps people alive. When a person fell so ill that they stopped eating maize, they were said to be incurable and already dead. The Maya say that when a person falls ill, they should eat only maize, the plant with the greatest life energy. Many Indians also use maize pistils and leaves as medicines. They use dried kernels as oracles and wear them as amulets. In former times, some Aztec magicians were so specialized that they functioned solely as maize oracles. Today, the Lacandon Maya hang ears of corn on the walls on their houses for protection. Benevolent spirits live in the kernels which are able to dispel demons.

Many South American Indians use maize to brew an inebriating and healing **Beer** known as *chicha*.

> 'Not just the use, but also the preparation of chicha was a sacred act and a duty of the virgins of the sun. The maize was chewed and spit into an earthen vessel to ferment. The sun's power had been collected in the ripe corn, and its inebriating power was distilled into the chicha. Mixing the maize with saliva, which was also attributed with magical powers, gave it extra power. A person who drinks chicha is literally drinking the essence of the sun, concentrated in the plant during the course of the summer. And thus, chicha was the appropriate drink at the high festivals, for they were all dedicated to the highest god of the sun' (Wedemeyer 1972:100f.).

Although copious quantities of chicha were consumed at cultic orgies, the use of chicha was not restricted to religious occasions alone. Chicha was also said to be a good remedy for pain and suffering and was reputed to be an aphrodisiac. Before drinking chicha, a person would spit out the first draught as an offering to Mother Earth. Chicha is used in conjunction with most magical acts, and is often combined with other magical plants: **Angel's Trumpet, Coca, San Pedro Cactus, Thorn-apple, Villca.**

Pharmacology: Maize pistils contain glycosides, saponins, essential oil, fat, resin, tannin, vitamins C and K, alkaloids, allantoin, potassium salts, and phytosterol. Chicha has a low alcohol content.

Literature: Ma'ax & Rätsch 1984; Moore 1989; Rätsch 1987f; Wedemeyer 1972.

MANACA (Brunfelsia spp.). There are some 25 varieties of manaca root in the New World. These grow wild in the Amazonian rain forests and on several Caribbean islands. Many South American Indians cultivate them for their beauty and their medicinal qualities. They call the violet, yellow, or white blooming shrubs *chiricaspi, chiricsanango*, or 'cold tree', and occasionally **Borrachero**. Columbian Indians consider it a sister of **Angel's Trumpet**; botanically, both plants are members of the nightshade family. Indians utilize the root to treat snakebite and as a medicine to remedy yellow fever. Throughout the Amazon, manaca is used as an aphrodisiac, anti-syphilitic agent, and as a diuretic, purgative, and abortifacient. The Kofán Indians of Columbia drink a tea made from the bark. They say that it cools the body so greatly that demonic fevers are forced to flee. The plant is also used for psychedelic or narcotic reasons. Further research, however, is necessary to clarify the precise details of such use. The shamans and magicians of the Jíbaro and Kofán add manaca roots to **Ayahuasca** drinks so that they are able to discern the nature of their patients' ailments when they are in the clairvoyant state.

Pharmacology: The root contains atropine-like alkaloids (brunfelsin, manacin, mandargorine, cuscohygrine, and franciscaine) and the cumarin scopoletine.

Literature: Rätsch 1987f; Schultes 1979; Schultes & Hofmann 1980.

MANDRAKE (Mandragora spp.). Many species of mandrake are native to the Eastern Mediterranean, the Middle East, and the Indian subcontinent. All varieties are very similar in appearance, with the leaves growing directly out of a long, often anthropomorphic root. In the regions where it is indigenous and in many areas beyond, mandrake is considered to be *the* magical root. Probably no other magical plant is so steeped in myth and has been the object of such desire as the mandrake. Entire libraries have been written about its history as a magical and medicinal plant, amulet and talisman, 'little man of the gallows' ('Galgenmännlein'), and plant spirit.

The Sumerians referred to mandrake as *nam-tar*, 'plague god plant'. The ancient Egyptians used mandrake (*Mandragora officinarum*) to increase potency, as an aphrodisiac, and to ensure fertility. A mandrake beer was very popular (**Beer**). One Coptic name of the plant was 'devil's testicle'. Even today, the mandrake is a sacred plant among the Bedouins of Israel.

To improve its effectiveness, mandrake was often mixed with **Wine**. The magicians of Mesopotamia also considered it a magic charm. The mandrake was one of the plants of the gods, a food of the satyrs, and a magical weapon with miraculous power. The famous rituals involving rhizotomes began in antiquity. It was said that a spirit lived in the root who could kill the careless rhizotome when they pulled out the root. For this reason, dogs were often enlisted to remove the roots from the earth, the dark realm of Hecate. Frequently, the ground around the root was consecrated with urine, menstrual blood, or sperm. In Rumania, sexual magical rituals for excavating the root have continued into the twentieth century. A person who possesses a mandrake root can awaken love, will have good fortune in both business and play, be fertile (potent), remain healthy, be protected from harmful spells and ghosts, be able to divine the future and make prophecies, and may attain eternal life. Among the Hebrews, the mandrake was the most important magical plant of all, as it later was for the Arabs and a number of Asian peoples as well.

> 'The Moslems had acquainted the Chinese with the mandrake in Central or Western Asia by the thirteenth century at the latest. The Chinese name (*ya-pu-lu*) is a transcription of *yabrûh*. According to the classical instructions for its use: a tunnel was dug in the ground until it reached the root, which was then dug out by dogs, which of course died afterwards as a result of the poisonous airs surrounding the plant. The plant was then hidden in the ground for a year so that it dried out. Even one small taste was sufficient to render a man senseless and like dead for three days' (Eberhard 1983:20).

Mandrake was also a very popular ingredient in love potions and **Witches' Ointments**.

Many famous magical plants of antiquity have been associated or even identified with mandrake: **Belladonna, Ginseng, Haoma, Jangida, Lakshmana, Moly, Scopolia, Soma.** Since mandrake was both rare and perilous to collect, it was also extremely expensive. As a result, the roots of other plants were often sold as mandrake: **False Mandrake, Ginger, Ginseng, May Apple, Orchids,** Celandine (*Chelidonium majus*; cf. Mitrovic 1907:233) and the English Mandrake (*Bryonia spp.*; cf. Dahl 1985).

Pharmacology: All mandrake species contain up to 0.4% alkaloids (scopolamine, atropine, apotropine, hyoscyamine, hyoscine, cuscohygrine, solandrine, mandragorine, and other active tropane alkaloids). These constituents have strong psychoactive effects, and can produce hypnotic

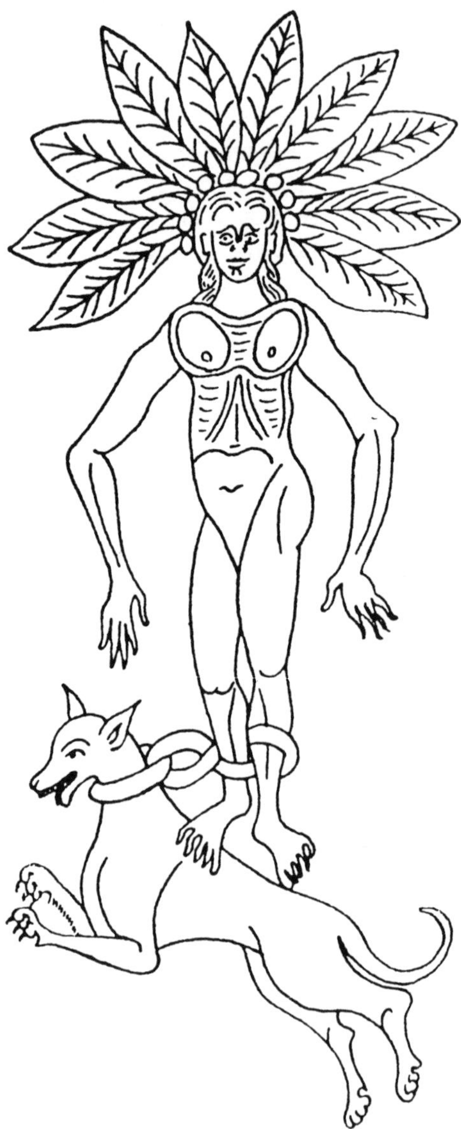

Fig. 15: Medieval representation of the mandrake as the Galgenmännlein, *or 'little man of the gallows' (England, 13th century).*

states. Higher doses can induce delirium and lead to death by respiratory paralysis. Reports concerning its aphrodisiac properties are ambiguous.

Literature: Berry & Jackson 1976; Eliade 1942, 1982; Jackson & Berry 1979; Khlopin 1980; Kreuter 1982; Manniche 1989; Marzell 1927; Mehra 1979; Müller-Ebeling 1987; Rätsch 1990a; Rahner 1957; Schlosser 1986; Schmidbauer 1968, 1984; Starck 1986; Tercinet 1950; Thompson 1968.

MATÉ (Ilex paraguariensis). Maté is a name given to the dried or roasted leaves of the maté yerba shrub. It has been used ritually in South America for thousands of years. Maté leaves have been recovered from pre-Columbian graves in the Andes region. A number of graves discovered in Argentina were found to contain *cuyas* (gourd vessels lined with silver). These were left with the dead so that they could make stimulating maté tea and remain awake during their journey to the heavenly afterworlds.

The Guaraní Indians venerate the spirit (called *ka'a yary*) of the maté yerba shrub. According to legend, the plant was originally a young maiden who was transformed into a shrub. This spirit must be honored and esteemed. The Guaraní also believe that the plant spirit will protect respectful persons but will punish anyone who exploits it immoderately with sickness and death. The spirit often appears as a beautiful young woman who seductively entices men. Any man who gives in to her call will vanish into the forest forever. Guaraní shamans also use maté tea. They prepare a potent decoction from the leaves which, when imbibed, produce the magical effects which enable a shaman to enter a clairvoyant trance. Maté is also used in communal ritual circles. Unfortunately, we have no precise information about the use of maté as a magical plant. We do know, however, that there are many parallels to the use of **Guayusa**.

Pharmacology: Maté leaves contain bound caffeine, theobromine, theophylline, chlorogenic acid, aromatic substances (including theophylline, chlorogenic acid, aromatic substances (including traces of vanillin), fatty oil, tannins, and resins. Maté has mild stimulating effects and is a weak purgative, diuretic, and appetite suppressant. It seems likely that the stimulating effects which maté has upon the central nervous system aided shamans to open their consciousness to other worlds.

Literature: Melzer 1985, 1987; Rätsch 1987f.

MAY APPLE (Podophyllum peltatum). The may apple, known also as American mandrake, is indigenous to eastern North America. It thrives in the moist undergrowth of shadowy deciduous forests. The Indians of the area used the root as a highly effective agent to treat intestinal parasites and for inducing abortions. The woodland tribes used the plant as a purgative and anthelmintic. The rootstock was apparently used as an amulet and magical agent as well, for the early European settlers named this New World plant after the **Mandrake**. With this, they also brought Old World beliefs about the mandrake into the New World.

Today, may apple root is an important love charm and amulet in the North American voodoo or hoodoo religion. Pieces of the plant are sold in Voodoo Drug Stores, which are primarily frequented by blacks. They say that a piece of the root should be carried as a talisman or amulet, preferably in the pocket of a person's pants. So that the 'vibrations' are not disturbed, a may apple should not be touched by anyone except its possessor. The root is said to make one desirable, lucky in love, provide wealth, and protect from evil magic, magical spells, the evil eye, and demons. If a person looses their root, they must reckon with misfortune.

There is evidence that the may apple also played a role in ancient Chinese magic (cf. **Hemp**).

Pharmacology: The rootstock contains a resin, podophyllin. Podophyllin contains podophyllotoxin and α- and ß-peltatins, which have drastic purgative effects. These stimulate intestinal peristalsis and the secretions of the large intestine and kill intestinal parasites. Podophyllotoxin also appears to inhibit the growth of certain tumors. Podophyllum contains drugs which are effective in treating certain virus and skin cancer diseases (venereal warts). Psychotropic effects are unknown.

Literature: Emboden 1974; Rätsch 1987a; Riva 1974.

MEAD. Mead is a generic term used to refer to drinks made from honey, water, and other ingredients. Mead may be humanity's oldest alcoholic beverage. It was originally made and consumed solely in conjunction with religious rituals in order to establish contact with the gods. The meads made by the Germanic tribes (*met*; cf. **Beer**) are renowned; a variety of 'bitter herbs' were used as additives, including **Henbane, Poppy, Wild Rosemary**, and perhaps also **Belladonna, Hemp**, or **Mandrake**. It has been suggested that prehistoric Africans made a type of mead using mushrooms which contained psilocybin (cf. **Mushrooms, Teonanacatl**). The Maya added a number of magical plants and toads to their mead (cf. **Balche'**).

Pharmacology: The general inebriating effects of mead are a result of its alcohol content. Depending upon the other ingredients, the finished mead may have specific psychedelic, psychotropic, or other effects. Some of the arieties of honey used to make mead may have themselves had psychoactive effects. The subject of mead still presents many questions for research. One especially interesting puzzle is to reconstruct the skaldic mead of old Nordic Europe.

Literature: Hartwich 1911; Höfler 1990; Huber 1929; Schlosser 1987.

MISTLETOE (Viscum album). Mistletoe is a parasitic plant which grows on trees. The Germans considered it a terrible magical weapon which brought death. With **Vervain**, it was the most important of the Celtic druid's sacred plants, and was their most mysterious magical plant. They used it to prepare magical drinks which gave strength, courage, and invincibility, healed all illnesses, rendered all poisons ineffective, and made both humans and animals fertile. Mistletoe was used as an apotropaic amulet, talisman, and a blessing for marriage and love. An evergreen plant which bears fruit in winter, it became a symbol of the winter solstice and the festival of the new year. In Tyrolia, mistletoe is known as *Drudenfuss* ('pentacle') and is said to protect against witches and devils. It has also been referred to as 'witch's broom' and used as an oracular plant.

The North American mistletoe (*Phoradendron flavescens*) is carried as a love charm and amulet by adherents of the voodoo religion. It is sacred to Erzulie, the goddess of love.

Pharmacology: Mistletoe contains glycosides, alkaloids, poisonous viscotoxins, sugar, lectins, and phenethylamine. Extracts of mistletoe have anticarcinogenic properties and strengthen the immune system. Psychoactive effects like those described in the ancient literature have not been observed with mistletoe.

Literature: Becker & Schmoll 1986; Markale 1989; Riva 1974.

MOLY (not yet identified). Moly is the famed Hermetic magical plant which Hermes, the mediator between above and below, gave Odysseus so that he could defend himself against the magic of Circe. Its earliest botanical mention is in Theophrastus: 'Moly grows in the area of Pheneus and in the mountains of Cyllene. It is used in antidotes and in magic.'

The authors of antiquity disagreed as to the botanical identity of the plant. But a variety of evidence suggests that moly was both an abstract term for magical plants in general as well as a common name for several plants sacred to the peoples of Persia and Egypt: **Syrian Rue**, the hôm or **Haoma**, and besasa, the sacred plant of the god Bes (cf. **Syrian Rue**). Dioscorides, who came from a region in which this plant grew and was used for religious and magical purposes, indicated that moly was Syrian rue. In the course of history, however, moly has also been identified as black **Hellebore, Garlic, False Mandrake**, squill, and the magic leek (*Allium moly*). Plutarch described the Persian cult surrounding the plant omomi (an incorrect spelling of moly): 'While invoking Hades and the darkness, the Persians crush in a mortar a certain plant which they call omomi, mix this with the blood of a slaughtered wolf, and then throw it away at a place which the sun does not shine upon.'

Hermes, the inventor of magical practices, was knowledgeable in Thessalian magic and was viewed as the leader who used his staff to point the human souls towards the light or the darkness; he was the 'leader of all magicians' (Parisian magical papyrus). Moly is the plant of the Cyllenic Hermes, and is thus a magical mediator between the world of light and world of darkness; moly joins god and demon and stands at the beginning of alchemy. This Hermetic plant provides knowledge, uncovers the hidden

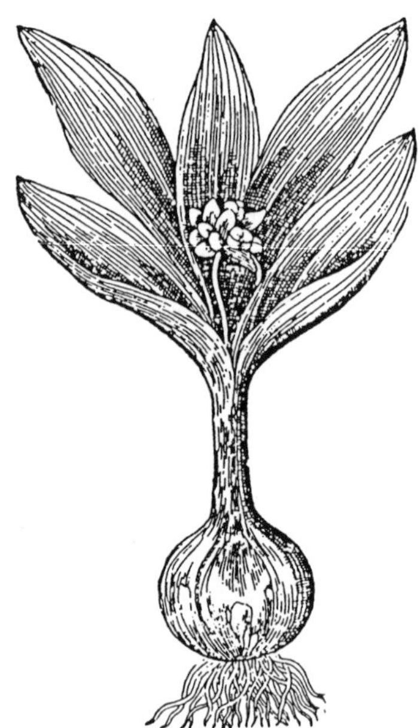

Fig. 16: Many of the old herbals claimed that the true identity of the legendary moly was the squill, a non-European species of onion. The illustrations in these books reflect this erroneous interpretation (woodcut from Tabernaemontanus).

secrets of existence, and gives insight into a divine wisdom which only strong persons are able to bear. Moly is the 'beneficial pharmacon'. The mystical qualities of moly are described in the Homeric verse of Maximo: 'I see the moly, and I become conscious of its secret: for I know very well how difficult it is to find the path to the good.' But it is also said that digging for the root of the moly could bring death to the unwary (unaware!) rhizotome (cf. **Mandrake**). The flower of Hermes or Mercury entered the folk medicine of the Middle Ages in the form of rue. One medieval rue spell included the following passage: 'I bless you, creature of the rue, so that you may serve to eradicate the devil and all of his fellows' (cf. **Rue**).

Pharmacology: The sources make no mention of any pharmacological effects of moly. If the interpretation as Syrian rue is in fact correct, then moly would have had psychotropic properties which conform well to Hermetic symbolism.

Literature: Rahner 1957.

MORNING GLORY (Ipomoea spp.). Vines and creepers are found throughout the world. Some have gained cultural significance as decorative plants, others as medicinal or magical plants (cf. **Borrachero, Lakshmana, Ololiuqui, Woodrose**). The Aztecs referred to the violet-blossomed morning glory (*Ipomoea violacea*) as *tlitliltzin*, and utilized it in the same manner as the **Ololiuqui** vine. The Spanish physician Fernando Hernandez wrote: 'When the Indians made an offering and asked something of their gods and wanted to obtain an answer, they ate so much of this plant that they became senseless and, dancing, saw phantoms and visions brought about by the demon which lingered around them.' Even today, healers and diviners in Oaxaca and Chiapas (Southern Mexico) ingest the seeds of *Ipomoea rubrocaerulea* and *Ipomoea tricolor*. The vines are fairly common at ancient ritual sites, Mayan ruins, and places of power.

Midwives give seeds of the white morning glory (*Ipomoea violacea* var. *Pearly Gates*), which the Maya called *xtóntikin*, 'dry penis', to women in labor to ease birth. The Yucatán Maya smoke the leaves of this plant as an aphrodisiac.

The Iroquois call the root of Ipomoea pandurata 'manroot' (cf. **Ginseng**). Their medicine men warned of the power of the root. A person who rubbed it on their finger could kill another merely by touching them. Hunters carried the root on their expeditions. It gave them the strength to carry two deer. When taken as a medicine, the root provided strength and healed all diseases. It was used in the various initiatory rites of the secret longhouse societies. Because of their strict code of silence, however, we do not know how it was used. The root can also be misused for the dark intrigues of witches. For this reason, it was itself also considered a 'witch' and viewed with fear.

Pharmacology: Identical or similar to **Ololiuqui**. Most *Ipomoea* seeds contain indole alkaloids (lysergic acid). The average dosage ranges from 3-40 seeds. The alkaloid content of the seeds is somewhat variable.

Literature: Herrick 1983; Hofmann 1983; Schultes & Hofmann 1980; Wasson 1962.

MUSHROOMS (Agaricaceae). Since antiquity, people have both honored and feared mushrooms. Because of their unusual appearance, manner of growth, and effects upon humans and animals, mushrooms have been viewed both as manifestations of the divine and embodiments of the demonic. In some cultures, mushrooms were taboo; the Pharaohs forbade normal mortals to even touch them. The ancient Hebrews found these entities so eerie that they also imposed taboos on them.

Throughout history, mushrooms have been used as magical devices, foods, poisons, medicines, and sacraments. Poisonous mushrooms (*Amanita phalloides, Inocybe spp., Boletus satanas*) were used for harmful magic. Other varieties were used in making elixirs of immortality (**Ling-Chih**). Many mushrooms have been associated with the activities of witches and fairies ('fairy rings', 'toadstools', etc.; cf. **Ergot**).

The phalloid fungi (*Phallus impudicus, Phallus spp.*), the puff-ball (*Elaphomyces cervinus*), and the panther mushroom (*Amanita pantherina*) are all valued as aphrodisiacs. Many psychoactive mushrooms were and still are used as sacraments and plants of magic and prophecy: **Fly Agaric, Jambur, Laughing Mushroom, Teonanacatl.**

A large number of mushrooms, especially from the genus *Psilocybe*, have psychedelic effects. The 'liberty cap' (*Psilocybe semilanceatus*) grows in almost every region and continent in the world. Frequently referred to simply as the 'magic mushroom', it is collected and eaten for its psychedelic effects (a psychedelic dose is 4-8 grams). We know of no traditional use of this species. Mushrooms with psychedelic effects also occur in the genera *Panaeolus, Pholiotina, Panaeolina, Geronema, Hygrocybe, Psathyrella, Inocybe, Gymnopilus, Pluteus, Stropharia*, and *Mycena* (none of which have been used as psychedelics in a traditional context).

It has been claimed that several species of the genus *Boletaceae* can effect a 'mushroom madness' which is known in Papua New Guinea as *kuma* or *amok*.

Pharmacology: Most mushrooms can be consumed without adverse effects. They seldom possess harmful substances. Some *Agaricaceae*, however, can be deadly. Mushrooms of the genera *Stropharia, Psilocybe, Geronema, Hygrocybe, Psathyrella, Pholiotina, Panaeolina, Gymnopilus, Pluteus, Mycena, Panaeolus*, and from the family *Coprinaceae* contain

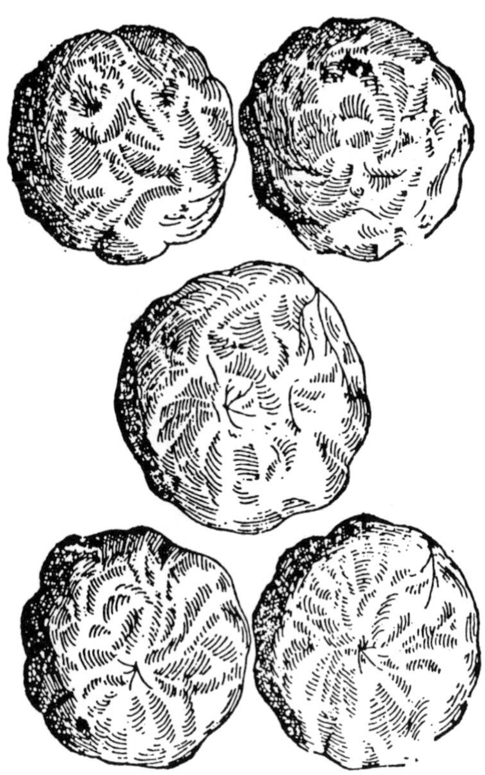

*Fig. 17: Truffles (*Tuber *spp.) have long been used as aphrodisiacs and in love magic, and they are still highly esteemed as a culinary delicacy. Evidence from recent studies into the chemistry of the truffle suggest that its reputation is not unjustified. The subtle aroma of the truffle is chemically analogous to human pheromones, the chemical lures which provoke the sexual interest of the partner (after Tabernaemontanus 1731).*

pyschedelically active tryptamines (psilocybin, psilocin, baeocystin). No active substances have been detected in *Boletus* species, said to be the cause of 'mushroom madness'.

Much work into the pharmacology of mushrooms used as aphrodisiacs and sacraments is still required.

Literature: Allegro 1970; Castaneda 1968, 1971; Festi 1985; Findlay 1982; Gartz 1985, 1986, 1987; Gartz & Drewitz 1985; Haard 1980; McGuire 1982; Ott 1976a; Ott & Bigwood 1978; Pollock 1975, 1977; Reko 1945; Remann 1989; Rubel & Gettelfinger-Krejci 1976; Stamets 1978; Vetterling n.d.; Wasson 1980.

MWAMFI (Erythrophloeum judicale). The mwamfi tree grows in West and Central Africa. It provides a poison used in ordeals (cf. **Calabar Bean**) and is an ingredient in magical medicines. Mwamfi is also known by the names *sassy, n'kassa, muawi, nga, nka,* and *nkasa*. The bark is used for ordeals and for medicinal and magical drinks. To treat malaria, diarrhoea with vomiting, and head aches, a decoction of the bark is taken together with **Tobacco**. When a member of a tribe is accused of sorcery, the fetish priest will make him drink a decoction of mwamfi. The accused must stand and consume the drink in public. If he collapses, he is declared guilty. If he vomits the drink, he is innocent. The Safwa consider mwamfi a sacred tree. They say: 'The people greatly venerate this tree, it incites their amazement; for they must vomit when they drink mwamfi, and therefore it is much sought after.' The tree is used as an oracle and a medicine. Its bark is collected according to an ancient ritual. To ensure that the bark's effects will be beneficial, offerings are first made to the spirit of the tree. When bark is required for an ordeal, then it is prepared the night before with the aid of spells. When an accused person dies, they are dragged to their grave with a rope. 'The magical doctors take possession of a rope which has been used to tie a person killed by mwamfi; it becomes a good and effective magical aid for the hunter, for they make it into an allegory: just as the rope pulled the dead man, so will it also pull forth animal flesh out in the wilderness when they go hunting' (Lewin 1929:8). If a chieftain wishes to determine how many sorcerers and witches live in his village, then he places a kettle with mwamfi bark and water on the fire. All the inhabitants of the village must then reach into the boiling brew. Whoever scalds their hand is shown to be a sorcerer. Those whose hands remain unscathed have no evil spirit within.

Pharmacology: The bark contains toxic substances with effects similar to those of digitalis.

Literature: Engel 1982; Lewin 1929.

NIANDO (Alchornea floribunda). The niando tree grows in Liberia, Nigeria, and Uganda. Its root cortex is added to palm wine and allowed to sit for several days; the resulting liquid is then imbibed as an aphrodisiac. Like love itself, it is said that niando can provide the greatest joy as well as the deepest sorrow. Niando may be combined with **Iboga** and **Yohimbe**. The Gabonese secret cult of Byeri uses it like **Iboga**. The bark is said to have magical powers, and is thus popular with warriors and fetish priests. Research into niando is just beginning.

Pharmacology: The bark contains several not yet identified alkaloids. Older studies have suggested that it contains yohimbine (cf. **Yohimbe**). The alkaloids have hallucinogenic effects; they also stimulate the sympathetic nervous system and increase its sensitivity to ephedrine (cf. **Ephedra**, **Qat**).

Literature: Scholz & Eigner 1983; Rätsch 1990a; Schultes & Hofmann 1980.

NIGHTSHADE (Solanum nigrum). As the name implies, the black nightshade is a member of the nightshade (*Solanaceae*) family. The ancient Greeks knew it by the names *strychnos halikakabos* (cf. **Nux Vomica**), *physalis*, 'bladder plant', and *apollinaris minor*, 'little plant of Apollo'. It was closely associated with **Henbane** and Apollo, the god of oracles. The Thessalian witches used nightshade to make a magical drink which, according to Pliny, evoked 'obscene desires, forms, and images'. Although the nightshade was a common ingredient of **Witches' Ointments**, we know very little about its use as a magical plant. In Africa, the nightshade was used in criminal telepathy and rain magic. It was also ingested in order to locate lost or stolen objects. The nightshade is sacred to the Vodun and Santería gods Oggún and Yemayá and is one of the 21 plants used to make the elixir of life (cf. **Canella**).

Pharmacology: Solanine, an alkaloid mixture with six constituents, is present throughout the plant. Solanine has toxic effects and, although seldom lethal, can be dangerous. No psychedelic components have been detected. On the other hand, many toxic substances can themselves induce trance-like states.

Literature: Andoh 1986; Engel 1979; Mehra 1979; Rätsch 1986b, 1990b.

NUTMEG (Myristica fragrans). The nutmeg tree is one of humankind's oldest cultivated plants. Originally from Asia, it has long been esteemed as a source of spice and as a medicinal and magical plant. In ancient India, the nutmeg (which is actually the seed of a fruit) was called *mada shaunda*, 'narcotic fruit'. It was used as an inebriant and aphrodisiac, added to **Betel** packets, and mixed into curries. In Malaysian magic, possessed persons were given nutmeg to drive out their demons. Arab physicians prescribed nutmeg as an aphrodisiac, potency agent, and provider of fertility. In the Middle Ages, it was one of the most popular of all spices, for it could incite 'commerce with Venus'. In Germany, one love charm was still being used in the nineteenth century: 'like the peppercorn, the nutmeg is used for an unsavory love magic: a girl swallows it, and after the nut has passed out again, she crushes it and mixes it into the food of her beloved (Franconia). As a result of this physical mingling, the aphrodisiac focused the boy's newly kindled desire for love toward that girl alone' (Aigremont 1986:II,83). Since the beginning of the present century, nutmeg has been smoked and eaten as a substitute for marijuana (cf. **Hemp**). It can elicit powerful psychedelic effects: 'Dreams gain in intensity and color' (Henglein 1985:174).

Pharmacology: Nutmeg contains an essential oil comprised of myristicin and safrole (cf. **Sassafras**). The oil has stimulating — and in high doses, toxic — effects. When myristicin is chemically altered through amination, the amphetamine derivative MDA results. When safrole is aminated, MDMA is produced (both MDA and MDMA have gained fame as 'love drugs'; cf. also **Qat**). Presumably, these two oils are metabolically aminated in the body. This biochemical process explains both the inebriating effects of nutmeg and its reputation as an aphrodisiac. High doses of nutmeg can result in unpleasant toxic effects.

Literature: Drury & Drury 1987; in Efron 1967; Rätsch 1990a; Warburg 1897; Weil 1976.

NUX VOMICA (Strychnos nux-vomica). Nux Vomica are the seeds of the strychnine tree, which has been under cultivation since ancient times and is now indigenous to all of the tropical zones of Asia. The fruits and seeds, known as 'crow's eyes' because of their appearance, were primarily used in the production of poisoned arrows, although there was also some medicinal use. These seeds were also important magical objects, and many sorcerers used them as poisons in toxic harmful magic. In smaller doses, however, they were also used in aphrodisiac love magic. In India and Persia, a number of aphrodisiac beverages, electuaries, and pills (*Gandschakini*) contain nux vomica. An Indian recipe for Majun contains crow's eyes together with **Hemp** leaves, **Poppy** leaves, **Thornapple** flowers, sugar, and milk. In Persia, 'orthodox Musulmen' consumed a beverage made of

Hemp, crow's eyes, kali, and **Wine** or a tea (known variously as *bangue, baeng*, or *beng*) of **Hemp, Poppy** leaves, and crow's eyes as an aphrodisiac. Nux vomica is an active ingredient in certain of the famous Oriental joy pills, which are known to produce a sensuous and erotic ecstasy.

Pharmacology: The seeds of nux vomica contain a number of alkaloids and glycosides. The two chief alkaloids are the indole strychnine and its analog brucine. In adults, 2-3 mg of strychnine is sufficient to cause death. Strychnine poisoning is frequently accompanied by strong erections. In small doses (maximum single administration 0.1 g; maximum daily dose 0.2 g), the seeds are an effective aphrodisiac (cf. Stark 1980). Doses about twice this amount can produce mild psychedelic states characterized by increased sensory acuity, involving especially the visual, olfactory, and gustatory faculties. Because of these effects, strychnine and nux vomica have occasionally been sold on the illegal market as LSD. Adolf Hitler is said to have been addicted to strychnine and to have taken large doses to enter a 'euphoric trance'. An effective antidote to nux vomica or strychnine poisonings is **Kava-Kava**.

Literature: Majupuria & Joshi 1988; Müller-Ebeling & Rätsch 1989; Rätsch 1990a; Stark 1980.

OLOLIUQUI (Turbina corymbosa). The ololiuqui vine is a **Morning Glory** which grows almost everywhere in Mexico and adjoining countries. An important magical plant in the Aztec, Mayan, and Zapotec cultures, it was first described by the Spanish physician Francisco Hernandez:

> 'In Mexico, there is a plant which is called snake plant, a creeper with arrow-shaped leaves which is thus also called arrow plant. The seed is used in medicine. Ground and drunk with milk and Spanish pepper, it takes away pain, heals all manner of disturbances, inflammations, and growths. When the priests of the Indians wish to contact the spirits of the dead, they partake of these seeds so that they may become senseless and then see thousands of devilish forms and phantoms around them.'

Ololiuqui seeds were among the most important magical tools of the Aztec divination priests (*naualli*):

> 'They consult them (i.e. the seeds they have ingested) like oracles and converse with them in order to find out what they wish to know, often things that human reason is not capable of recognizing, such as the course of future life or the location of lost or stolen objects. When a person ingests the seeds, they withdraw, shut themselves in, and may not be approached. They believe that a demon resides in the seeds who,

> after they have been eaten, comes out and reveals to the asker whatever he wanted to know' (Ruiz de Alarcon).

The Aztecs attached the same importance to the use of ololiuqui seeds as they did to the use of **Peyote** and **Picietl** (cf. **Teonanacatl**).

The Maya of Yucatán still use the seeds of the ololiuqui vine, which they call *xtabentum* (literally, 'precious stone cord'), for divination and for medicine.

> 'Especially when they are gathered fresh, ground, and ingested in a drink; and when one drinks enough of it, he sees thousands of spirits, has contact with the devil and with hell... When someone loses something valuable, we give him xtabentum to drink. Before he falls asleep, we repeatedly say into his ear: "Where is the lost object". And we describe it. In the sleep of xtabentum which follows, he becomes clear-sighted and sees where the object is. And if it was stolen, he recognizes the thief. Since the sleep is not deep, we can call to him repeatedly and speak with him, like a person who has been hypnotized. He will give clear answers, but slowly and falteringly' (Leuenberger 1979:83,84).

Mayan healers use the seeds of the vine like they use **Thornapple** seeds. The healer falls into a trance after ingesting several seeds. Once in this state, he can make the diagnosis and cure the patient. This trance also aids him in detecting the spirits which cause illness and determine measures to counter them.

In the Zapotecan culture, *piuleros* (professional diviners) ingested *piule* (the Zapotecan name for ololiuqui) so that they could divine and prophesy. Even today, Zapotecs still use the plant to induce a clairvoyant state to recover objects which have been lost, misplaced, or stolen.

Many Indian healers use ololiuqui seeds to treat women's disorders, infertility, fever, and as an aphrodisiac.

Pharmacology: Ololiuqui seeds contain various alkaloids which also occur in **Ergot**, in **Woodrose**, and in several **Morning Glory** species: lysergic acid amide, chanoclavine, elymoclavine, and lysergole. Higher doses of especially lysergic acid amide produces effects similar to those of lysergic acid diethylamide (LSD). The other alkaloids have strong effects upon the uterus (powerful uterine contractions).

Literature: Fields 1968; Hofmann 1964, 1983; Rätsch 1986b, 1987f; Ruiz de Alarcon 1984; Wasson 1971.

ONYCHA (not yet identified). Onycha is one of the legendary magical incenses of antiquity. It is mentioned frequently in the Bible (cf. **Incense**).

According to Dioscorides, onycha was onyx, the keratinous operculum of a marine snail. In the Middle Ages and the early modern period, onycha was listed in pharmacopoeia and herbal books as incense claws or *Unguis odoratum*. The following gastropods were said to provide onycha: *Ampullaria sp., Babylonia spirata, Murex inflatus, Murex brandaris, Murex trunculus, Strombus spp., Turbinella pyrum.* Animal claws or hoofs have also been suggested as sources of onycha, as have a number of plants: bdellium (*Balsamodendron mukul*), labdanum (*Cistus creticus, C. ladaniferus*), clove (*Eugenia caryophyllata*), and **Benzoin**.

Pharmacology: Unknown.

Literature: de Waal 1984; Vinci 1980.

ORCHIDS (Orchidaceae). The earth is home to over 30,000 species of orchids. Most live symbiotically or epiphytically upon other plants and form tubers and magnificent flowers. Many species of orchids are used as magical plants, aphrodisiacs, and amulets. The most renowned magical plant from the orchid family is the satyrion, which was most likely an orchis (*Orchis sp.*). Thought to be the aphrodisiac food of the satyrs, it was believed that anyone who ate of the satyrion would themselves become a satyr, an ithyphallic companion of Dionysos. The plant was thus a love magic *per se*, and considered a sibling of the **Mandrake**. The lady's slipper (*Cypripedium*) was a plant of Aphrodite which incited 'commerce with Venus'. The ancient Germans used orchis species as aphrodisiacs, love charms, and protective amulets. The gypsies called the speckled orchis (*Orchis maculata*) *karengro*; they collected the root tubers, which were viewed as effective love amulets and fertility promoters, in a manner not unlike that used to collect **Mandrake**.

In Northern Mexico, the Tarahumara Indians use a yellow-flowered orchid (*Oncidium cebolleta*) as a substitute for **Peyote**. The Chinantecs use two orchid species to help them determine the sex of an unborn child. A pregnant woman drinks a tea of *Clidemia setosa* when she wishes to have a daughter, and a tea of *Pleurothallis cardiothallis* when she wants to have a son. She can also wear the root tuber as an amulet. Vanilla (*Vanilla planifolium*), an orchid which grows wild in southern Mexico, is also thought to be able to effect love magic. The Indians of South America view orchids as love charms and sexual symbols as well.

In Asia, and especially in China, many species of orchids (e.g., *Dendrobium linawianum*) are used as aphrodisiacs, tonics, and elixirs for long life. Before divining, Tantric magicians ingested tubers of *Vanda tesselata* and *Ephemerantha macraei*. In Africa, the species *Ansellia gigantea*, *Lissochilus arenarius*, and *Lissochilus arenaris* are eaten as aphrodisiacs and love charms. Adherents of the North American voodoo religion offer root tubers of the Adam-and-Eve root (*Aplectrum hyemale*) to the goddess Erzulie when they wish to perform powerful love magic.

Pharmacology: All orchid tubers contain starches and various mucous drugs. Some species also contain glycosides. Alkaloids appear to be quite uncommon in this plant family. Such aromatic substances as vanillin are also rare. *Oncidium cebolleta* has been found to contain alkaloids which may possibly have hallucinogenic effects. *Dendrobium linawianum* contains three alkaloids, one of which — dendrobine — has a known structure. Narcotic substances have been detected in the species *Arethusa bulbosa, Goodyear pubescens*, and *Cymbidium devonianum*.

Literature: Brondegaard 1985; Emboden 1974, 1976; Rätsch 1987a, 1987f; Schultes & Hofmann 1980.

*Fig. 18: Because the root tubers of the orchid (*Orchis *spp.) bear such a striking resemblance to testicles, they have often been viewed as magical aphrodisiacs (woodcut from Tabernaemontanus).*

PEDILANTHUS (Pedilanthus itzaeus, Pedilanthus tithymaloides). Pedilanthus species, which belong to the spurge family, are indigenous to the American tropics. They have straight stalks with stemless, fleshy leaves arranged in pairs. The Yucatán Maya call the plant *yax halal che'*, 'green arrow tree' (*Pedilanthus itzaeus*). They plant it before the entrances to their houses and in their yards to protect against evil sorcerers. Sorcerers are said to perceive the bush as a collection of deadly arrows. The plant is also planted upon graves to protect the souls of the deceased. The sap of the stalk is used medicinally to dispel the evil winds which eat their way through the flesh in the form of invisible snakes or worms. The leaves heal all ailments caused by the evil eye.

In Peru, *Pedilanthus tithymaloides* is added to the hallucinogenic cimora drink (cf. **San Pedro Cactus**). This same species has spread as far as the islands of the Indian Ocean. The Creoles call it *bois malgache*, 'tree of the bad winds'. Healing drinks are prepared from its leaves, which must always number seven. On the Seychelles, the leaves are used as an antidote against the poisons of sorcerers (**Jequirity**). Planted by the house, they protect against magicians, who cannot cross the threshold. The plant protects against all types of black magic. To break a spell cast against him, a person who has been charmed must simply carry a couple of leaves or a stalk into the house of the magician who cast the spell.

Pharmacology: Unknown.

Literature: Müller-Ebeling & Rätsch 1989; Rätsch 1986a.

PEYOTE (Lophophora williamsii). In the desert regions of northern Mexico and Texas, a number of species of cactus and other plants occur which the Indians of this region call *peyotl, peyote, híkuli*, etc. There are also a number of plants which the Indians name 'false peyote', *peyotillo, híkuli brava*, etc. (see Table). In general, however, the name peyote is reserved for a small, spineless, tuberous cactus (*Lophophora williamsii*). Both the actual peyote cactus and its substitutes have been used as magical plants and sacraments since pre-Columbian times. In his natural history of New Spain, the Spanish physician Francisco Hernandez wrote about peyote:

> 'This root is attributed with wondrous properties, if you will believe what is said about it. Those who partake of it receive the divine gift of prophecy and can see future things like prophets... The Chichimecs (a tribe of hunters who live in the desert) believe that the power of this root makes this possible.'

Many documents of the church attest to the important role which peyote had as a plant of prophecy. One question asked in confession was: 'Have you

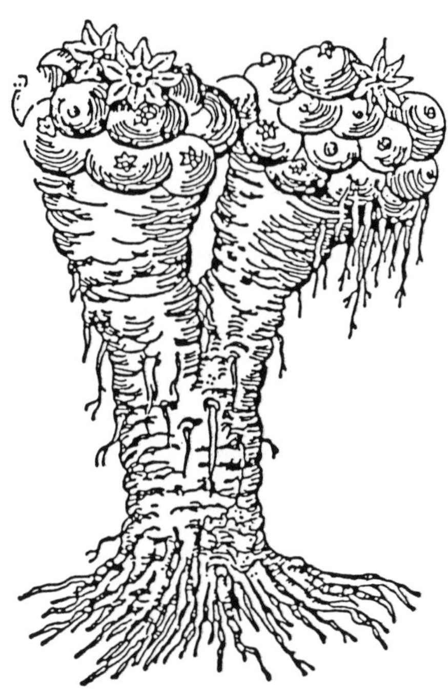

Fig. 19: Because the root of the peyote cactus is so long and fleshy, many of the early Spanish sources referred to the entire cactus as a 'root'. According to Fra Diego de Landa, the Maya produced their sacred inebriating drink by combining honey mead with a 'root' (cf. Balche'*). It is interesting to speculate whether this 'root' may in fact have been peyote. We know that the Maya maintained trade contacts with groups living far up in the northern highlands, and that these routes were one of their primary sources of ritual paraphernalia (contemporary woodcut).*

given others peyote in order to find out secrets or to recover what was stolen or lost?' In the Aztec culture, peyote was a type of god, and was used especially by the prophets and magicians (*naualli*). It was considered sacred and had the same importance as **Ololiuqui** and **Picietl**. The fantastic visions evoked by the plant could divulge the future, disclose the actions of the gods, and reveal one's own fate as well as that of the cosmos. Aztec physicians used peyote as a remedy for many different ailments, especially fever and headaches. They used low doses for such purposes; it was also given as an enema. Brews of peyote, water, and unknown ingredients, presumably pulque (cf. **Agave**) were offered and consumed communally during temple festivals. These rituals were said to have culminated in orgies which were particularly anathematic to the Spanish missionaries. Peyote drinks were also given to humans being readied for sacrifice. Warriors wore pieces of peyote as amulets; these amulets offered the best protection against sorcery and treacherous attacks and gave a warrior superhuman strength. Some sources also refer to peyote as a fetish. Tarahumara runners ingested peyote prior to their ritual races as a doping agent.

Peyote buttons are still used today for religious festivals, to treat the sick, and to divine. In ancient times, the Tarahumara used peyote in order to ward off evil sorcerers, thieves, and enemies and to divine the future. They also ingested them communally to become inebriated, an act which emphasized the mystical nature of the experience. The Huichol Indians of the Sierra Madre go on an annual peyote hunt. During these excursions, they ritually collect and ingest the cactus in order to obtain visions of their past and future life and to ascertain the causes of illnesses and hardships.

Towards the end of the nineteenth century, the peyote cult crossed the border of Mexico and entered the rest of North America. Since this time, many Indian tribes (beginning with the Apaches and Comanches) have integrated the ritual circle, a ceremony in which varying amounts of the cactus are consumed, into their traditional culture ('peyote way of worshipping', 'Half Moon Way of the Peyote Religion'). This even led to the establishment of a native church, known variously as the *Native American Church*, the *Native American Church of Jesus Christ*, the *Peyote Church*, *The Church of Father Peyote*, and *Pejuta yuta okolakiciye* ('Medicine-Eating Church'), with the peyote cactus as its sacrament. Many North American Indians refer to the cactus simply as 'medicine' or 'God's plant' or 'Divine Herb' and attribute it with special healing powers and magical abilities. Many Mexican Indians and Mestizos also use dried peyote buttons as amulets to protect against the evil eye and to ward off all forms of destructive magic and witchcraft. Today, tinctures of peyote are still used as aphrodisiacs.

Pharmacology: The peyote cactus contains mescaline, the main active ingredient, together with 43 other alkaloids. Mescaline and several of the other alkaloids (anhalonidine, lophophoridine) affect the central nervous system and produce exceptionally colorful visions and mystical experiences. The pharmacological activity of the alkaloid peyocatine or hordenine is similar to that of the hormone adrenaline; it also has antibiotic effects.

Table of Peyote Substitutes and Magical Plants Associated with Peyote

Botanical species	*Popular name*	*Contents*
Lophophora diffusa	Peyote	peyotine, lophophorine
Lophophora fricii	Chiculi hualala	peyotine, lophophorine
Ariocarpus fissuratus		
Ariocarpus retusus		
Obregonia denegrii	Híkuli sunami	phenylethylamines
Pelecyphora aselliformis		
Pelecyphora pseudopectinata		
Epithelantha micromeris	Chilito, Híkuli mulato	triterpenes, alkaloids
Mammillaria craigii	Peyote de San Pedro	alkaloids (?)
M. grahamii	Híkuli, Peyote	alkaloids (?)
M. heyderii		dimethoxyphenethylamine
Mammillopsis sensilis	Peyote christiano (?)	alkaloids (?)
Coryphanta compacta	Bakana	DMPEA
Coryphanta macromeris		DMPEA, macromerin
Echinocereus tri-glochidiatus	Híkuli, Pitallita	3-hydroxy -4-methoxy-phenethylamine
Pachycereus pecten-aboriginium	Chawe', Cardón	phenethylamines
Carnegia gigantea	Saguaro	(?)
Cacalia cardiofolia	Peyote	
Cacalia decomposita	Peyote	
Senecio canicida		
Senecio cardiophylus	Palo bobo	sequiterpene-lactones
Senecio grayanus	Palo loco	pyrrolizidines
Senecio praecox	Quantlapatzinzintli	
Senecio tolucanus		
Scirpus spp.	Bakana	alkaloids
Lycoperdon spp.	Kalamota	
Oncidium cebolleta	Híkuri	alkaloids

Literature: Anderson 1980; Bruhn *et al.* 1971, 1973, 1976; Bye 1979; Deimel 1985; Diaz 1979; Haan 1988; La Barre 1989; Mount 1988; Müller-Ebeling & Rätsch 1987; Rätsch 1987f; Rosenbohm 1991; Rouhier 1986; Schultes & Hofmann 1980; Stewart 1987.

PICHI-PICHI (Fabiana imbricata). The evergreen fabiana plant grows in the Andes of northern Chile, where the natives call it *pichi-pichi* or *k'oa.*

The fresh or dried herbage is thrown onto fires or burned as incense during religious ceremonies and when curing illnesses. The resulting smoke dispels spirits and demons and wards off disease. The aromatic plant also has many folk medicinal uses. Pichi-pichi is one of the least studied of all magical plants.

Pharmacology: The entire plant contains a pleasant smelling essential oil with fabinol, the alkaloid fabianine, up to 10% resin, various tannins, glycosides, and fats. The twigs contain scopoletine. In higher doses, the alkaloids appear to have inebriating effects.

Literature: Rätsch 1987f.

PICIETL (Nicotiana glauca (?)). Usually, picietl is identified as 'Turkish tobacco' (*Nicotiana rustica*; Wasson 1971). Picietl was an Aztec term for an inebriating magical plant which is related to and similar to **Tobacco**, but whose effects are more like those of **Ololiuqui** and **Peyote**. The Aztec diviners and magicians used picietl just as they used other psychedelic magical plants (according to Ruiz de Alarcon). It thus seems more likely that picietl refers to an unknown or little studied *Nicotiana sp.*

Today, Indian healers use Turkish tobacco, which they call *pisiete*, for magical purposes. They grind dried, unfermented leaves and mix these with slaked lime. This powder has the power to dispel diseases caused by evil winds (*aires*) from the body and to protect people from sickness and harmful magic. To do this, the Indians rub the powder on the skin. The powder may also be rolled into a tobacco leaf and chewed as a stimulating quid (cf. **Coca**).

Pharmacology: Nicotiana rustica contains the same active ingredients as common **Tobacco**. Hallucinogenic properties like those ascribed to picietl in the literature have not been observed with Turkish tobacco, although they have been found with other *Nicotiana spp.* Further research is needed into the entire picietl complex. It is possible that *Nicotiana glauca* either contains or produces (through empyromatic reactions) the fantasy-enhancing compound harmaline (**Syrian rue**).

Literature: Baer 1986; Ruiz de Alarcon 1984; Wasson 1971.

PITURI (Duboisia hopwoodi, Datura leichardti, and Nicotiana spp.). In its broadest sense, pituri (or pitjuri) refers to all plants which the aborigines of Australia chew or smoke for hedonistic or magical purposes. Various wild tobacco species (*Nicotiana ingulba, N. gossei, N. stimulans, N. benthamii, N. velutina, N. megalosiphon,* and *Goodenia lunata*) are chewed for primarily hedonistic purposes, while *Duboisia* and *Datura* are chewed in a magico-religious context. Usually, pituri leaves are mixed with plant ash and chewed as a quid. 'The aborigines are said to also place the chewed mass in their ears, their eyes then take on a strange luster and their pupils become greatly dilated' (Hartwich 1911:834f.). Pituri stills hunger and thirst, has inebriating effects, and evokes passionate dreams. This is presumably the reason why the aborigines use pituri as a magical plant. Entering the dreamtime, the transcendental primeval state of being, is a central activity of aboriginal magic. In the dreamtime, it is possible to determine and carry out all the magical activities which affect the normal state — which is itself considered unreal.

Pharmacology: Duboisia contains a number of alkaloids: piturine, duboisine, d-nor-nicotine, and nicotine. These alkaloids have powerful stimulating as well as toxic effects. The main active substance in all the tobacco species is nicotine (**Tobacco**). For the pharmacology of *Datura*, see **Thornapple**.

Literature: Hartwich 1911; Peterson 1979; Rouhier 1986.

POPPY (Papaver somniferum). Because the genuine poppy or opium poppy is now cultivated over a very wide geographic area and is widely used as a remedy and source of food, it is very difficult to determine where the plant first originated. Poppy capsules have been recovered at archaeological

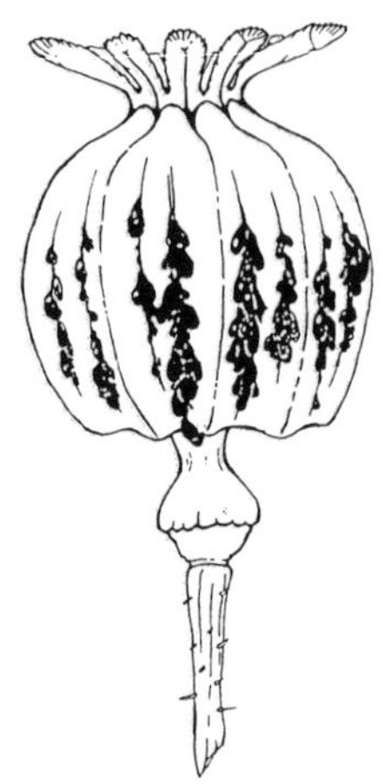

Fig. 20: Making incisions into unripe poppy capsules causes opium, 'the poppy's tears', to ooze out (illustration by Sebastian Rätsch).

excavations of lake dweller sites in Switzerland which date to over 4,000 years old.

The poppy is the source of opium, the thickened sap obtained by slitting the unripened seed capsule. Opium has a long history as an inebriant and an instrument of magic. It can either be eaten or smoked. When opium is intended for ingestion, it is simply consumed together with fat and other substances (resins, plant extracts). When the opium is intended to be smoked, on the other hand, a number of complicated steps are required to transform it into smoking opium, or chandu.

Opium has been used as a remedy since at least 2,500 BC. In Assyrian medicine, the poppy was known as the 'plant of joy'. Opium was used in ancient Egypt as well as in Greece (Thorwald 1985:61). According to one legend, the poppy grew from the tears of Aphrodite. Burnt offerings of poppy seeds and opium were offered to Hypnos, the god of sleep. Poppy capsules and opium were sacred to Demeter, the goddess of fertility. Opium may have also been used in her mysteries (cf. **Ergot**). The famed 'wine of Cleopatra' was composed of wine, 30% opium, and **Thornapple** (seeds). Most likely, it was the Arabs who brought knowledge about the production and the properties of opium to India and China. Opium had great importance as an inebriant among the Arabs and the Persians. They combined it with **Coffee, Hemp**, or **Wine**. Some Sufi sects used opium to induce mystical ecstasy. In Oriental alchemy, it was viewed as a means for transforming consciousness: 'Opium breathed its plant soul into me, it breathed its plant soul into me with barely perceptible movements, and I lived and moved in the midst of the world of plants; I had become a plant myself' (Hedayat, in Gelpke 1982:46). In Thailand and Southeast Asia, opium was used to produce clairvoyant states and as an offering to the spirits of the trees and rocks. The shamans of the Miao (a tribe in the Golden Triangle) smoke opium before and during every ceremony. This allows them to more readily fall into trance and journey to the heavens.

Opium (*ahiphena*) has long occupied a firm place in the Indian medical tradition. The Unani system lists it as a remedy, poison, and an antidote. Since the earliest times, however, it has especially been considered a potent aphrodisiac (Penzer 1952:32,35). Opium's aphrodisiac use was quite widespread. Frequently, opium was also combined with **Hemp** and consecrated to Shiva.

Opium was associated with sexuality in China as well. Pressed into the form of small fish and sold under the name *ying-tsu-su*, opium was not merely an aphrodisiac, but also a veritable symbol of sexuality. Taoist aphrodisiacs, elixirs of life, and magical drinks often consisted of a combination of opium with **Ginseng** and musk.

In the Middle Ages, opium was an important ingredient in theriacs used as cure-alls, antidotes, and to extend life (cf. **Garlic**). It was mixed into magical powders for burning, and was an ingredient in **Witches' Ointments** and laudanum. Opium is rarely used alone. It is often combined with other substances (olibanum, cumin, spices, alcohol, snake meat, etc.) and magical plants (**Bay Laurel, Belladonna, Betel, Ginseng, Hemp, Henbane, Mandrake, Nutmeg, Nux Vomica, Saffron, Tea,** and **Thornapple**). This is done both to improve its primary effects and to avoid its principle side-effect: constipation.

Pharmacology: Opium contains a number of alkaloids which are characteristic in their synergistic and antagonistic effects. Some 40 alkaloids are subsumed under the label opium alkaloids. A distinction is made between those of the morphine type (morphine, codeine, thebaine) and those of the benzylisochinoline type (papaverine, noscapine = narcotine, narceine, nor-laudanosine, reticulin). The main active ingredient is morphine, which has sedative, hypnotic, narcotic, antitussive, respiratory suppressing, and constipating properties.

> 'The effects of opium are much more complex than those of morphine, for it contains not insignificant amounts of many other alkaloids. Among these are thebaine, a stimulant which counteracts morphine. Papaverine and noscapine moderate the suppressing effects which morphine has upon breathing. And finally, the opium alkaloids codeine and the above-mentioned noscapine strongly suppress the urge to cough. In short, opium is not as suppressing as morphine and is more effective against coughs. The relation of morphine to opium is like that of alcohol to wine...' (Pelt 1983:70).

Literature: Geddes 1976; Gelpke 1982; Hayter 1988; Rätsch 1990a; Seefelder 1987; Wagner 1985.

PRICKLY POPPY (Argemone mexicana). We are not certain of the role which the yellow or reddish blossomed prickly poppy played in the pre-Hispanic cultures of Central and South America. The cosmology of the Aztecs encompassed a number of realms of the dead which were associated with the prickly poppy:

> 'All poisonous plants are eaten in the underworld, and all who go there eat prickly poppy. In short, everything which is not eaten on earth is eaten in the underworld, and it is said that nothing else is eaten. Great poverty and need prevails in the underworld. Obsidian knives whirl about, sand, trees, thorny plants, splinters of flint, wild **Magueys**, earth cacti and round cacti (**Peyote**), and it is bitterly cold. Hardships rest upon the dead...' (Sahagún).

The prickly poppy was sacred to Tlaloc, the Aztec god of rain who was also guardian of a water paradise. Aztec and Mayan physicians used the prickly poppy as a medicinal plant to treat a variety of afflictions: head aches, migraines, ear aches, bad breath, bad teeth, snake bites, asthma, influenza, bronchitis, tightness of the chest, chest pains, heart palpitations, liver disorders, lack of appetite, kidney stones, anuria, dropsy, constipation, pestilence, fever, dizziness, and side aches. It is also good for the brain and an effective amulet against the evil eye. The Chinese who immigrated to Mexico in the nineteenth century developed a technique for using prickly poppy to produce a type of opium (chicalote-tamales). This technique is now unknown, and poses an unsolved puzzle for botanists and pharmacologists:

> 'But what the chemists and botanists do not know, the Chinese do, namely: that this prickly poppy, when grown in a tropical climate in fields in which only a few opium poppies (cf. **Poppy**) grow, mixes slightly with these and produces capsules from which, in an unripe state, a product can very certainly be obtained that, like opium, causes blissful self-forgetfulness and a complete absence of wants' (Reko 1986:94).

Today, the dried leaves are smoked in Mexico as an aphrodisiac. In Paraguay, the Guaraní brew the root together with Maté leaves to make a medicinal and stimulating tea. Among the Mapuche, the prickly poppy appears to be a magical plant.

The North American Prickly Poppy (*Argemone polyanthemus*) has strong irritant and narcotic properties. Feared as a poison, it is only infrequently used for ritual or magical purposes. On Hawaii, fresh Puakala prickly poppy (*Argemone glauca*) is used for medicinal purposes. There have been suggestions that *Argemone spp.* are ethnobotanically significant in Southeast Asia as well.

Pharmacology: The latex of the plant contains two alkaloids, berberine and protopine, which have mild narcotic properties. Morphine has not been detected. The roots also contain another alkaloid, sanguinarine. Little is known concerning the pharmacology of prickly poppy drugs. *A. polyanthemus* also contains several active alkaloids. *A. glauca* has psychoactive and narcotic properties.

Literature: Cutts 1985; Emboden 1972; Kepler 1983; McBride 1988; Ownbey 1961; Rätsch 1987f; Reko 1986.

PUKUSA (Allium victorialis var. platyphyllum). This north Asian onion is used medicinally and magically by the shamans of the Ainu, the original inhabitants of Japan. Through the spells of the shamans, the onion, whose scent is reminiscent of **Asafoetida**, develops magical powers which can ward off all infectious diseases and disease demons. The leaves can also be eaten to treat infectious diseases (cf. **False Mandrake**).

Pharmacology: Probably similar to Garlic.

Literature: Mitsuhashi 1976.

QAT (Catha edulis). The tree-high qat bush grows wild or cultivated in plantations in the 'lands of the gods', the fertile plains and mountain regions of the Upper Nile, the humid primeval forests of Carelia in what is now Ethiopia, in southern Arabia, and in Yemen. The nomads of these regions view the small oval leaves and tender twigs of the bush as 'keys to a special paradise. They chew a few leaves, and then open sesame' (Leuenberger 1970:188).

In ancient Egypt, a mummy's grave was known as the 'chamber of transformation'. There, the embalmed corpse was to prepare itself for eternal life, rebirth into a new life, or an astral journey to Sirius, the Dog Star. At the same time, the tombs were a symbol of human consciousness. The human mind was also considered a 'chamber of transformation', for it was the site where impressions of the visible world were transformed into knowledge about the internal relationships of the world, the humans and gods, the animals and plants. The Egyptians possessed a number of techniques for activating this process of transformation (cf. **Cedar, Mandrake, Water Lily**). They practised meditations, fasted, inebriated themselves with pomegranate **Wine** and **Beer**, and ingested the sacred plants, which they referred to as 'nourishment of the gods', 'divine food', and the 'essence of being'. The sacred plants which contained the divine powers of transformation grew in the 'land of the gods' on the Upper Nile (Abyssinia; Thorwald 1962:69). Recently, a painstaking study of hieroglyphics, ethnoarchaeology, and comparative ethnopharmacology led Charles Musès, an American scientist and consciousness researcher, to identify the plant as *kht* (qat).

Today, Yemen is the center of qat use. Usually, fresh leaves and twigs are chewed. But they can also be made into a paste with honey or sugar and eaten or imbibed in **Coffee**. The fresh flowers are brewed as tea and consumed in great quantities. Dried leaves, which are not as highly valued because of their weaker effects, are not chewed but smoked with several **Hemp** flowers instead.

In the thirteenth century, the stimulating effects of qat became a tool for creating mystical experiences. Ethiopian Sufis venerated the plant, for it 'served them in facilitating their religious duties. Mystical experiences were accelerated and intensified. The use of the leaves brought them closer to God, and qat thus became sacrosanct' (Schopen 1981:496). Presumably, qat was also used to intensify the Sufi *heart-chakra meditation*. Later, use of the sacred plant spread to the aristocracy. Qat meditation rituals emerged in which the leaves were chewed in groups. With the leaves, they drank **Tea**, later **Coffee**, and smoked hashish (**Hemp**) and, later, **Tobacco**, in large water pipes. During a qat session, interpersonal relationships were established which bound together those present.

Surprisingly, the use of qat was not restricted to the Orient. Gerald B. Gardner, a chronicler of modern witches' cults, has convincingly argued that qat was one of the sacred plants of the witches:

> 'I was told that in earlier times witches knew a plant called qat. Together with **Incense** (olibanum), it opened the inner eye, the unconscious. Mixed with another plant, sumac (*Toxicodendron* ?), it produced hallucinations and thus should not be taken often. When both plants were used correctly, a person obtained the ability to leave his body. Unfortunately, witches no longer know which herbs these were, although both are said to grow in England (?). It is also said that a woman appears more beautiful when a man inhales incense mixed with qat. Magicians use similar things for the same purpose. Their mixture contains **Hemp** and many other ingredients used for tonics' (Gardner 1965:109).

Pharmacology: Along with vitamin C, qat leaves, flowers, and twigs contain the main active alkaloids cathine and cathidine. Cathine is identical to ephedrine, which is also present in **Ephedra**. Qat also contains a number of methylated amphetamines and methamphetamines whose chemical structures are quite similar to those of MDA and MDMA. Chemists are looking for an isomer of MDMA which is thought to be present in fresh — but not dried — plant material (Musès 1989). This work is still in progress. Recent findings indicate that the substance α-aminopropiophenone plays an essential role in the effects of qat. This substance remains stable for only a few hours after the harvest, and is completely absent from the dried leaves. This substance has even stronger amphetamine-like stimulant effects upon the central nervous system than cathine/ephedrine. Qat has potent euphoriant and dream-inducing effects. It makes a person more cheerful and talkative, and dispels sleep.

Literature: Geisshüsler & Brenneisen 1987; Leuenberger 1970; Musès 1989; Remann 1984; Schopen 1978, 1981.

QUEBRACHO (Aspidosperma quebracho-blanco). The tall, yellow-blossomed quebracho tree grows in central South America. Its wood is as hard as rock. For this reason, the Indians esteem it as an aphrodisiac and potency agent. In Paraguay, the tree was formerly used to brew a magical drink. The seeds of the molle tree (*Schinus molle*) were mixed into a paste of maize. After fermentation was complete, several pieces of quebracho bark were added. In the folk medicine of the Indians, decoctions of the bark were drunk as remedies for respiratory problems, coughs and feverous colds, malaria, and liver pains. The ground bark was often boiled with **Maté** leaves. The Mocoretas Indians of the Alto Paraná consider quebracho a magical tree. Female shamans use living trees to carry out divination rituals. They start a fire under the tree, and then dance around the flames while singing incantations. These shamans use the position of the moon and the manners in which its rays penetrate through the branches to divine.

Pharmacology: The bark contains several yohimbine-like alkaloids (up to 1.5%). Both yohimbine and its analogs lower blood pressure and stimulate the sexual centers located in the sacral vertebrae. This leads to an increase in the flow of blood to the lower abdomen. This can produce strong erections of long duration in men and awaken strong sexual desires in women. In large doses, yohimbine also has psychedelic effects. (**Yohimbe**).

Literature: Rätsch 1987f, 1990a; Zech 1982:21.

REED (Arundo donax). In ancient times, the reed, a native of the Mediterranean region, was used to make shawms and other wind instruments (aerophones) which were often played in magical or mystical contexts. The reed is an Orphean plant associated with the underworld. It was sacred to the gods Priapus and Silvanus and was thus closely tied to the realms of sexuality and aphrodisiacs. An ancient legend describes how Pan pursued a nymph who, just as he was about to catch her, stopped and was transformed into a reed. Pan cut off a stalk and, using beeswax, made it into the first pipes of Pan. The lusty god used this pipe to call out the 'panicky' terrors. The leaves and roots were used to manufacture a variety of medicines.

Pharmacology: The root contains up to 3% DMT. The reed thus has powerful psychedelic effects. We do not, however, know whether it was ever used for this purpose. Reed also contains gramine, sugar, starch, and resin.

Literature: oral communication from Terence McKenna 1989; Baumann 1982; Smith 1977.

RUE (Ruta graveolens). Rue, also known as the common rue, is a very ancient magical plant. It has long been a popular spice, and a house remedy as well. Because it was believed to counteract the effects of poisons, it was often added to **Wine**. Since antiquity, rue has been associated with the Roman moon goddess Diana and her daughter Aradia (cf. **Artemisia**). Rue was a common plant in folk gynaecology, and thus became associated with the midwives, who were often discredited as witches. In the late Middle Ages, rue was burned or hung in a house to magically protect against the intrigues of witches and the madness of devils (cf. **Haoma, Syrian Rue**). Curiously, witches were believed to use rue to brew magical drinks for causing harm. In Italy, rue was an effective device for protecting against the evil eye and the evil spirits which can make a man impotent and a women infertile. Rue was also a popular means of safeguarding against the reprehensible desires of the flesh, and it was recommended to Christians as an anaphrodisiac. The pagan followers of the orgiastic cult of Diana, however, used it as a love charm. In England, rue was planted to protect against the plague. When the Spanish brought the plant into the New World, Indian healers and magicians immediately integrated it into indigenous medical systems as a new magical and medicinal agent. It is considered a 'woman's plant', for it can heal all women's complaints and bring about fertility. In the voodoo cult, rue is sacred to Erzulie, the goddess of love. When used together with the proper incantations, it can effect an irresistible love magic.

Pharmacology: The entire plant contains an essential oil (with phenols, methylketones, terpenes), alkaloids (skimmianine, kokusaginine, graveoline, graveolinine, γ-fagarine, dictamine, ribalinine, arborinine, and harmaline; cf. **Syrian Rue**). The essential oil has sedative and the alkaloids abortifacient and psychoactive effects. It is said that the plant enhances fantasy and stimulates an active imagination.

Literature: Flattery & Schwartz 1989; Mercatante 1976; Rätsch 1987f.

SAFFRON (Crocus sativus). Saffron is a cultigen which as been grown in the Orient since antiquity. In ancient Egypt and Greece, saffron was said to have great healing powers. Greek soothsayers and prophets attributed almost god-like powers to saffron, which they called the 'blood of Hercules'. For this reason, saffron was also worn as an amulet to protect against disease. It was also mixed into **Wine** for use as an antidote and added to mixtures for producing smoke for magical or medicinal purposes. Only the yellow, sun-dried stigmas are used. Saffron (*keshar*) is used to make *tika* or *tilakha*, the spot of color which pious Hindus apply to their brow (at the third eye) as a sign of their religious devotion. In both Ayurvedic and Islamic medicine, saffron is used to soothe the nerves and as an aphrodisiac. It was said that saffron could incite sexual desires especially in women, and it was thus used in love magic, often in combination with **Betel, Hemp, Poppy,** and **Thornapple** (so-called 'Oriental Joy Pills'). In late Medieval Europe, saffron was also employed as a powerful magical device to combat St Anthony's fire (cf. **Ergot**) and was an ingredient in the **Witches' Ointments**. In more recent times, saffron has been used as an opium-like (cf. **Poppy**) inebriant. 'Too much saffron, however, was dangerous, for one was in danger of dying from excessive joy' (Henglein 1985:52).

Pharmacology: Saffron is very rich in riboflavin (vitamin B), contains an essential oil, the yellow dye α-crocine, picrocrocine, and safranal. Saffron has a narcotic effect upon the brain, promotes sleep, can produce headaches and uterine bleeding, and can be lethal for children. Saffron also has estrogenic effects. The psychotropic activity has never been investigated.

Literature: Basker & Negbi 1983; Henglein 1985; Majupuria & Joshi 1988.

SALVIA DIVINORUM (Salvia divinorum). This 'sage of divination', which is also known as *Yerba de la Pastora* ('Herb of the Shepherdess') or ska María Pastora, is found only in the Mexican state of Oaxaca. Mazatec shamans use its leaves when they are unable to obtain magic mushrooms (**Teonanacatl**). The Mazatecs consider *Salvia divinorum* a sibling of **Coleus**. Before they collect parts of the plant, they must carry out a ritual ablution, make an offering to the living plant, and offer a prayer to the spirit of the plant.

The leaves are ingested to find lost objects or to clear up thefts. *Salvia divinorum* is one of many Mexican plants of prophecy used in this manner (cf. **Morning Glory, Ololiuqui, Thornapple, Zacatechichi**). It may be that the plant is identical to *pipiltzintzintli*, an Aztec magical plant mentioned in the ancient sources.

Pharmacology: The plant extract contains nonalkaloidal constituents called Divinorin A and Divinorin B, whose psychoactive effects have been experimentally verified. Large quantities of fresh leaves (appr. 60) must be chewed to produce these effects.

Literature: Emboden (oral communication); Hofmann 1983; Mayer 1977; Rätsch 1986a, 1991; Valdes et al. 1984; Wasson 1962.

SAN PEDRO CACTUS (Trichocereus pachanoi, Trichocereus spp.). This tall, columnar cactus grows along the Peruvian coast, where it is known by the names *Huando, cuchuma, cardo, hermoso, agua-colla, San Pedrillo,* and *San Pedro*. The tribes of the coast and highlands have long used it for magical, medicinal, and ritual purposes. The numerous artistic portrayals of this magical plant on pre-Columbian ceramics and stelae provide an indication of its historical importance. Father Bernabé Cobo, a Spanish missionary, wrote:

> 'It is a plant with whose aid the devil is able to strengthen the Indians of Peru in their idolatry; those who drink its juice loose their senses and are as if dead; they are almost carried away by the drink and dream a thousand unusual things and believe that they are true. The juice is good against burning of the kidneys and, in small amounts, is also good against high fever, hepatitis, and burning in the bladder'.

The cactus was and still is the most important magical device used by Peruvian shamans. They drink decoctions of the cactus flesh so that they may travel to normally unseen worlds to help their patients. It is used in all types of healing and witchcraft (*brujeria*). It is also used in both white and black magic, and especially for transforming a person into an animal. A sixteenth-century Spanish text notes that

> 'among the Indians, there is also a class of magicians whom the Incas tolerate to a degree. They can assume any shape desired and in a short time cover large distances through the air; and they can see events before they occur. They speak with the devil, who answers them using certain stones or through other objects which they venerate' (after Schultes & Hofmann 1980).

To induce psychedelic effects, slices of San Pedro are usually boiled for several hours together with seeds of **Angel's Trumpet**, club moss (*Lycopodium sp.*), **Pedilanthus, Villca**, and a plant named *hornamo* (not yet identified). San Pedro is often ingested in conjunction with **Coca**, chicha (cf. **Maize**), and **Tobacco**. It is said that these substances make a person clean and open for the powers of San Pedro.

Pharmacology: The main active ingredient is mescaline (an average of 1.29 grams per kilo of fresh cactus). Low doses (ca. 1-3 gram of dried material) of San Pedro have stimulating effects and are beneficial for treating stomach and intestinal problems. Larger doses (10 grams of dry matter) produce psychedelic effects which are quite similar to those of **Peyote** and its substitutes. Clarity of consciousness and an increased ability to concentrate, both of which often last for days, are especially noteworthy effects.

Literature: Andritsky 1988; Dobkin de Rios 1968a, 1968b, 1980; Donnan & Sharon 1977; Furst 1972; Jimenez 1977; Schultes & Hofmann 1980; Sharon 1978, 1982. Jimenez (1977:91) has identified 16 mescaline-

Fig. 21: The feline oracle god from Chavín de Huantar (Peru) is shown holding a psychedelic San Pedro Cactus. The priests of this god used extracts of the cactus to produce an altered state of consciousness, during which they travelled upon the cosmic spiral into a psychedelic reality in which past, present, and future merged into a single point. Today, many suburban shamans use the cactus in the same manner. The ritual use of this columnar cactus, which has been found to contain mescaline, can be traced back for several thousand years.

containing columnar cacti which grow in Peru at altitudes between 1,000 and 2,500 meters:

Trichocereus pachanoi	Cereus sp. (?)
Trichocereus santaensis	Opuntia pachiypus
Trichocereus cuzcoensis	Opuntia sp.
Trichocereus peruvianus	Cephalocereus melanostele
Trichocereus tulhuyacencis	Cephalocereus sp. (?)
Cereus macrostibus	Melocactus peruvianum
Cereus acranthus	Neoraimondia macrostibus
Cereus peruvianum	Epiphyllum sp.

Sharon (1982) has claimed that there are over forty Trichocereus species which contain alkaloids.

SASSAFRAS (Sassafras albidum, S. officinale). The sassafras tree, a slender member of the *Lauraceae* family which can attain a height of 35 meters, grows in the south of North America. Many Indian groups venerated the tree as a *good medicine* which could effect love magic. All parts of the tree were used medicinally. The dried root cortex was added to many of the **Tobacco** mixtures which the Indians smoked in ritual contexts. The Ojibwa boiled the root pulp and used it as a narcotic. One reason for the respect accorded the tree had to do with its ability to kindle the fires and awaken the tools of love. This *good medicine* was thus both an aphrodisiac and a love drug. The early white settlers and the black slaves integrated this Indian love tree into their own folk medical systems. The black adherents of the hoodoo cult view sassafras as a tree of love and have consecrated it to Erzulie.

Pharmacology: The entire plant contains an essential oil composed of 70% safrole. Safrole has antiseptic, mildly toxic, carcinogenic, and diuretic properties and affects the central nervous system (stimulating, mood-improving, antidepressive). In the stomach, safrole is presumably aminated into a variety of amphetamine derivatives (e.g. 3,4-methylendioxy-methamphetamine; MDMA). This would explain the psychological effects of sassafras oil (cf **Nutmeg**).

Literature: Rätsch 1987f; Stafford 1983.

SCOPOLIA (Scopolia carniolica). Scopolia is a nightshade indigenous to Central and Eastern Europe, especially in the Carpathian Mountains. Its folk medicinal and magical uses are similar to those of **Belladonna** and **Henbane**. Scopolia was often misused for poisonings and harmful magic.

Since the Middle Ages, it has been an important ingredient in many recipes for **Witches' Ointments** and love drinks. A popular aphrodisiac, it was often spread over dance floors at rural festivals. According to one folk tradition, any person who danced over it would be filled with desire and amenable to any type of sexual activity. In Romania, scopolia roots were used as substitutes for genuine **Mandrake**.

Pharmacology: Tropane alkaloids, especially *l*-scopolamine (cf. **Henbane**, **Thornapple**), hyoscine, hyoscyamine as well as cuscohygrine, tropine, and pseudotropine, are present in all parts of the plant. Plant extracts have potent psychoactive effects. Overdoses can produce death through respiratory paralysis.

Literature: Rätsch 1990a; Römpp 1950; Schultes & Hofmann 1979.

SHANG-LU (Phytolacca acinosa or Phytolacca esculenta). A relative of the pokeberry (*P. americana*), shang-lu grows throughout the tropical zones of Eastern Asia. Its leaves are edible, and the flowers and roots have medicinal value. Because the roots are extremely poisonous, they are only used externally. According to Su Sung: 'The magicians used them a great deal in ancient times.' The ancient Taoist magicians used the roots to make a medicine to treat 'worms in the stomach' and to make spirits appear. They differentiated between two types of shang-lu roots: 'There are two forms of this medicine, a red and a white. The white form is used in the healing arts. The red form can be used to call forth spirits; it is very poisonous. It can otherwise only be used externally for inflammations. If it is eaten, it is very terrible: it causes bloody feces. It can be deadly. It causes spirits to be seen' (Su Ching). In modern Chinese herbal medicine, the poisonous root is used as a harsh expellant (cathartic).

Pharmacology: Most *Phytolacca* roots contain toxic triterpensaponines, phytolaccine, and potassium nitrate. The toxic effects are manifested as gastrointestinal cramps which can be lethal.

Literature: Bensky & Gamble 1986; Li 1978.

Fig. 22: The shang-lu plant (from the Chêng-lei pên-ts'ao, *1249 AD).*

SINICUICHE (Heimia salicifolia). The Indians of the Mexican Highland use the leaves of a plant known variously as *jarilla, sinicuitl, cuauxihuitl, huauchinolli, anchinol, rosilla de Puebla*, and *yerba de las ánimas* to prepare a drink known as sinicuiche, a 'magical drink which makes one forgetful' (Reko). The slightly wilted leaves are allowed to steep in water for a day, after which they are pressed. The resulting liquid is then allowed to ferment. The drink is reportedly used for journeys into memory (i.e. journeys intended to recollect experiences which took place prior to birth).

Healers in Tamaulipas and Veracruz drink sinicuiche in order to divine and prophesy. A healer from Veracruz prepared the drink in a manner similar to that which the Maya use to prepare the **Balche'** drink. He added the leaves to water and honey and allowed the solution to ferment (cf. **Mead**). The drink produced the desired effects after just a few days.

Pharmacology: The plant contains the alkaloids cryogenine, heimine, lythrine, lythridine, sinine, vesolidine, and cryofoline. Cryogenine, which is anticholinergic, sedative, and antispasmodic, presumably has the strongest pharmacological effects. The effects of the pure alkaloid, however, differ from those of the fermented sinicuiche drink. The ethnobotany and ethnopharmacology of sinicuiche requires further study.

Literature: Diaz 1979; Reko 1986; Scholz & Eigner 1983; Schultes & Hofmann 1980.

SNUFF. Psychedelic snuffs enjoy wide ritual use throughout South America and the Caribbean, and especially in the rain forests. Many of the shamans of the tribes in the Amazon and adjacent areas use sacred plants to manufacture very powerful magical concoctions. These powders are invariably sniffed when a shaman wishes to discern the cause of an illness, heal someone who is sick, visit the lord of the animals, carry out hunting magic, establish contact with his animal and helping spirits, transform himself into a jaguar or eagle, predict the future, detect evil magic, or himself cause harmful magic. Shamans usually keep their methods for manufacturing these powders secret. Most persons who are not shamans greatly fear the effects of such powders. A person who uses them without adequate preparation can become mad. Women are usually not allowed to use these snuffs because they can provoke miscarriages.

The Indians of these regions have developed a variety of devices for sniffing their powders. Some use very short, others very long tubes for taking snuff. The Yanomamö use extremely long tubes, and one of their shamans will use the tube to blow the snuff directly into the nose of another.

In South America, a number of plants are used to make snuffs: *Anadenanthera peregrina* (cf. **Villca**), *Virola* (*V. theidora, V. elongata, V. calophylla, V. calophylloidea*), *Elisabetha princeps*, *Justicia pectoralis* var. *stenophylla, Psychotria viridis* (?). The snuffs themselves are known widely by many names, including *epená, cohoba, curupa, hatax, jatay, niopa, yopo, yupa, paricá*. These snuffs are all characterized by the same pharmacology (other magical plants are also used to prepare snuffs, including: **Angel's Trumpet, Ayahuasca, Calamus, Coca, Guayusa, Hemp, Koribó, Tobacco, Villca**; also chili (*Capsicum spp.*), rape dos

Indios (*Maquira sclerophylla*), manusukata (*Pagamea macrophylla*), and tetsi (*Piper interitum*)).

Pharmacology: The tryptamine derivatives (DMT, 5-Meo-DMT, bufotenine) contained in all snuff drugs have extremely potent psychedelic effects and elicit a completely different state of consciousness for approximately 10 to 15 minutes. This state is typified by ego dissolution, fantastic multidimensional visions, experiences of death and rebirth, transformations into animals, erotic ecstasies, experiences of flying, and powerful eruptions. Because these tryptamine derivatives are not orally effective (cf. **Ayahuasca**), they must be either sniffed or smoked (cf. Appendix: DMT-containing Plants).

Literature: Brewer-Carias & Steyermark 1976; Höhle et al. 1987; Prance 1970; Schultes & Hofmann 1980; Smet 1985.

Snuff Plants of the New World

Indigenous Name	*Botanical Name*	*Reference*
ai-amo	?	Seitz 1967:315
a'ku:duwha	*Anadenanthera sp.* (?)	Wassén 1967:265
áma-asíta	*Elizabetha princeps*	Brewer-Carias & Steyermark 1976:63
ama asita	*Trichilia sp.*	Seitz 1967:318
angíco	*Anadenanthera sp.*	Schultes 1967:293
bolek-hena	*Justicia sp.*	Schultes 1967:303
buhenak	*Justicia pectoralis*	Smet 1985:90
cebil	*Anadenanthera macrocarpa*	Wassén 1967:268
cébil	*Anadenanthera colubrina* var. *Cébil*	Schultes 1967:300
chopó	*Elizabetha princeps*	Brewer-Carias & Steyermark 1976:65
coca	*Erythroxylon coca* *E. coca* var. *ipadu*, *E. fimbriatum*, *E. macrophyllum*, *E. novogranatense*, *E. n.* var. *truxillense*	Schultes 1967:293 Smet 1985:82
cohoba	*Anadenanthera peregrina*	Wassén 1967
coro	?	Wassén 1967:269
curupá	*Mimosa acacioides*	Wassén 1967:268
epéna	*Virola callophylloidea*	Seitz 1967: 317
épena	*Virola elongata*	Brewer-Carias & Steyermark 1976:60

epéna-kési	*Virola sp.*	Schultes 1967:303
hakúdufha	*Virola sp.* (?)	Wassén 1967:265
hatax	?	Rätsch 1988:132
hisioma	*Anadenanthera peregrina*	Schultes 1967:303
huilca	*Anadenanthera sp.*	Schultes 1967:299
jatay	?	Rätsch 1988:132
ka'/vi	?	Wassén 1967:268
kokoime	?	Wassén 1967:265 Schultes 1967:304
koribó	*Tanaecium nocturnum*	Prance et al. 1977 Rätsch 1988:93
manacá	*Brunfelsia hopeana*	Wassén 1967:268
manusukata	*Pagamea macrophylla*	Smet 1985:94
mashihiri	*Justicia pectoralis* var. *stenophylla*	Brewer-Carias & Steyermark 1976:58
masho-hara	*Piper sp.*	Schultes 1967:303
morí	(*Nicotiana sp.* ?)	Wassén 1967:267
niopa	?	Wassén 1967:266
niopo	*Anadenanthera sp.*	Schultes 1967: 293
ñope	*Acacia niopo*	Wassén 1967:266
pa-ree-ká	?	Wassén 1967:267
paricá	*Virola calophylloidea* *Mimosa acacioides*	Seitz 1967:335 Wassén 1967:265
petun	*Nicotiana tabacum*	Wassén 1967:273
poschi-have-moschi	?	Seitz 1967:326
rapé dos indios	*Olmedioperebea sclerophylla* *Maquira sclerophylla*	Wassén 1967:271 Smet 1985
sayri	*Nicotiana sp.* ?	Wassén 1967:269
tabaco-rapé	*Anadenanthera sp.*	Wassén 1967:265
toloachi	*Datura inoxia*	Smet 1985:81
vilca	?	Wassén 1967:269
vilca bejuco	*Banisteria leiocarpa*	Reis Altschul 1967:308
villca	*Anadenanthera colubrina*	Reis Altschul 1967:307
wee-kees	*Acorus calamus*	Smet 1985
yakee	*Virola* (*V. calophylla, V. calophylloides*)	Schultes 1967:300
yauardi-hena	*Piper sp.*	Schultes 1967:303
yopa	?	Wassén 1967:265
yopo	*Anadenanthera sp.*	Wassén 1967:265; Schultes 1967:293

* * *

Plants Used to Make Psychedelic Snuffs

Botanical Name	*Indigenous Name(s)*	*Active Principle(s)*
Acorus calamus	wee-kees	essential oil asarone
Anadenanthera		
colubrina	villca, vilca	DMT, MMM, 5-Meo-MMT 5-Meo-DMT, bufotenine
colubrina var. *Cébil*	cébil	
macrocarpa	cebil, cevil	
peregrina	cohoba, khoba cogioba, cohobba cahoba cajoba, cohiba, coiba hisioma	
peregrina var. *falcata sp.*	paricá yopa, yopo, niopa tabaco-rapé, angíco	
Brugmansia spp.	toé, huacacuchu, tonga, borrachero	tropane alkaloids
Brunfelsia hopeana	manacá	tropanes
Cecropia sp.	?	?
Datura inoxia	toloachi, xtohk'uh miyaya	tropanes
Elizabetha princeps	ama-asita áma-asíta chopó	'some active principle'
Erythroxylon coca	coca	cocaine
îlex guayasa	guayasa	caffeine
Justicia pectoralis var. *stenophylla*	mashihiri mashahari buhenak	DMT (?), cumarin, benzopyranes
Lecythidacea sp.	yopo (?)?	
Maquira sclerophylla	rapé dos indios	cumarins
Mimosa acacioides (syn. *Anaden-anthera*)	curupá paricá, niopo	tryptamines
Nicotiana		
rustica	k'uts	nicotine
sp.	sayri	nicotine
tabacum	petun	nicotine

Olmedioperebea sclerophylla (syn. *Maquira*)	rapé dos indios	?
Pagamea macrophylla	manusukata	?
Piper		
interitum	tetsi	
sp.	masho-hara yauardi-hena	piperidines ?
Tanaecium nocturnum	koribó, hutkih	hydrogen cyanides, saponins
Theobroma		
sp.	?	?
subincanum	?	theobromine (?)
Trichillia sp.	ama-asita	?
Virola		tryptamines
calophylla	yakee, paricá	DMT, 5-Meo-DMT
callophylloidea	paricá, yakee epéna, epená	tryptamine derivatives
cuspidata		6-methoxy-harmane, 6-methoxy-harmalane, 6-Meo-tetrahydroharmane
elongata	épena, (yakee)	DMT, 5-Meo-DMT, MMT MTHC, tryptamine
rufula		DMT, 5-Meo-DMT
sebifera		DMT, 5-Meo-DMT, MMT
theiodora		DMT, 5-Meo-DMT

SOLANDRA (Solandra brevicalyx). A member of the nightshade family, solandra grows in the tropical and temperate zones of Central America. Lacandon women adorn themselves with its large yellow flowers, and rub the inebriating scent onto their clothes as an aphrodisiac perfume. In ancient Mexico, the Aztecs referred to solandra as *tecomaxochitl*. They boiled the leaves with cacao and drank the mixture as a love drink. They warned, however, against overdose: a person would dry out and might die of an excessive sex drive. Today, small branches are used to make teas for love magic.

Among the Huichol Indians, solandra is one of the *kieli*, the 'plants of the gods'. It is the counterpart to **Thornapple**, which is considered a *kielitsa*, a 'plant of the bad gods'. At the beginning of the world, solandra was a god which was born of the union of the cosmic snake and the rain. Later, for the good of humanity, he transformed himself into a plant. This plant is so powerful that it is utilized in every form of magic. The Huichol say that anyone who disturbs or insults the plant will be punished with madness or death.

The plant is offered objects which are otherwise reserved for **Peyote**: ceremonial and magical arrows, corn tortillas, tequila, yarn paintings, coins, tobacco flasks, jewelry, and miniature sandals. Initiates require a five-year period of training under an experienced shaman before they are allowed to use the plant for magical purposes. It is said that the visions it produces are similar to those of peyote, although they may be slightly terrifying. The leaves of the solandra are considered to be a potent weapon and amulet against all forms of black magic. On the other hand, the plant can also be misused for black magic (death magic).

Pharmacology: The entire plant contains the tropane alkaloids hyoscyamine, scopolamine, atropine, noratropine, and cuscohygrine, all of which produce psychedelic effects (cf. **Angel's Trumpet, Thornapple**).

Literature: Knab 1977.

SOLOMON'S SEAL (Polygonatum canaliculatum). Named after King Solomon, this liliaceous plant was the most important magical plant in the culture of the Kickapoo Indians (Northern Mexico). Only the clan leaders may collect the plants in the Sierra Santa Rosa or in Utah. During the festival of the New Year, the clan leader must give a piece of the root to each of the other members of the clan. It is said that the root magically heals many afflictions and diseases, protects its possessor from witches and magic, joins spouses together, and effects love magic. When a woman leaves a man, the root ensures him of a speedy replacement. When a hunter goes hunting, he places a small piece of the root in his mouth, allows it to become softened with saliva, and then smears himself with the saliva. This protects him from rattlesnakes during the hunt. Other species (*Polygonatum multiflorum, P. commutatum*) are eaten and used as all-round house remedies (cf. **Fo-Ti**).

Some ethnobotanists have equated Solomon's seal (*Polygonatum odoratum*) of the Old World with the mysterious 'spring plant', which was said to open doors and locks and blow up boulders which stood in the way of hidden treasures. It blooms only on Midsummer's Eve. It is easily recognized because it shatters scythes and horses' hoofs bounce off it. Similarly, legend tells that another plant (the botanically unknown *shamir*) was used to blow up stones during the construction of Solomon's temple.

Pharmacology: The root contains acetidine-2-carbonic acid, chelidonic acid, and saponines as well as unknown substances. These constituents have toxic effects (nausea, diarrhoea, disturbances of cardiac rhythm).

Literature: Engel 1978; Latorre 1977.

SOMA (not yet identified). The Rig-Veda and the Atharva-Veda, the two sacred books of the ancient Aryans, contain numerous passages which refer to a sacred magical plant called soma. In these works, soma is the name of the plant, of a sacred drink ritually prepared from this plant and milk, and the name of a golden, phallic moon god. The Vedic religion had no temples and no pompous ceremonial displays. Instead, religion manifested itself within a person in the form of mystical experience. To achieve this, they imbibed the soma drink, which effected an ecstatic merging with eternity and the divine. It provided visions of the real, heavenly world; gave paradisiacal joys; made one immortal and undefeatable; fostered art, poetry, and creativity; granted eternal youth and health; promoted fertility; and enhanced the experience of the blissful delights of love. In the post-Vedic period, many of the elements of the soma ritual were adopted by the Tantrics. The objects used in the ritual (the stones used to press the soma stalks, as well as musical instruments and conch trumpets), the soma plant, and the drink made from this were used as powerful instruments of magic.

Unfortunately, it is no longer possible to identify with certainty the soma plant described in the Vedas, for knowledge of the original plant had already been lost by the post-Vedic period. A number of researchers have worked on the problem and have variously suggested that soma was **Fly Agaric, Hemp, Mandrake, Rue**, or **Syrian Rue**. Even certain succulents have been proposed, as has the horsetail (*Equisetum sp.*). Soma was apparently a generic term used to refer to a variety of psychoactive plants. Terence McKenna's view that the term soma referred to a species of *Stropharia* which grows in the Himalayas (cf. **Mushrooms, Teonanacatl**) certainly has merit. From the post-Vedic period until today, the following (magical) plants have been utilized as soma substitutes: **Ephedra** (*E. gerardiana*), **Hemp**, *Sarcostemma acidum, Periploca aphylla, Calotropis gigantea, Vitex negundo, Basella cordifolia, Andropogon sp., Caesalpinia bonduc, Bacopa monnieri.* Today, vestiges of the soma ritual live on in the practices of several Indian sects and in the Tibetan tradition of offering chang beer whose potency has been increased by the addition of certain 'bitter herbs' or 'medicinal roots'. The resulting drink, which is known as *bdud rtzi* (literally, 'devil's juice'), is offered to the gods before it is consumed (Hermanns 1980:74). The Lepchas have a comparable ritual. The Vedic soma is probably the same as the ancient Iranian **Haoma**. It has also been associated with **Ling-chih**.

Pharmacology: Unknown.

Literature: Aero 1980; Ajaya 1980; Flattery & Schwartz 1989; Hermanns 1980; Khlopin 1980; Majupuria & Joshi 1988; Müller-Ebeling & Rätsch 1986; Schlosser 1987; Stutley 1980; Wasson 1972.

Soma Candidates and Substitutes

(? = unknown; not yet chemically identified)

Plant	*Active Principle(s)*	*Effect(s)*
Arjunnâni (*Andropogon sp.*)	essential oil	stimulant
Ephedra (*Ephedra gerardiana);*	ephedrine pseudoephedrine	CNS stimulant, hypertensive
Fly Agaric (*Amanita muscaria*)	ibotenic acid muscimole	synaesthetic narcotic
Hemp (*Cannabis indica*)	THC	euphoriant stimulant
Horsetail (*Equisetum sp.*)	?	(tonic)
Hyssop (*Bacopa monnieri*)	?	?
Magic Mushroom (*Stropharia cubensis*)	psilocybin psilocin	psychedelic visionary
Mandrake (*Mandragora turcomanica*)	tropane alkaloids	sedative, hypnotic, excitant
Negundo Tree (Indrasura) (*Vitex negundo*)	?	(anaphrodisiac) febrifuge
Pûtîkâ (*Basella cordifolia*)	latex	?
Rue (*Ruta graveolens*)	essential oil alkaloids harmaline	sedative abortifacient MAO inhibitor
Somalata (*Sarcostemma acidum*	latex	thirst-quenching
Periploca aphyla	latex	toxic (?)
Calotropis gigantea	latex	emetic
Caesalpina bonduc)	?	febrifuge
Succulents (not identified)	?	?
Syrian Rue (*Peganum harmala*)	harmaline harmine	MAO inhibitor stimulates the fantasy

SYRIAN RUE (Peganum harmala). Syrian rue grows in the Mediterranean countries, the Near East, the Himalayas, and across to Manchuria. Almost all the groups who live in these regions use Syrian rue as a medicinal and magical plant. Dioscorides may have been the first to mention the plant, and he also suggested that Syrian rue may have been **Moly**, the renowned magical plant of ancient times: 'Some also call the same Harmala, the Syrians Besasa, but the Cappadocians Moly, for in most respects it shows a similarity with Moly, as it has black roots and white flowers. It grows on hilly and fertile soil' (1902:294). Its most common names are *hermel, harmel, harmal, Peganon, besasa, epnubu, churma*. The Egyptians called the plant Besasa and esteemed it for its magical properties. It stood under the protection of the misshapen god Bes. This dwarf god with the face of an old man was especially beloved among the Egyptian folk and was venerated as a protector against all evil. Attributed with many animal features, Bes' image appeared on countless amulets which were used to decorate headrests, beds, mirrors, and cosmetic jars (to preserve magical cosmetics for warding off sorcery). Bes, like his magical plant — Syrian rue — was believed to protect against the evil eye. There is evidence that Syrian rue was burned as an incense before his image. In North Africa, vestiges of this ancient Egyptian use of Syrian rue have been retained into the present day. Today, Egyptians can purchase oil made from Syrian rue seeds from any herb dealer. Called *Zit-el-Harmel*, this oil is used as an aphrodisiac and to protect against black magic. In Morocco, the seeds are used medicinally and magically. Inhaling the smoke is said to ease birth, make one clairvoyant, protect against the evil eye, inebriate, heal headaches, purify the house of evil spirits, aid in clearing the mind, calm agitated children, and provide help against devils. The seeds are often smoked together with **Hemp** flowers to foster clairvoyant states. A mixture of Syrian rue seeds, **Rue** (*Ruta montana*), coriander, *Corrigiola telephiifolia*, *Nigella sativa*, **Juniper**, and **Asafoetida** is burned in a mezmer (charcoal incense stove) to dispel devils and demons (de Vries 1985).

In Turkey, the seeds are available in any herbal shop under the name *Üzerlik*. They are burned as incense to protect against the evil eye. The seeds have also long been used to obtain the dye known as Turkish red.

Syrian rue is one of the sacred plants of the Hunza. The *Bataiyo* (shamans) burn seeds of the plant in order to enter their clairvoyant shamanic trances. Under the influence of Syrian rue, the *Bitaiyo* initiate close, lusty, sexual contact with the fairies (cf. **Juniper**).

Some scholars have suggested that Syrian rue was the legendary **Haoma** mentioned in the Avesta (Flattery). Because this plant is still used cultically by the Parsi people of the Hunza, this theory has some merit. Syrian rue seeds are also burned to produce smoke during the Iranian Spring festival of Nauruz.

Pharmacology: Syrian rue seeds contain the ß-carbolines harmaline, harmine, and harmalol. These function as MAO inhibitors, enhance free association, bolster the fantasy and imagination, and enormously augment the effects of

Fig. 23: Syrian rue (after Tabernaemontanus 1731).

other psychotropic substances (e.g. of cannabinoles and tropane alkaloids). These effects have certainly contributed to the plant's magical reputation (**Ayahuasca**).

Literature: Felmy 1986; Flattery 1984; Flattery & Schwartz 1989; Plies & de Vries 1987; de Vries 1984, 1985.

TAGETES (Tagetes lucida). In Mexico, this small, aromatic, yellow-blossomed plant is a widely used house remedy and medicinal plant. It is known variously as *pericón, anisillo, curucumín, hierba de Santa Maria, yerba de nube,* and *tzitziqi*. Many ailments are treated by imbibing decoctions of the plant or adding these to the bath water. Ill persons may smell the scent of tagetes or inhale its smoke during healing ceremonies in order to support the effects of the magic or the remedy. Its herbage is woven into the shape of a cross and nailed to houses to repel all the devils which pass by. The flowers are used as part of pastoral ceremonies. Urban healers use the plant during the *limpias* (cleansings) to percuss their patients. This dispels negative influences and evil winds from the patient. The plant is also used in Zapotecan purification rituals.

The Huichol combine the plant with **Tobacco** (*Nicotiana rustica*) when making a smoking mixture for use during their **Peyote** rituals. Shamans smoke the same mixture to help clarify the causes of a problem or an illness.

Ancient Mexican sources refer to a magical plant known as *yauhtli*, which was given to captives before they were sacrificed, smoked to aid clairvoyancy, burned as incense, and drunk as an aphrodisiac and to heal insanity and the terror produced by thunder. Since one of the Huichol names for tagetes is *yahutli*, and because the early descriptions fit the appearance of the plant, it seems likely that tagetes is that plant which the Aztecs knew as *yauhtli*.

In Nepal and India, tagetes flowers (*Tagetes erecta*) are sacred to Shiva, the Hindu god of ecstasy (**Hemp, Thornapple**), and to the goddess Bhagwati. Many different types of offerings are made to this plant.

Pharmacology: The herbage contains an essential oil, tannic acid, and alkaloids. Neither the medicinal nor the psychoactive effects which Indians have described can be explained on the basis of the known constituents. Further ethnobotanical and pharmacological research is needed.

Literature: Diaz 1979; Majupuria & Joshi 1988; Siegel et al. 1977.

TAMARISK (Tamarix spp.). The red-blossomed, gracile tamarisk grows along river beds and in marshes in the Eastern Mediterranean and the adjoining areas of the Near East. Its gall-like fruits provide the raw material for the coveted manna. The ancient Egyptians used these for medicinal (and perhaps magical?) purposes. In Mesopotamia, they were seen as a powerful magical weapon which could dispel all evil. It was the weapon of Anu, the god of the heavens, and was hung on door bolts as an apotropaic agent along with branches from the **Date Palm**. The Sumerians and their successors believed that illnesses were due to gods, demons, or sorcerers. Consequently, they had to be treated with magical means. As the following recipe for treating an eye disease illustrates, their techniques were often quite elaborate:

> 'You should pound tamarisk leaves, add these to strong vinegar, and allow this to stand outside under the stars; in the morning, press these in a helmet: white alum, storax, "Accadian salt", fat, corn meal, black caraway, "copper gum", should be ground separately: take equal parts thereof and mix; pour this into the helmet into which you have pressed the tamarisks; you should knead in curds and sunis mineral; open his eyelids with the finger and rub it into his eyes. You should apply this to his eyes as long as they are dull, you should do this for nine days' (after Sigerist 1963:103).

In ancient times, the tamarisk (Greek *myriki*) symbolized beauty and youth. It was sacred to Aphrodite, the goddess of love. The wild tamarisk (*Tamarix africana*) was sacred to Apollo, the god of oracles. It is possible that it may have been used as a magical plant in divination. Manna (or *tamarisk manna*), which had many uses as an ingredient in incenses and as a medicine, is obtained from *Tamarix mannifera*.

Pharmacology: Tamarisk manna contains cane sugar and invert sugar, dextrin, and trace elements. Manna has anti-inflammatory effects.

Literature: Manniche 1989; Sigerist 1963; Thorwald 1962.

TEA (Thea sinensis). The tea shrub was probably originally from China or Assam. Many legends are associated with its discovery. Originally used as a medicinal plant as well as a magical agent, tea soon became a sacred drink as well, for it was a 'spiritual' plant which could dispel tiredness and awaken the 'benevolent life spirits'. A person who made tea and allowed it to flow over an image of a god as an offering before it was drunk was cured of all afflictions. In a classical Zen Buddhist text from 1211 AD, tea is referred to as a special medicine which prolongs life and, because it possesses mystical effects, is a sacred plant which must be venerated. Taoist magicians and alchemists used tea as well, for it increased concentration during the long magical practices and meditations. In China and Japan, the preparation and consumption of tea eventually evolved into the tea ceremony, a ritual which still enjoys great prestige today. Tea has also been used in Taoist sex magic as an aphrodisiac and as a stimulant when using **Hemp**, opium (cf. **Poppy**), Han-Shi (**Aconite**) and **Wine**.

Pharmacology: Tea leaves contain the stimulant theine, which is chemically identical to caffeine, the active ingredient of **Coffee** (cf. **Guayusa, Maté**).

Literature: Aleíjos 1977; Goetz 1989; Staufenbiel 1981.

TEONANACATL (Psilocybe spp., Stropharia cubensis). Ancient Mexico had a number of cults whose members ritually ingested magic mushrooms as sacraments, plants of prophecy, and for magical purposes (cf. **Jambur, Mushrooms**). One Aztec text recorded by Friar Bernardino de Sahagún describes their medicinal and magical properties:

> '*Nanacatl.* They are called *Teonanacatl*, "flesh of the gods". They grow in the plains, in the grass. The head is small and round, the stalk long and slender. It is bitter and scratches, it burns in the throat. It makes one foolish; it confuses one, distresses one. It is a remedy for fever, gout. Only two or three are eaten. It makes one sad, gloomy, distressed; it makes one flee, scares one, makes one hide. A person who eats much sees many things which frighten him and amuse him. He flees, hangs

Fig. 24: Pre-Columbian mushroom stone (Late Formative Period, 300 BC- 200 AD) made by Mayan Indians from the area of what is now El Salvador. This stone may be intended as a depiction of the spirit of the mushroom, who is capable of foretelling the future (illustration by Sebastian Rätsch).

himself, throws himself from a cliff, screams, is afraid. They are eaten with honey. I eat mushrooms; I take mushrooms. Of one who is haughty, impertinent, conceited, it is said: "He has bemushroomed himself".'

The secret of the magic mushrooms was well-guarded into the middle of the twentieth century. Until María Sabina, a Mazatecan curandera, introduced Gordon Wasson to the secret cult, it was long believed that these psychedelic mushrooms were identical with **Fly Agaric** (e.g., Reko). Mushrooms are eaten to aid clairvoyance, to recognize and to dispel diseases, and to strengthen the vigor of persons who are healthy. In the psychedelic state, 'small persons' and wild animals (jaguars, crocodiles, octopods, etc.) may appear alongside giant anthropomorphic mushrooms — spirit allies. The magicians and healers converse with these beings, who bestow upon them the powers they need for healing. In pre-Columbian times, the Highland Mayan tribes manufactured so-called mushroom stones. Apparently, these were used during psychedelic rituals of knowledge.

Teonanacatl **species in Mexico (after Guzman 1978:109-116 and 1980:30f.)**

Species	*Common name*	*Distribution*
Psilocybe aztecorum	niños de las aguas niñitos	Estado de México
P. bolivarii		Sinaloa
P. bonetii		Estado de México
P. caerulescens	derrumbe	Oaxaca, Puebla
P. candiceps		Oaxaca
P. cordispora		Oaxaca
P. cubensis	sanisidro	Oaxaca, Veracruz, Chiapas, Puebla
P. hoogshageni	derrumbito	Oaxaca
P. mexicana	pajarito	Jalisco, Morelos, Oaxaca, Puebla, Veracruz
P. muliercula		Estado de México
P. yungensis		Oaxaca, Veracruz
P. zapotecorum	derrumbe de monte	Oaxaca

Pharmacology: The magic mushrooms contain the tryptamines psilocybin and psilocin, which have hypotensive, anti-pyretic, and, in high dosages (10-30 fresh or 5 g dried mushrooms), psychedelic effects. These evoke extremely colorful visions which often incorporate Mexican motifs.

Literature: Emboden 1982; Estrada 1980; Hofmann 1983; McKenna 1989; Ott & Bigwood 1978; Roldan 1975; Rosenbohm 1991; Rubel & Gettelfinger-Krejci 1976; Wasson 1980.

THORNAPPLE (Datura spp.). The tropical regions of the New and Old Worlds are home to a number of different datura species. In the cultural history of humanity, few other plants have gained as much prominence as a magical plant as has thornapple.

The Asian thornapple is known as *Datura metel*. It is found in all of the warmer and tropical zones of South and Southwest Asia. The varieties of this herbaceous plant are distinguished by the colors of their flowers. The white-blossomed *Datura metel* was formerly also known as *Datura alba*. The yellow or purple variety was also called *Datura fastuosa*. The most common type has whitish flowers which are tinged a light violet at the edge. The fruits, thorny apples not unlike chestnuts (also known as *nux metel* or metel nuts), are identical in all three varieties.

The first known mention of *Datura metel* was by the Arabian physician Avicenna (Abu Ali Ibn Sina, 980-1037 AD), who noted that the Arabs used the plant for medicinal purposes and that low doses had inebriating effects, while larger doses could be lethal. It was called *jous-matehl, datora*, or *tatorah* (Avery 1959:3). For the Arabs, the thornapple was one of the *mokederrat*, or narcotica (Ainsle 1979:446). *Datura metel* is certainly one of the oldest remedies in India. It is known by the Sanskrit names *dhustura* or *unmata*, 'divine craziness', as well as the East Indian names *dhatura, dutra, unmata*, or *unmeta*. One of Lord Shiva's many names is *unmatta*, the 'crazy one'; this refers to his incarnation as the datura plant. The Thugs (worshippers of Kali) use of datura seeds for criminal purposes is widespread in Asia (Gimlette 1971: 204-221; Penzer 1924:160). In East India, women fed datura leaves to a certain type of beetle (the species is unknown). They then collected the beetle's excrement, which they mixed into the food of their unfaithful husbands.

In India, the thornapple is sacred to the god Shiva. According to the *Vamana Purana*, the datura plant grew from Shiva's breast. Instructions given in the *Garuda Purana* state that datura flowers should be offered to the god Yogashwara (= Shiva) on the thirteenth day of the waxing moon (Mehra 1979:163f). To honor Shiva, yogis and sadhus smoke the leaves, flowers, or seeds of thornapple mixed with **Hemp**:

> 'Both plants are sacred to Shiva.... The smoking mixture of ganja and dhatura corresponds to one of the cosmological principles of the god, namely his androgyny. Ganja is the female aspect and dhatura the male;

> the mixture of the two is the perfect primordial unity and cosmic creative energy of Shiva, the androgynous.... The smoking blend must be ignited with two small pieces of wood. These represent his feminine and his masculine aspects and, when transformed by Shiva's aspect as the god of fire, awaken the aphrodisiac creative power and activate the kundalini snake (**Lakshama**) which is rolled up and resting in the pelvis. When the kundalini has been unleashed, it snakes along the spinal chord through the seven chakras, the non-material energy centers, and causes them to blossom like the flowers of the lotus. The universal consciousness of the unity of the cosmos pervades the being. In this way, the plant of the god becomes the sacred aphrodisiac of man' (Müller-Ebeling & Rätsch 1986a:19,20f).

The use of datura as an inebriant is widespread in India. A popular way of ingesting the plant is to mix its seeds with alcoholic beverages (**Beer**). We have evidence that datura seeds have long been used as an aphrodisiac in Indian folk medicine. Indian medicine also prescribes datura preparations for a number of ailments: head aches, mumps, poorly-healing wounds, pains, nervous disorders, insanity, rheumatism, muscle tension, epilepsy, cramps, convulsions, syphilis and other venereal diseases, asthma, bronchitis, chickenpox, boils, and opium poisoning (cf. **Poppy**). In China, *Man-t'o-lo (Datura alba)* is used medicinally for a number of diseases and, combined with **Hemp** or **Wine**, as a narcotic. Li Shih-chên, the author of the famous *Pents'ao kang-mu*, wrote: 'According to tradition, it is said: if a person laughs when the flowers are being picked to use with wine, the wine will evoke laughter in everyone who partakes of it. If the flowers are picked while someone dances, then the wine will evoke dancing.' Moroccans add six flowers to **Coffee** preparations or use these to decoct an inebriating and erotic tea. In West and Central Africa, the species *Datura fastuosa* is used as an inebriant and plant of prophecy. 'Criminal telepathists' ingest it to locate stolen objects and to solve murders and other crimes (cf. **Nightshade**). Among the Shagana-Tsonga of the North Transvaal, *Datura fastuosa* is used to evoke religiously meaningful visions in a female initiation ceremony at puberty. The plant is given to the girls so that they may enter into communication with the ancestor gods who grant fertility (**Iboga**). Johnston (1972) has pointed out that the context in which this psychedelic plant is used is culturally patterned to produce stereotypical visions in which the young initiates hear ancestral voices assuring them of fertility.

First introduced into Europe in modern times, the thornapple immediately gained notoriety as a witches' plant. While it was allegedly used as an ingredient in **Witches' Ointments**, it was also utilized to thwart the schemes of witches, harmful magic, and the hordes of the devil.

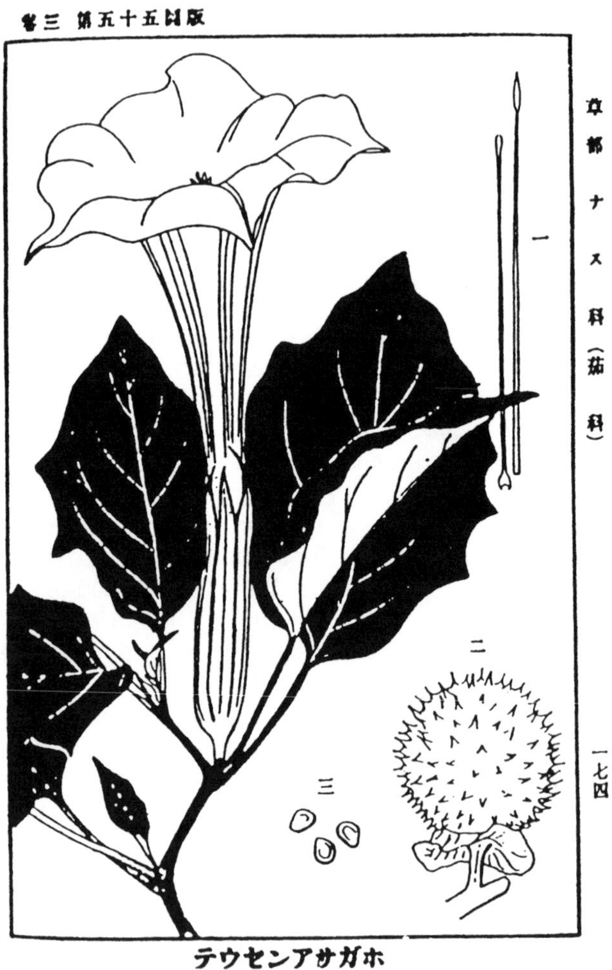

Fig. 25: One of the earliest illustrations of the Asian Datura metel *or* D. alba *is this Japanese woodcut by Siinuma Yokusai. In Japanese, this variety of thornapple is known as* chosen-asagao, *'Korean morning beauty'. The Chinese Buddhists gave the plant a non-translatable name from a passage of a sutra* man t'o lo hua. *Because glimmering dew drops once rained from heaven onto these flowers as the Buddha was speaking, Buddhists consider the plant sacred. And in fact, this plant, when used correctly and respectfully, can indeed grant paradise on earth.*

The Indians of the New World venerated the thornapple species indigenous to the region (*Datura inoxia, D. stramonium, D. tatula, D. ferox, D. discolor*). Although these plants were primarily used for magical purposes, they were also utilized as medicines and in ritual sacrifices.

In the Andes, the thornapple is known as *chamico* (cf. **Angel's Trumpet**). It is one of the oldest medicinal plants in the region. The physicians of ancient Peru were quite familiar with the effects of different dosages. They were able to prepare medicines for narcotic and analgesic purposes, to induce clairvoyant visions, and to kill. Thornapple seeds were apparently crushed and taken in *chicha* (cf. **Maize**). In ancient Peru, thornapple was used along with **Coca** during skull trephinations. The fact that many trephined skulls healed well provides an indication of the success of these operations. Thornapple was also given to initiates when their ears were pierced during their initiation. The Mapuche, a group living in the southern Andes, still retain this custom. They use *miyaya* preparations of *Datura ferox*. They smoke the leaves, drink flower teas to induce shamanic trances, and place fresh flowers upon painful parts of the body as a local anesthetic. Thornapple drinks are also given to children who are disobedient and 'play crazy'. The Mapuche trust the power of the plant and its abilities to show their children 'the proper way to live'. The Jíbaro Indians of Ecuador have a similar custom.

The Aztecs, who were very knowledgeable about plants, were familiar with a number of thornapple species. These plants were associated with the other 'plants of the gods', including **Morning Glory, Ololiuqui, Peyote,** and **Teonanacatl**, and were used for medicinal and magical purposes. Rectal application was very popular among the Aztec physicians and magicians. They either administered a datura tea or a suppository made from a datura leaf.

Datura ceratocaula, whose fruits lack thorns, was called atlinan. It was considered to be a sister of the **Ololiuqui** vine and was sacred. Only the magician priests were allowed to use it. They invoked the spirit of the plant with a prayer:

> 'I call to you, my mother, for you are the beautiful water!
> Who is the god or who has the power, that he can break and consume my magic?
> Come over, sister of the green woman Ololiuqui, from whom, through whom I go, and I leave behind the green pain, the brown pain, that he conceals himself.
> Go and destroy the entrails of the possessed with your hands, that you will test his power and he will fall into disgrace.'

The thornapple is still widely used in modern Mexico. Usually, the leaves are smoked, although they are also made into teas for inebriant and analgesic purposes. The flowers are utilized as aphrodisiacs and love charms. There is even a *Santo Toloache*, the patron saint of the thornapple, who is invoked in order to awaken the love of another.

Many North American tribes, especially the peoples of California, the Pueblo, the Apache, and other tribes of the Southwest, venerate the thornapple and know of its medicinal and magical powers. The Chumash developed a shamanic cult around the ritual use of thornapple. The Navajo consider the plant sacred, and call it *Decoction of the Beautiful Path, Small White Hair, Great Flower of the Sun,* but also *Imbecile-Producer*. They use all parts of the plant. Collecting the holy plant is a ritual activity. When a person encounters a plant, he kneels down and scatters maize pollen over its leaves. He then addresses the plant:

> 'Forgive me for taking you.
> I do not do this out of pride.
> I want you to heal me.
> I will only take as much as I need.'

A person is allowed to take as much from the living plant as he needs, but he must leave enough to ensure its survival. If a person takes too much, and the plant perishes and its soul dies, then the collected material will loose its healing power. When a piece of the root is collected, then several leaves of another thornapple plant must be placed into the hole. The spirit of the plant is especially grateful when a person places a small piece of turquoise, the most sacred stone of the Indians, next to the root. The thornapple is also used for harmful magic, to transform a person into an animal, and for frenzy witchcraft.

Thornapple grows on most Caribbean islands as well. It is known as *concombre-zombí*, 'zombie cucumber', or *herbe aux sorciers*, 'plant of the magician'. It is greatly feared for its toxic and paralyzing properties, while it is an esteemed medicine and a popular aphrodisiac among the Exumas and the Bokors, the black magicians and healers of Haiti and Jamaica.

Pharmacology: The various thornapple species (*D. stramonium, inoxia, discolor, ceratocaula*, etc.) all contain identical or similar active ingredients. The highest alkaloid concentrations are in the seeds. The main active constituents are tropane alkaloids: hyoscine (= *l*-scopolamine; the principle alkaloid in Datura metel), *l*-hyoscyamine, atropine (= *l*/*d*-hyoscyamine). The drug also contains smaller amounts of nicotine, flavonoglycosides, and the cumarin scopoletine. The pharmacological effects are of two types: a centrally stimulating and a peripherally inhibiting. Increasing doses cause excitation, gaiety, flight of ideas, the urge to talk and to move, restless movement, desire to dance, cheerfulness, forced laughter, and finally states of confusion and deliriant hallucinations. The effects of the alkaloid complex are thus both stimulating and subduing (cf. **Angel's Trumpet**).

Literature: Adovasio & Fry 1976; Alegre 1980; Applegate 1975; Dobkin de Rios 1974; Furst & Myerhoff 1966; Hansen 1981; Hill 1938; Johnston 1972; Kennedy & Rätsch 1985; Li 1978; Litzinger 1981; Munizaga A. 1960; Rätsch 1987f, 1990a; Rätsch & Probst 1985; Weil 1977.

TOBACCO (Nicotiana tabacum, N. rustica, N. ondulata, N. spp.). There are some 70 varieties or species of tobacco, one of the oldest and most important cultivated plants of the American Indians, which grow throughout the New World (cf. **Picietl**). The religious, medicinal, and hedonistic use of tobacco is very ancient. Tobacco has been found among pre-Columbian grave goods, and images of the plant and images of smoking gods decorate Mayan temples and pyramids (e.g. Palenque). In addition to their medicinal use, a number of tobacco species were also used by religious and ecstatic cults. The shamans of many South American tribes smoke, chew, or sniff large amounts of tobacco, drink tobacco decoctions, or administer themselves tobacco enemas so that they may travel to the world of the spirits, recover the souls of the sick from the 'house of tobacco', and bring these back to earth. Often, a shaman will be referred to as 'one who is inebriated by tobacco'.

Tobacco is a magical plant known to all Mesoamerican Indians. Its leaves are used to defend against evil spirits and diseases, and cigars and cigarettes are deposited on paths and in houses and farms as protection against snakes. The Lacandon use cigar stumps to ward off the snake spirit which brings death. Medicine men blow the smoke of cigars or pipes over the skin of sick persons; this allows their magical healing powers to penetrate the skin. Tobacco smoke may also be blown across the genitals for aphrodisiac love magic. Tobacco is an important article of trade, is presented to guests, and serves as a symbol of friendship and affection. An additional reason why the gods gave humans tobacco was so that they could protect themselves from blood-sucking insects and crawling animals.

Tobacco smoke is also used for ritual purification, while decoctions of the plant are consumed as part of the preparations for ingesting more potent magical drinks (**Ayahuasca, San Pedro Cactus, Villca**). Among North American Indians, many kinds of tobacco (*Nicotiana attenuata, N. bigelovii, N. quadrivalvis, N. rustica, N. trigonophylla*) are venerated as sacred plants and used ceremonially in rituals of the sacred pipe.

After the Europeans arrived in the New World, tobacco spread throughout the world as a recreational drug. But it was also eagerly taken into the repertoire of Asian shamans, who use tobacco to induce shamanic trances, enter ecstatic states, and to dispel disease-causing spirits with its smoke. The shamans of Siberian and Manchurian tribes inhale tobacco smoke in the same manner as they inhale the smoke of their other magical plants (cf. **Juniper, Syrian Rue, Wild Rosemary**).

Native American shamans and magicians seldom smoke, sniff, or drink tobacco alone. Usually, they add it to any of a number of other herbs and magical items: **Aloe, Angel's Trumpet**, birch bark (*Betula spp.*), **Coca**, coneflower roots (*Echinacea angustifolia*), cornel bark (*Cornutum spp.*), **Henbane, Koribó**, papaya leaves (*Carica papaya*), shredded **Peyote**, **Sassafras** root cortex, styrax resin (*Liquidambar styraciflua*), tacamahaca buds (*Protium heptaphyllum*), **Tagetes** herbage, **Thornapple** leaves and flowers, uva-ursi leaves (Kinnikinnick), willow bark, and yarrow flowers (*Achillea millefolium*).

Pharmacology: The entire plant contains the pyridine alkaloids nicotine, nornicotine, anabasine, and nicotyrine. The main active substance is nicotine; depending upon the species, the leaves may contain up to 10%. Tobacco plants also contain piperidine, pyrrolidine, rutin, kaempferol-rhamnoglucaside, free amines, flavones, and cumarines. In small doses, nicotine stimulates the central nervous system; in moderate doses, it has inhibitory effects; and in large doses, it is lethal (50-100 mg). Recently, the ß-carbolines harmane and norharmane (cf. **Ayahuasca, Syrian Rue**) have been detected in tobacco smoke (but not in the plant). The concentrations of harmane present in the smoke of different tobacco species and preparations varies. The harmane content may be the reason why shamans use tobacco or may at least favor its use (Janiger & Dobkin de Rios 1976). The various species of *Nicotiana* most likely exhibit different effects.

Literature: Baer 1986; Janiger & Dobkin de Rios 1973, 1976; Mehra 1979; Moerman 1986; Rätsch 1987f; Robicsek 1978; Siegel et al. 1977; Wilbert 1979, 1987.

TULASI (Ocimum sanctum). The tulasi plant is found in India and Nepal, where it is planted around temples as an apotropaic agent and is venerated in domestic cults. According to legend, the plant arose from a former lover of Krishna, the god of love. Its scent is said to ward off demons and to heal. The plant is also used for medicinal purposes. Its juice is consumed as a rejuvenant (*rasayana*). Tulasi leaves are boiled with **Orchid** roots and cardamom to produce an aphrodisiac love drink. Pulverized leaves are sniffed to treat suppurations of the nasal sinuses.

The Brahmans consider Tulasi sacred, and the plant is consecrated to the gods Vishnu and Shiva. A person who cares for the plant with the reverence it deserves will attain happiness and health and will obtain a momentary glimpse of god and receive eternal blessing and youth. Drinking water to which tulasi leaves have been added is considered to be an effective panacea. The cult of death uses tulasi as a transformative plant. Dying persons are given tulasi to drink, and the plant is also placed in the grave. This enables the soul of the deceased to immediately rise to heaven.

In the Nepalese cult of Vishnu, the plant is married to a saligram (an ammonite from the Himalayan Kali-Gandhi valley). Here, the plant is considered an incarnation of Lakshmi, and the stone to be Vishnu himself.

Pharmacology: Tulasi contains an essential oil (composed of terpene derivatives, thymol, and camphor) with expectorant, antiseptic, and insecticidal properties. Psychoactive effects have not been observed.

Literature: Henglein 1985; Knecht 1985; Majupuria & Joshi 1988; Rätsch & Guhr 1989.

VACCINIUM (Vaccinium uliginosum). Vaccinium is a small bush quite similar to the blueberry (*Vaccinium myrtillus*). Found throughout Eurasia, its berries are edible but are said to produce a mild state of inebriation. Its German name, 'drunken berry' (*Trunkelbeere*), may reflect its use in a Siberian drink in which extracts of **Fly Agaric** were mixed with the juice of crushed vaccinium berries.

In Tyrolia (Austria), it is said that children can loose their wits if they eat 'dizzy berries' (*Schwindelbeeren*). We have no precise details concerning the use of vaccinium as an inebriant and a magical plant. It may be that vaccinium berries, like blueberries, were an additive in some old Germanic **Beers** and **Meads**. Another small bush, *Empetrum nigrum*, was known by the name 'inebriating berry' (*Rauschbeere*).

The Hawaiian ohelo plant (*Vaccinium reticulatum*) was sacred to Pele, the goddess of volcanos. Berries of this plant were offered to the goddess.

Pharmacology: Vaccinium berries contain tannins, fruit acids, vitamins, and minerals. They may also contain glycosides. No toxic constituents have been detected. The reports on its toxic effects are quite contradictory. No inebriating, narcotic, or psychedelic substances have been found. At least some of the properties attributed to vaccinium may be due to a parasitic fungus (*Sclerotinia megalospora*).

Literature: Engel 1982:109; Hartwich 1911:257; Kepler 1983.

VERVAIN (Verbena officinalis). The Romans knew this plant as *verbenaca* or *Veneris herba*, 'herb of Venus', and used it during rituals of love. Vervain was one of the sacred plants of the Celts, a fact which accounts for another of its names, Druid's Weed. The druids used it for healing purposes and to prepare magic drinks. Pliny has provided us with a description of the magical use of vervain among the Gauls: they

> 'would use the *verbenaca* for divination and the *magi* (druids) would make pure nonsense with it. When rubbed into the skin, a person can attain everything he desires: the herb dispels fever, promotes friendship and heals all diseases. It should be collected when the dog star (Sirius) rises, when neither the sun nor the moon are shining, but placate the earth beforehand by offerings of wax and honey. Use iron to make a circle around the plant and then immediately dig it up with the left hand.'

It is possible that the use of vervain was also associated with the magical practices of the blacksmiths. The Germans used vervain as an amulet during peace treaties and to protect against the evil eye and the temptations of witches. Vervain was said to give strength ('tough as iron', 'hard as steel') and to act as an aphrodisiac (the hardness of iron was said to be transferred to the penis).

In Central Europe, vervain has been venerated as a magical plant even in recent times. It was thought to dispel ghosts and evil spirits, kindle burning love ('like glowing iron', 'an iron in the oven'), give wondrous, prophetic dreams, and refresh the mind. The plant was worn as an amulet to protect against demons, and yet was also one of the ingredients of the **Witches' Ointments**. Vervain was considered a cure-all in the folk medical traditions of Europe.

Pharmacology: Vervain contains various glycosides (verbenalin, hastatoside), essential oil, bitter agents, and mucilage. The pharmacology is still unknown (!). Animal experiments have demonstrated parasympathetic effects.

Literature: Andoh 1986; Engel 1978; Gessmann n.d.; Schöpf 1986.

VILLCA (Anadenanthera colubrina). In pre-Columbian times, the magicians of the Peruvian coastal regions and the countries of the Andes often added villca fruits or seeds to their chicha (**Beer, Maize**). The resulting beverage was very potent, and opened doors to invisible worlds to which the magicians could then fly to meet their animal spirits and collide with the divine and the demonic powers. They would partake of this drink whenever they needed advice, wanted to see into the future, or wished to aid the sick. Villca also played a central role in one purification ritual. The fruits were used to prepare a liquid, half of which was drunk, while the other half was administered as an enema. The instrument used to administer the enema was named after the fruit: *villca-china*, the 'villca fruit servant'. Villca was also sniffed (**Snuff**).

The aromatic seeds of the *espingo* plant (*Quararibea sp.*) had a similar use and importance.

Pharmacology: Villca contains the potent psychoactive tryptamine derivatives DMT, 5-Meo-DMT, and bufotenine, none of which are orally effective (cf. **Snuff**). For this reason, the information contained in the older sources is certainly incomplete. In chicha, the psychoactive effects of villca can only become manifest when an MAO inhibitor is added as well (cf. **Ayahuasca**). The constituents and pharmacology of the *espingo* plant have not yet been determined.

Literature: Dobkin de Rios 1980; Rätsch 1987d; Smet 1985; Wassén 1979.

VOACANGA (one or several plants from the family of the Apocynaceae; Voacanga dregei, V. spp.). Voacanga is a shrub found in the tropics of Western Africa. Its root is used ritually in a similar manner as **Iboga**, whereby its effects are said to be more pronounced. In Ghana, voacanga is considered a magical medicine and a powerful aphrodisiac. Drummers are said to use it to increase their endurance and enhance their technical expertise. This plant is one of the best guarded secrets of West Africa. Its investigation promises an exciting adventure.

Pharmacology: The root contains an alkaloid named voacangine, which has a completely new chemical structure. It is reported to have potent psychedelic effects. Dosages as low as 0.3 grams are active. Voacangine is said to be a 'heart tonic'.

Literature: oral communication from Ralph Metzner; Schultes & Hofmann 1980:366.

WATER LILY (Nymphaea spp., Nuphar luteum). To the ancient Egyptians, the blue water lily (*Nymphaea caerula*) was a magical plant closely related to the **Lotus**. The blue water lily was a symbol of death and rebirth and was sacred to Osiris. After Osiris was murdered by Seth, his wife and sister Isis, the goddess of magic and medicinal plants, brought him back to life. According to one myth, she re-created him as a blue water lily. The blue water lily was also a symbol of divination, and was often portrayed together with **Mandrake**, **Poppy** capsules, and the toad. The Egyptian Book of the Dead contains a text known as the 'Transformation into the Water Lily' which describes a shamanic or alchemical transformation: 'I am the sacred water lily, which came out of the light, which belongs to the nostrils of Ra and to the head of Hathor. I am the pure water lily, which came from the field of Ra.' Ra was associated with **Mandrake** beer and was presumably also associated with the magical flights and visions produced by the water lily (?). The flowers of the blue water lily were also strung together with mandrake fruits and poppy capsules and worn as amulets and talismans. Additional research is still needed to fully clarify the significance which the blue water lily had for the culture of ancient Egypt. The white water lily (*Nymphaea lotus*) was said to ward off demons and incite love. Its flowers were offered to the gods.

According to the ancient Greeks, the white water lily (*Nymphaea alba*) had a divine origin, having arisen from a nymph who died of jealousy. It was added to **Wine** and taken for medicinal purposes. It was also known as an anaphrodisiac. Known as the 'flower of chastity', the white water lily was a popular means for Medieval monks and nuns to suppress their 'devilish desires'. Strangely, however, the water lily was also used in love magic. For this purpose, the flower had to be plucked during a night of a full moon. The collector had to plug his ears, lest he be seduced by the bewitching songs of the water nixes and pulled into the depths. After he had obtained the flower, he wore it on his body as a love amulet.

Water lilies also possess magical and ritual meaning in the New World. The Iroquois refer to the yellow pond lily (*Nuphar luteum variegatum*) as 'great root' or 'seat of the bullfrog'. The root is good medicine against all forms of witchcraft and protects from demons. In order to dispel irritating spirits, several slices of the root tuber are placed in water. This water is then sprinkled about those places where the spirits like to linger. To protect against witches, the Iroquois hang the root over the entrances to their houses. Any witch who then passes below loses her eyesight. When a person wishes to discover the source of some harmful magic, they must make and drink a decoction of the root. They will then see the cause. If a person is suspected of practising harmful magic, he is given a drink made from the root and four other (unknown) plants. If the suspect vomits, or if he speaks in an unknown tongue, he is considered guilty (cf. **Mwamfi**).

The white water lily (*Nymphaea ampla*) played an important role in the Mayan religion. It was often depicted in conjunction with animal transformations and visions. It was presumably added to the **Balche'** drink in order to produce ecstatic states. Many magical spells refer to it as a magical device. There is also evidence that the water lily is still being used in Chiapas (in Southern Mexico) as a plant of prophecy. The significance of the water lily for the culture of the Maya also requires additional investigation.

The Guaraní Indians know of the magical power of the water lily Irupé (*Nymphaea sp.*). The scent of the flower can enchant a person. Irupé was originally a beautiful girl who cast herself into the water after learning that her future husband had fallen in battle. Upon her death, she was transformed into the water lily.

Pharmacology: Nymphaea caerula may contain several narcotic alkaloids whose chemistry must still be investigated. A decoction made from 3-6 buds or flowers which are just beginning to open has hypnotic effects. *Nymphaea alba* contains the alkaloid nupharine and the glycoside nymphaline. An extract of the plant causes states of excitation, but also respiratory paralysis. The principle alkaloid in *Nuphar lutea* is desoxynupharidine; it also contains nupharine and nupharidine. The spasmolytic and hypotensive effects of nupharine are similar to those of atropine and papaverine (cf. **Belladonna, Poppy**). Desoxynupharidine has tonic and hypertensive effects. The total extract has anaphrodisiac effects. *Nymphaea ampla* contains aporphine and quinolizidine alkaloids, which have psychoactive effects. The leaves of *Nymphaea lotus* are said to have narcotic effects. Unfortunately, we have no dependable reports about these effects.

Literature: Dobkin de Rios 1978b; Emboden 1978, 1979a, 1981a, 1981d, 1982, 1983, 1989; Emboden & Dobkin de Rios 1980; Herrick 1983; Manniche 1989; Melzer 1987:35-37; Müller-Ebeling & Rätsch 1986; Rätsch 1987a.

WILD ROSEMARY (Ledum palustre). Wild rosemary, which grows in Northern Europe and Northern Asia, appears to have played an important role as a magical plant and remedy. However, this role has not yet been sufficiently investigated. The Germans used the plant (known by the name *Porst* or *Sumpfporst*) as a bittering agent in **Beer**. Beer which was treated in this way (*Grutbier*) also had strong inebriating properties and could cause frenzy and deliria. And in fact, the madness of the Berserkers has been linked to excessive consumption of beer made with wild rosemary (cf. **Fly Agaric**). In Siberia, wild rosemary is a popular medicinal plant which is effective in protecting against insects. Besides **Juniper**, the shamans of the Tungus and Giljacs use especially wild rosemary to produce shamanic trances in which they can prophesy and heal the sick. While they usually inhale the smoke of the plant, they may also chew the root. They also

Fig. 26: Wild rosemary (after Tabernaemontanus 1731).

massage the needle-like leaves into their knees. Ainu shamans use the plant to make a tea for treating dysmenorrhea. During shamanic healing rituals, they imbibe a salted drink of spruce, wild rosemary, and mint.

Pharmacology: The entire plant contains the aromatic essential oil ledole, palustrole, myrcene, quercetin, hyperoside, arbutin, and several alkaloids. The oil has psychoactive and inebriant effects. Larger doses have toxic effects upon the gastrointestinal tract; they can also induce miscarriage.

Literature: Chamisso 1987:169; Greve 1938; Knoll-Greiling 1959; Mitsuhashi 1976; Ohnuki-Tierney 1980; Rätsch 1990b; Sandermann 1980.

WINE (Vitis vinifera). Although wine has been known in the eastern Mediterranean region and in Mesopotamia since the earliest recorded history, it is difficult to state precisely when and where the wine grape was first cultivated or when the first wine was pressed. In ancient times, wine was one of the sacred drinks associated with the gods ('drink of the gods') and which made it possible to contact them. The ancient Egyptians considered the grapevine one of the trees of life. When Isis, the goddess of magic and herbal lore, ate grapes, she became pregnant and bore Horus. Osiris, her brother and spouse, became the lord of wine and made the drink into an instrument of magic. Wine was a life-sustaining food for the dead, and was consumed at temple festivals and used in practical magic. The Egyptians added many highly active magical plants to the wine they pressed from grapes, including **Henbane, Mandrake**, and possibly **Thornapple**; they may have also added opium (cf. **Poppy**), **Qat**, and the blue **Water Lily**.

To the ancient Greeks, wine was the 'blood of the earth'. They used it as a universal remedy, aphrodisiac, and antidote. It was recommended to treat the toxic effects of such plants as **Aconite, Hellebore, Mistletoe, Mushrooms,** and **Poppy**, and for snake bites and scorpion stings. A number of herbs were also added to Greek wine to produce certain specific effects: **Belladonna, Hellebore, Henbane, Mandrake, Poppy, Saffron,** and **Incense**, balsam, myrrh, cyclamen (*Cyclamen*), oleander (*Nerium*), etc. Prior to consumption, Greek wine was diluted with water (1:3). This made it easier to control the stimulating effects of wine during the *symposion*, the ritual 'drinking bouts', while avoiding becoming drunk too quickly.

Wine was the inebriating drink consumed during the Aphrodisia and Dionysia to inflame the ecstatic orgies staged to honor the gods. In all likelihood, Dionysos was a god of shamanic origin who came from Asia and introduced an ecstatic/erotic cult into Greece. He was the god of ecstasy and thus the god of those magical plants which produced ecstasy. As one of his symbols, the grapevine consequently became an instrument of magic. The god was always present in wine. The wine was his blood and the carrier of his life energy.

The grapevine was attributed with magical properties which have been preserved in a Slavic custom. If a maiden wants to be visited by her lover in her dreams, she should place a grapevine under her pillow. When a person wishes to break an unwanted love spell, they are told to pull up a white grapevine and throw it into a stream. Wine itself was also used for love magic: 'When a maiden places water in the cellar or in the parlour on Thomas' Night and pours wine into it from a height, she can see her future husband' (Aigremont 1987:94). In medieval times, it was said that the love potion of Tristan and Isolde was a type of wine. Even today, wine continues to enjoy a reputation as an aphrodisiac.

Pharmacology: Wine contains over 250 active ingredients, including vitamins, minerals (iron and phosphorus), trace elements, and, of course, alcohol. In low doses, wine has stimulating, invigorating, slightly anti-bacterial, anti-inflammatory, and diuretic effects. The powerful inebriating and ecstatic effects of wine that are described in the ancient sources resulted from the alkaloids and other psychotropic constituents present in the additives.

Literature: Emboden 1977; Hagenow 1972; Lurker 1987; Müller-Ebeling & Rätsch 1986; Rätsch 1990a; Ruck 1982; Wasson et al. 1978.

WITCHES' OINTMENTS. The case histories of the witchcraft trials of the Middle Ages and early modern times repeatedly refer to witches' flying, and love ointments. Cited as the cause of the nocturnal departures for witches' sabbaths, it was said that these ointments enabled the person who used them to go on an inner journey to magical worlds. They were also reputed to be the most important tool of the witches and sorcerers. Unfortunately, these case histories usually do not give recipes or only hint at them. It was said that they were manufactured from human fat, the boiled corpses of children, etc. We also occasionally find mention that the ointments contained 'Thebaicum, Smyrna paste, dragon's blood, sleeping oil (a medieval synonym for opium; cf. **Poppy**) and **Asafoetida**. The recipes for witches' ointments remained a secret into modern times. Nevertheless, many scholars and physicians (!) — especially during the sixteenth century — recorded a number of recipes which they claimed provided a pharmacological basis for the reports of witches' flights, the sabbath, and the associated erotic excesses and orgies. Amazingly the recipes for witches' ointments were remarkably similar to recipes for poplar bud ointments (*Unguentum populi*) (de Vries 1986).

All of the recipes which have been passed down to us are composed of several magical plants: **Aconite, Artemisia, Asafoetida, Belladonna, Betel, Calamus, Garlic, Hellebore, Hemp, Henbane, Lettuce, Mandrake, Nightshade, Nux Vomica, Orchids, Poppy, Saffron, Scopolia, Thornapple, Vervain, Water Lily, Wine,** as well as **Hemlock**, Spanish fly, **Incense** (olibanum), household spices, parsley, celery, watercress, pastinaca, corn poppy, and salad. We do not know whether these recipes for witches' ointments were in fact invented by the persons accused of being 'witches' and 'sorcerers', or whether they represented an ancient tradition of a Central European pagan fertility cult, or whether they were simply put together by the early apothecaries. We do know that the philters or love drinks of the sixteenth century which the apothecaries compounded did contain a great many of the 'Satanic plants and forces'. They — like the 'witches' ointments' — contained mandrake, Spanish fly (*Lytta vesicatoria*), saffron and other spices (cinnamon, marjoram, lavender, pepper), myrrh, mastic, wolves' fat, and **Vervain**. In the eighteenth and nineteenth century, many recipes similar to those for the witches' ointments and intended especially for use in sexual magical circles appeared in France.

Ointments are known from Mexico which the *brujas* ('witches') use for aphrodisiac love magic. These ointments are primarily composed of extracts of **Thornapple** in pig lard.

Pharmacology: The folklorist Will-Erich Peuckert has provided a dramatic description of the effects produced when witches' ointment is smeared on the naked body: 'We had wild dreams. Faces danced before my eyes which were at first terrible. Then I suddenly had the sensation of flying for miles through the air. The flight was repeatedly interrupted by great falls. Finally, in the last phase, an image of an orgiastic feast with grotesque sensual excesses.' The effects of the witches' ointments are probably due to a synergism between the components: 'The witches' ointment may be psychopharmacologically interesting because we apparently have here the only toxic technique of ecstasy in the world in which the specific components of the experience are achieved by the way the psychopharmacological agents are added together. This principle of selective effects by combining substances has not yet been investigated scientifically' (Leuner 1981:67). Witches' ointments contain a mixture of tropane alkaloids, glycosides, cannabinols, opiates, and essential oils.

Literature: de Vries 1986; Hansen 1981; Harner 1973; Hauschild 1981; Marzell 1964; Müller-Ebeling & Rätsch 1986; Peuckert 1960; Römpp 1950; Rose 1972; Schrödter 1981; Spilmont 1984; Urchs 1986; Wedeck 1966.

WITCH HAZEL (Hamamelis virginiana). The Indians of North America have long used witch hazel for a variety of medicinal purposes: as an analgesic, cold remedy, febrifuge, dermatological aid, gynaecological aid, throat aid, tuberculosis remedy, emetic, eye medicine, antidiarrheal, antirheumatic, heart medicine, kidney aid, and venereal aid. The Iroquois venerated witch hazel as a panacea. The Menominee used its seeds as sacred beads in their medicine ceremony. However, it apparently only became a magical plant after the arrival of the European settlers, who saw in it a relative of the European hazel (*Coryllus avellana*), which was renowned as a magical and sacred plant of the ancient Germans and was used for manufacturing divining rods. The settlers attributed the witch hazel with even greater occult powers, and made its branches into divining rods which they used to search for water and gold.

Pharmacology: Hamamelis leaves contain ß-hamamelitanine as well as other tannins, saponines, flavonglycosides, and some essential oil. The precise pharmacodynamics of the substances contained in witch hazel are still unknown; they are mildly astringent and antiseptic and influence the venous circulation. The plant's use as a divining rod is probably due to the elasticity of its branches rather than any pharmacological effects.

Literature: Aigremont 1987; Engel 1979; Moerman 1986; Weiner 1972.

WOODROSE (Argyreia nervosa, Argyreia tuberosa and A. spp.). The woodrose is a member of the family of the **Morning Glory**. Found chiefly on Hawaii, it also occurs in Asia. In former times, the seeds of this vine were used in Hawaii as a poor man's inebriant. Today, we can only guess whether the indigenous Huna religion used the plant in a cultic or magical context. In the Californian subculture, it is possible to obtain herbal tablets made from five woodrose seeds, damiana (*Turnera diffusa*), **Ginseng, Fo-Ti** and bee pollen. These *Utopian Bliss Balls* are used in modern sexual magic practices. Ethnobotanical research into the woodrose is still in its beginnings.

Pharmacology: The seeds of the woodrose contain 0.3% lysergic acid amide and ergoline. The effects are comparable to those of **Ololiuqui** (see also **Morning Glory**). Up to thirteen seeds can be taken at one time. Initial sensations of nausea and dizziness are followed by magnificently colored visions with mystical contents. 'As little as two grams of seeds produces hallucinogenic effects not unlike LSD, which persist for 8 hours or more. The seeds must be ground prior to ingestion, for if swallowed whole poor digestion and absorption will vitiate the effects' (Ott 1979:58). Euphoric and aphrodisiac effects have also been observed (Stark 1980).

Literature: Emboden 1974; Ott 1979; Smith 1985; Stafford 1983; Stark 1980.

YOHIMBE (Corynanthe yohimbe). Traditional fetish priests have used the West African yohimbé tree for magical purposes since ancient times. They use its bark to brew love drinks, to promote potency, and as an aphrodisiac. Bantu-speaking peoples utilize the inner cortex of the bark as a sacrament when they marry. Reports from dubious sources suggest that the bark was also used to make virgins tractable for chiefs, who had the right to the first night with a woman. It is also said that great amounts of yohimbé were consumed during tribal orgies which lasted for ten days. It was also used in ritual contexts for initiations and divinations:

> 'In Africa, the black magicians have their followers drink yohimbé and

> **Iboga** to introduce them to the inebriation of the great fetish initiations. The candidates are given a great amount of iboga, either in its natural state or as a decoction. Shortly thereafter, all of their nerves tauten in an unusual manner; they are overcome by an epileptic madness, while they utter words unconsciously which, if one of the initiated can pick them out, have a prophetic meaning and prove that the fetish lives within them' (Rouhier 1986:8).

Although the yohimbé tree is famous throughout the world because of its effects, little is known about its ethnobotanical status. Yohimbé bark is a popular sacrament in modern witches' cults and sexual magical circles. The bark of a related West African tree, *Corynanthe pachyceras*, is used to increase the potency of fermented drinks such as sorghum **Beer**. In tropical Africa, it too is considered an aphrodisiac.

Pharmacology: The principle active constituent of yohimbé bark is yohimbine, an indole alkaloid (cf. **Niando, Quebracho**). Yohimbine is an

Fig. 27: The yun-shih plant (from the Chêng-lei pên-ts'ao, *1249 AD).*

MAO inhibitor (cf. **Ayahuasca, Syrian Rue**) which has stimulating effects upon the sexual ganglion cells in the sacral medulla and is capable of producing strong, long-lasting erections. In higher doses (20-30 mg of the alkaloid), it also has mild psychedelic effects. The bark of *C. pachyceras* contains corynanthine alkaloids.

Literature: Andoh 1986; Gilg & Schürhoff 1926; Miller 1985; Müller-Ebeling & Rätsch 1986; Rätsch 1990a; Rouhier 1986; Stafford 1983.

YUN-SHIH (Caesalpinia sepiaria). Yun-shih enjoys one of the longest traditions of medicinal use of any wild plant in China. A herbaceous tendril from the family of the *Fabaceae*, yun-shih is found throughout southern China and Central Asia. Its roots, leaves, and seeds are used in traditional Chinese medicine. According to ancient texts, the flowers contain occult powers. In the *Pen Ts'ao Ching*, it is said that: '[The flowers] make it possible to see a spirit, but when they are taken in excess, you can become demented. If they are ingested over an extended period, they produce bodily levitation and promote communication with the spirits.' In another text, the *Tao Hun-ching*, one can read: '[The flowers] dispel the evil spirits. Placed in water or burned, they can conjure up spirits.... The seeds are like those of Lang-tang (**Henbane**); when they are burned, spirits can be conjured up.' It is unknown whether the plant is still used for magical purposes. The related plant *Caesalpina bonduc* was used as a substitute for **Soma**.

Pharmacology: Unknown.

Literature: Li 1978.

ZACATECHICHI (Calea zacatechichi). This yellow-blossomed shrub from the family of the *Asteraceae* grows throughout Central America. Its herbage is used in folk medicine as a purgative and antipyretic. The Mexican name *zacatechichi* is derived from Aztecan and means 'bitter grass' (a reference to its extremely bitter taste). This plant may be identical with the inebriating *chichixihuitl* described in colonial sources. The Chontal Indians, who live in the Mexican state of Oaxaca, refer to the plant as *thle-pelakano*, 'leaf of god'. Chontal healers make a potent, astringent decoction of freshly crushed leaves which they drink to produce visions and clairvoyant, dream-like states. After drinking this, they lay in a semi-darkened room and smoke a cigarette of dried zacatechichi leaves. In this state, they often perceive the voices of the gods and spirits who reveal the causes of diseases, decipher the future, and help them find lost objects.

Pharmacology: The plant contains various germacranolides (caleicines and their analogs) and an as yet structurally unknown alkaloid ($C_{24}H_{26}O_8$) with presumably mild hallucinogenic, antiatherogenic, and CNS depressing effects. According to Diaz (1979:79), there are both psychoactive and non-active varieties of the plant. Diaz *et al.* (1986) conducted a double-blind experiment using a placebo and found that the use of zacatechichi led to a significant increase in the number of meaningful dreams. The dried leaves can be smoked and may induce effects not unlike those of marijuana.

Literature: Diaz 1979; Diaz et al. 1986; Emboden 1979; Mayagioita et al. 1986; Schultes & Hofmann 1980.

Bibliography

Adamson, Sophia. 1985. *Through the Gateway of the Heart*, San Francisco: Four Trees.

Adovasio, J.M. & G.F. Fry. 1976. 'Prehistoric Psychotropic Drug Use in Northern Mexico and Trans-Peco Texas', *Economic Botany*, 30:94-96.

Aero, Rita. 1980. *The Complete Book of Longevity*, New York: Perigee.

Aigremont, Dr. 1917. *Volkserotik und Pflanzenwelt*, (two volumes), Leipzig: Krauss (reprinted 1986, Berlin: EXpress).

Ajaya, Swami. 1980. *Living with the Himalayan Masters*, Honesdale, Pennsylvania: Himalayan International Institute.

Albert-Puleo, Michael. 1978. 'Mythobotany, Pharmacology, and Chemistry of Thujone-Containing Plants and Derivatives', *Economic Botany*, 32:65-74.

Aldrich, Michael R. 1977. 'Tantric Cannabis Use in India', *Journal of Psychedelic Drugs*, 9(3):227-233.

Alegre, Dennis G. 1980. *Sagada: A Survey of the Folk Herbal Practices of the Sagada Igorots in Mountain Provinces and Some Important Implications*, Los Baños, College of Agriculture, University of Philippines (MS).

Aleijos. 1977. *T'u Ch'uan—grüne Wunderdroge Tee*, Vienna: Braumüller.

Allegro, John. 1970. *The Sacred Mushroom and the Cross*, London: Hodder & Stoughton.

Anderson, Edward F. 1980. *Peyote—The Divine Cactus*, Tucson: University of Arizona Press.

Andoh, Anthony. 1986. *The Science and Romance of Selected Herbs used in Medicine and Religious Ceremony*, San Francisco: North Scale Institute.

Andrews, George & David Solomon, eds. 1975. *The Coca Leaf and Cocaine Papers*, New York, Harcourt Brace Jovanovich.

Andrews, George & Simon Vinkenoog, eds. 1968. *The Book of Grass*, New York: Grove Press.

Andritsky, Walter. 1989a. *Schamanismus und rituelles Heilen im Alten Amerika*, (two volumes), Berlin: Clemens Zerling. 1989b. 'Sociopsychotherapeutic Functions of Ayahuasca', *Journal of Psychoactive Drugs*, 21(1):77-90.

Anonymous. 1974. 'Navajo Witchcraft', *El Palacio*, 80(2):38-43.

Antonil. 1978. *Mama Coca*, London: Hassle Free Press.

Applegate, Richard B. 1975. 'The Datura Cult Among the Chumash', *The Journal of Californian Anthropology*, 2(1):7-17.

Artaud, Antonin. 1975. *Die Tarahumaras — Revolutionäre Botschaften*, Munich: Rogner & Bernhard.

Ayala Flores, Franklin & Walter H. Lewis. 1978. 'Drinking the South American Hallucinogenic Ayahuasca', *Economic Botany*, 32:154-156.

Baer, Gerhard. 1986. 'Der vom Tabak Berauschte — Zum Verhältnis von Rausch, Ekstase und Wirklichkeit', *Verhandlungen der Naturforschenden Gesellschaft in Basel*, 96:41-84.

Baker, John Read. 1989. *The Emergence of Culture*, Dr.Phil. dissertation, Seminar für Völkerkunde, Universität Hamburg, Germany.

Baldwin, E. 1984. *Hawaii's Poisonous Plants*, Hilo: Petroglyph.

Barrios, Virginia B. de. 1984. *A Guide to Tequila, Mezcal and Pulque*, México, D.F.: Minutae Mexicana.

Basker, D. & M. NEGBI. 1983. 'Uses of Saffron', *Economic Botany*, 37(2):228-236.

Bastien, Joseph W. 1987. *Healers of the Andes*, Salt Lake City: University of Utah Press.

Baumann, Hellmut. 1982. *Die griechische Pflanzenwelt in Mythos, Kunst und Literatur*, Munich: Hirmer.

Becker, Hans & Helga Schmoll, called Eisenwirth. 1986. *Mistel: Arzneipflanze — Brauchtum — Kunstmotiv im Jugendstil*, Stuttgart: Wissenschaftliche Verlagsgesellschaft.

Beckmann, Dieter & Barbara Beckmann. 1990. *Alraun, Beifuß und andere Hexenkräuter*, Frankfurt/Main, New York: Campus.

Behr, Hans-Georg. 1980. *Weltmacht Droge*, Vienna: Econ. 1982. *Von Hanf ist die Rede*, Basel: Sphinx.

Bensky, Dan & Andrew Gamble. 1986. *Chinese Herbal Medicine — Materia Medica*, Seattle: Eastland.

Berge, Fr. & V.A. Riecke. 1845. *Giftpflanzen-Buch*, Stuttgart: Hoffmann'sche Verlagsbuchhandlung.

Berry, Michael I. & Betty P. Jackson. 1976. 'European Mandrake (*Mandragora officinarum* L. and *M. autumnalis* Bertol.); the Structure of the Rhizome and Root', *Planta Medica*, 30:281-290.

Betz, Hans Dieter. 1986. *The Greek Magical Papyri in Translation*, Chicago: University of Chicago Press.

Bibra, Ernst Freiherr von. 1855. *Die Narkotischen Genußmittel und der Mensch*, Nuremberg: W. Schmid.

Biedermann, Hans. 1972. *Medicina Magica: Metaphysische Heilmethoden in spätantiken und mittelalterlichen Codices*, Graz, Austria: Akademische Druck- u. Verlagsanstalt.

1974. *Hexen*, Graz, Austria: Verlag für Sammler.

1984. *Höhlenkunst der Eiszeit*, Cologne: DuMont.

1986. *Handlexikon der magischen Künste*, Graz, Austria: Akademische Druck-u. Verlagsanstalt.

Boland, Maureen & Bridget Boland. 1976. *Old Wive's Lore for Gardeners*, London: The Bodley Head.

1977. *Gardener's Magic*, London: The Bodley Head.

Boulos, Loutfy. 1983. *Medicinal Plants of North Africa*, Algonac, Michigan: Reference.

Bouquet, Armand. 1969. *Féticheurs et médecines traditionelles du Congo (Brazzaville)*, Paris: O.R.S.T.O.M. (Mémoires No. 36).

Bramley, Serge. 1977. *Im Reiche des Wakan*, Basel: Sphinx.

Brewer-Carias, Charles & Julian A. Steyermark. 1976. 'Hallucinogenic Snuff Drugs of the Yanomamo Cubriwe-Teri in the Cauaburi River, Brazil', *Economic Botany*, 30:57-66.

Brito, Silvester J. 1989. *The Way of a Peyote Roadman*, New York: Peter Lang.

Brondegaard, V.J. 1972. 'Artemisia in der gynäkologischen Volksmedizin', *Ethnomedizin*, 2(1/2):3-16.

1985. *Ethnobotanik*, Berlin: Mensch und Leben.

Bruhn, J.G. et al. 1971. '*Carnegiea gigantea*: The Saguaro and Its Uses', *Economic Botany*, 25(3):320-329.

1973. 'Alkaloids and Ethnobotany of Mexican Peyote Cacti and Related Species', *Economic Botany*, 27(2):241-251.

1976. 'Alkaloids of *Carnegiea gigantea*', *Lloydia*, 39(4):197-203.

Brunner, Theodore F. 1977. 'Marijuana in Ancient Greece and Rome? The Literary Evidence', *Journal of Psychedelic Drugs*, 9(3):221-225.

Bye, Robert A. 1979. 'Hallucinogenic Plants of the Tarahumara', *Journal of Ethnopharmacology*, 1:23-48.

Calderon, J.B. 1896. 'Estudio sobre el arbusto llamado Sinicuiche', *Anales del Instituto Médico Nacional (México)*, 2:36-42.

Camporesi, Piero. 1980. *Il pane selvaggio*, Bologna, Italy: Società Editrice il Mulino.

Castaneda, Carlos. 1968. *The Teachings of Don Juan: A Yaqui Way of Knowledge*, Berkeley: University of California Press.

1971. *A Separate Reality: Further Conversations with Don Juan*, New York: Simon & Schuster.

1972. *Journey to Ixtlan: The Lessons of Don Juan*, New York: Simon & Schuster.

Chamisso, Adelbert von. 1987. *Illustriertes Heil-, Gift-und Nutzpflanzenbuch*, Berlin: Reimer (reprint of the 1827 edition).

Chesi, Gert. 1989. *Die Medizin der Schwarzen Götter: Magie und Heilkunst Afrikas*, Vienna: Jugend und Volk.

Christensen, Bodil & Samuel Marti. 1979. *Witchcraft and Pre-Columbian Paper*, Mexico, D.F.: Euram.

Clifford, Terry. 1984. *Tibetan Buddhist Medicine and Psychiatry*, York Beach, Maine: S. Weiser

Cooper, J.C. 1984. *Chinese Alchemy: The Taoist Quest for Immortality*, Wellingsborough, Northamptonshire: The Aquarian Press.

Cooper, John M. 1949. 'Stimulants and Narcotics', *Handbook of South American Indians*, Washington, D.C.: Smithsonian Institute, 5:52 5-558.

Crowley, Aleister. 1979. *Energized Enthusiasm*, New York: S. Weiser.

Cunningham, Scott. 1983. *Magical Herbalism*, St. Paul, Minnesota: Llewellyn.

1989. *Cunningham's Encyclopedia of Magical Herbs*, St. Paul, Minnesota: Llewellyn.

Cutts, Gretchen S. 1985. *Potions, Portions, Poisons*, Estes Park, Colorado: Rocky Mountains Nature Association.

Dahl, Jürgen. 1985. 'Die Zauberwurzel der kleinen Leute...', *Natur*, 6/85:83-84.

Davenport, John. 1966. *Aphrodisiacs and Love Stimulants*, New York: Lyle Stuart.

Davis, E. Wade. 1985. *The Serpent and the Rainbow*, New York: Simon & Schuster.

1988. *Passage of Darkness*, Chapel Hill & London: University of North Carolina Press.

Degenhard, Armin von. 1985. *Das Klistier*, Flensburg, Germany: Carl Stephonson.

Deimel, Claus. 1985. 'Die Peyoteheilung der Tarahumara', *Schreibheft*, 25:155-163.

Deltgen, 1979. *Mit Flinte und Blasrohr*, Cologne: Rautenstrauch-Joest-Museum.

Devereux, Paul. 1990. *Places of Power*, London: Blandford.

De Waal, M. 1984. *Medicinal Herbs in the Bible*, York Beach, Maine: Samuel Weiser.

Diaz, José Luis. 1977. 'Ethnopharmacology of Sacred Psychoactive Plants Used by the Indians of Mexico', *Annual Review of Pharmacology and Toxicology*, 17:647-675.

1979. 'Ethopharmacology and Taxonomy of Mexican Psychodysleptic Plants', *Journal of Psychedelic Drugs*, 11(1-2):71-101.

Diaz, José L. *et al.* 1986. 'Psychopharmacologic Analysis of an Alleged Oneirogenic Plant: *Calea zacatechichi*', *Journal of Ethnopharmacology*, 18:229-243.

Dioscorides. 1959. *The Greek Herbal of Dioscorides*, Robert T. Gunther, ed., New York: Hafner (reprint of the 1934 edition).

Dittrich, Adolf & Christian Scharfetter, eds. 1987. *Ethnopsychotherapie*, Stuttgart: Enke.

Dobkin de Rios, Marlene. 1968a. 'Folk Curing with a Psychedelic Cactus in Northern Peru', *International Journal of Social Psychiatry*, 15:23-32.

1968b. '*Trichocereus pachanoi* — A Mescaline Cactus Used in Folk Healing in Peru', *Economic Botany*, 22(2):191-194.

1969. 'Fortune's Malice: Divination, Psychotherapy, and Folk Medicine in Peru', *Journal of American Folklore*, 82(324):13 2-141.

1970a. '*Banisteriopsis* Used in Witchcraft and Folk Healing in Iquitos, Peru', *Economic Botany* 24(35):296-300.

1970b. 'A Note on the Use of Ayahuasca Among Mestizo Populations in the Peruvian Amazon', *American Anthropologist*, 72(6):1419-1422.

1972. *Visionary Vine: Psychedelic Healing in the Peruvian Amazon*, San Francisco: Chandler.

1974a. 'The Influence of Psychotropic Flora and Fauna on Maya Religion', *Current Anthropology*, 15(2):147-164.

1974b. 'Cultural Persona in Drug-Induced Altered States of Consciousness', in *Social and Cultural Identity*, Thomas N. Fitzgerald, ed., Athens, Georgia: University of Georgia Press (SAS Proceedings No. 8), pp. 15-23.

1977. 'Plant Hallucinogens and the Religion of the Mochica', *Economic Botany*, 31(2):189-203.

1978a. 'A Psi Approach to Love Magic, Witchcraft and Psychedelics in the Peruvian Amazon', *New Directions in the Study of Man*, 2(1):22-27.

1978b. 'The Maya and the Water Lily', *New Scholar*, 5(2):299-307.

1980. 'Plant Hallucinogens, Shamanism and Nazca Ceramics', *Journal of Ethnopharmacology*, 2:233-246.

1981. 'Socio-Economic Characteristics of an Amazon Urban Healer's Clientele', *Social Science and Medicine*, 15B:51-63.

1982. 'Plant Hallucinogens, Sexuality and Shamanism in the Ceramic Art of Ancient Peru', *Journal of Psychoactive Drugs*, 14(1-2):81-90.

1984. *Hallucinogens: Cross-Cultural Perspectives*, Albuquerque: University of New Mexico Press.

1985. 'Schamanen, Hallucinogene und Erdaufschüttungen in der Neuen Welt, *Unter dem Pflaster liegt der Strand*, 15:95-112.

1989. 'A Modern-Day Shamanistic Healer in the Peruvian Amazon: Pharmacopoeia and Trance', *Journal of Psychoactive Drugs*, 21(1):91-100.

Dobkin de Rios, Marlene & David E. Smith. 1976. 'Using or Abusing? An

Anthropological Approach to the Study of Psychoactive Drugs', *Journal of Psychedelic Drugs*, 8(3):263-266.

1977. 'The Function of Drug Rituals in Human Society: Continuities and Changes', *Journal of Psychedelic Drugs*, 9(3):269-275.

Donnan, Ch. B. & Douglas G. Sharon. 1977. 'The Magic Cactus: Ethnoarchaeological Continuity in Peru', *Archaeology*, 30:374-381.

Donner, Florinda. 1982. Shabono, New York: Delacorte.

Dow, James. 1986. *The Shaman's Touch: Otomí Indian Symbolic Healing*, Salt Lake City: University of Utah Press.

Drury, Nevill. 1978. *Don Juan, Mescalito and Modern Magic*, London: Routledge & Kegan Paul.

1982. *The Shaman and the Magician*, London: Routledge & Kegan Paul.

1988. *Lexikon esoterischen Wissens*, Munich: Knaur (expanded German edition).

1989. *Vision Quest*, Bridport, Dorset: Prism .

1991. *The Visionary Human*, Shaftesbury, Dorset; Rockport, Massachusetts: Element.

1992. *Dictionary of Mysticism and the Esoteric Traditions*, Bridport, Dorset: Prism.

Drury, Nevill & Susan Drury. 1987. *Healing Oils and Essences*, Sydney: Harper & Row.

Eberhard, Wolfram. 1983. *Lexikon chinesischer Symbole*, Cologne: Diederichs.

Efron Daniel H., ed. 1967. *Ethnopharmacologic Search for Psychoactive Drugs*, Washington, D.C.: U.S. Department of Health, Education, and Welfare.

Eliade, Mircea. 1942. 'La Mandragore et les mythes de la "naissance miraculeuse"', *Zalmoxis*, 3:3-48.

1982. *Von Zalmoxis zu Dschingis-Khan: Religion und Volkskultur in Südosteuropa*, Cologne-Lövenich: Hohenheim.

Emboden, William A. 1972. *Narcotic Plants*, New York: Macmillan.

1974. *Bizarre Plants*, New York: Macmillan.

1976. 'Plant Hypnotics among the North American Indians', in *American Folk Medicine: A Symposium*, Wayland D. Hand, ed., Berkeley: University of California Press, pp. 159-167.

1977. 'Dionysus as a Shaman and Wine as a Magical Drug', *Journal of Psychedelic Drugs*, 9(3):187-192.

1978. The Sacred Narcotic Lily of the Nile', *Economic Botany*, 32(4):395-407.

1979a. '*Nymphaea ampla* and Other Mayan Narcotic Plants', *Mexikon*, 1:50-52.

1979b. *Narcotic Plants*, New York: Macmillan (revised and enlarged edition).

1981a. 'Transcultural Use of Narcotic Water Lilies in Ancient Egyptian and Maya Drug Ritual', *Journal of Ethnopharmacology*, 3:39-83.

1981b. 'The Genus Cannabis and the Correct Use of Taxonomic Categories', *Journal of Psychoactive Drugs*, 13(1):15-21.

1981c. 'Cannabis in Ostasien: Herkunft, Wanderung und Gebrauch', in *Rausch und Realität*, G. Vögler, ed., Cologne: Rautenstrauch-Joest-Museum, Vol. 1, pp. 324-329.

1981d. 'Seerose — literarische und bildische Zeugnisse von *Nymphaea* als rituellen Psychotogen', in *Rausch und Realität*, G. Vögler, ed., Cologne: Rautenstrauch-Joest-Museum, Vol. 1, pp. 352-357.

1982. 'The Mushroom and the Water Lily', *Journal of Ethnopharmacology*, 5:139-148.

1983. 'The Ethnobotany of the Dresden Codex with Especial Reference to the Narcotic *Nymphaea ampla*', *Botanical Museum* Leaflets, 29(2):87-132.

1985. 'The Ethnopharmacology of *Centella asiatica* (L.) Urban (Apiaceae)', Journal of Ethnobiology, 5(2):101-107.

1987. *Leonardo da Vinci on Plants and Gardens*, Portland, Oregon: Dioscorides.

1989. 'The Sacred Journey in Dynastic Egypt: Shamanistic Trance in the Context of the Narcotic Water Lily and the Mandrake', *Journal of Psychoactive Drugs*, 21(1):61-76.

Emboden, William A. & Marlene Dobkin de Rios. 1980. 'Narcotic Ritual Use of Water Lilies Among the Ancient Egyptian and Maya', in *Folk Healing and Medicine*, George Meyer, Kenneth Blum & John C. Cull, eds., Springfield, Illinois: Charles Thomas, pp. 275-286.

Engel, Fritz-Martin. 1979. *Zauberpflanzen — Pflanzenzauber*, Hannover: Landbuch.

1982. *Die Giftküche der Natur*, Hannover: Landbuch.

Escohotado, Antonio. 1989. *Historia de las drogas*, (three volumes), Madrid: Alianza Editorial.

Estrada, Alvaro. 1980. *Maria Sabina — Botin der heiligen Pilze*, (afterword by Albert Hofmann), Munich: Trikont.

Evans, Arthur. 1978. *Witchcraft and the Gay Counterculture*, Boston: FAG RAG.

Evans-Pritchard, E.E. 1976. *Witchcraft, Oracles and Magic among the Azande*, Oxford: Oxford University Press.

Fadiman, J. 1965. '*Genista canariensis*: A Minor Psychedelic', *Economic Botany*, 19:383-384.

Feilberg, H.F. 1897. 'Zwieselbäume nebst verwandten Aberglauben in Skandinavien', *Zeitschrift des Vereins für Volkskunde*, 7:42-53.

Fernandez, James W. 1972. 'Tabernanthe Iboga: Narcotic Ecstasis and the Work of the Ancestors', in *Flesh of the Gods*, Peter T. Furst, ed., London: Allen & Unwin, pp. 237-260.

1982. *Bwiti: An Ethnography of the Religious Imagination in Africa*, Princeton: Princeton University Press.

Ferré, Felipe. 1991. *Kaffee: Eine Kulturgeschichte*, Tübingen: Wasmuth-Verlag.

Festi, Francesco. 1985. *Funghi allucinogeni: aspetti psicofisiologici e storici*, Rovereto, Italy: Musei Civici di Rovereto (Publ. LXXX VI).

Fields, Herbert F. 1968. '*Rivea corymbosa*: Notes on Some Zapotecan Customs', *Economic Botany*, 23:2-209.

Fillipetti, Harvé & Janine Trotereau. 1979. *Zauber, Riten und Symbole: Magisches Brauchtum im Volksglauben*, Freiburg i.Br., Germany: Bauer.

Findlay, W.P.K. 1982. *Fungi: Folklore, Fiction, & Fact*, Richmond: Richmond.

Fink, Hans. 1983. *Verzaubertes Land: Volkskult und Ahnenbrauch in Südtirol*, Innsbruck, Vienna: Tyrolia.

Flattery, David Stophlet. 1984. 'Synopsis of Arguments for the Identification of "Soma" as *Peganum harmala* L.', Berkeley: Unpublished Paper.

Flattery, David Stophlet & Martin Schwartz. 1989. *Haoma and Harmalin*, Berkeley: University of California Press (Near Eastern Studies, Volume 21).

Fulder, Stephen. 1984. *Über Ginseng*, Bonn: Hörnemann.

Furst, Peter T. 1972a. *Flesh of the Gods*, ed., London: Allen & Unwin.

1972b. 'Ritual Use of Hallucinogens in Mesoamerica', *Religión en Mesoamerica, XII Mesa Redonda*, pp. 61-68, México, D.F.

1976. *Hallucinogens and Culture*, San Francisco: Chandler & Sharp.

Furst, Peter T. & Barbara G. Myerhoff. 1966. 'Myth as History: The Jimson Weed Cycle of the Huichols of Mexico', *Anthropología*, 17:3-39.

Gardner, Gerald B. 1965. *Witchcraft Today*, London: Rider & Co.

Gartz, Jochen. 1985a. 'Zur Analytik der Inhaltsstoffe zweier Pilzarten der Gattung Conocybe', *Pharmazie*, 40(5):366.

1985b. 'Zum Nachweis der Inhaltsstoffe einer Pilzart der Gattung Panaeolus', *Pharmazie*, 40(6):431.

1986a. 'Quantitative Bestimmung der Indolderivate von *Psilocybe semilanceata* (Fr.) Kumm.', 'Nachweis von Tryptaminderivaten in Pilzen der Gattungen *Gerronema, Hygrocybe, Psathyrella* und *Inocybe*', and 'Psilocybin in Mycelkulturen von *Inocybe aeruginascens*', *Biochemie und Physiologie der Pflanzen*, 181:117-124, 275-278, 511-517. 1986b. 'Untersuchungen zum Vorkommen des Muscarins in Inocybe aeruginascens Babo', *Zeitschrift für Mykologie*, 52(2):359-3 61. 1986c. 'Ethnopharmakologie und Entdeckungsgeschichte des halluzinogenen Wirkstoffe von europäischen Pilzen der Gattung Psilocybe', *Zeitschrift zur ärztlichen Fortbildung*, 80:803-805. 1987. 'Vorkommen von Psilocybin und Baeocystin in Fruchtkörpern von *Pluteus salicinus*', *Planta Medica*, 3:290-291.

Gartz, Jochen & G. Drewitz. 1985. 'Der erste Nachweis des Vorkommens von Psilocybin in Rißpilzen', *Zeitschrift für Mykologie*, 51(2):199-203.

Geddes, William Robert. 1976. *Migrants of the Mountains*, Oxford: Clarendon.

Geisshüsler, S. & R. Brenneisen. 1987. 'The Content of Psychoactive Phenypropyl and Phenylpentyl Khatamines in *Catha edulis* Forsk. of Different Origin', *Journal of Ethnopharmacology*, 19:269-277.

Gelpke, Rudolf. 1982. *Vom Rausch im Orient und Okzident*, Frankfurt/ Main: Ullstein.

Gentry, Howard Scott. 1982. *Agaves of Continental North America*, Tucson: University of Arizona Press.

Gessman, G.W. n.d. *Die Pflanzen im Zauberglauben*, Den Haag: J.J. Couver.

Gifford, Edward S. 1962. *The Charms of Love*, New York: Doubleday.

Gilg, E. & P.N. Schürhoff. 1926. *Aus dem Reich der Drogen*, Dresden: Schwarzbeck.

Gimlette, John D. 1971. *Malay Poisons and Charm Cures*, Kuala Lumpur: Oxford University Press.

Goetz, Adolf. 1989. *Teegebräuche*, Berlin: VWB.

Golas, Thaddeus. 1972. *The Lazy Man's Guide to Enlightenment*, Palo Alto: The Seed Center.

Golowin, Sergius. 1970. *Hexer und Henker im Galgenfeld*, Bern: Beuteli. 1974. *Die Magie der verbotenen Märchen*, Hamburg: Merlin.

Graves, Robert. 1961. *The White Goddess*, London: Faber and Faber.

Greve, Paul. 1938. *Der Sumpfporst*, Hamburg: Hansischer Gildenverlag.

Griffith, F.Ll. & Herbert Thompson. 1974. *the Leyden Papyrus: An Egyptian Magical Book*, New York: Dover.

Grof, Stanislav. 1981. *LSD-Psychotherapy*, New York: Hunter House.

Guerrero, Raúl. 1985. *El Pulque*, México, D.F.: INAH.

Guzman, Gastón. 1978. *Hongos*, México, D.F.: Limusa.
1980. *Identificación de los hongos*, México, D.F.: Limusa.
1983. *The Genus Psilocybe*, Beihefte zur Nova Hedwigia, No. 74, Vaduz, Liechtenstein.

Haan, Prem Lölia de. 1988. *Bei Schamanen*, Frankfurt/Main: Ullstein.

Haard, Richard & Karen Haard. 1980. *Poisonous & Hallucinogenic Mushrooms*, Seattle: Homestead (second edition).

Hagenow, Gerd. 1982. *Aus dem Weingarten der Antike*, Mainz: Zabern.

Hand, Wayland, ed. 1980. *American Folk Medicine*, Berkeley: University of California Press.

Hansen, Harold. 1981. *Der Hexengarten*, Munich: Trikont-Dianus.

Hargous, Sabine. 1976. *Beschwörer der Seelen: Das magische Universum der südamerikanischen Indianer*, Basel: Sphinx.

Harner, Michael. 1973. 'The Role of Hallucinogenic Plants in European Witchcraft', in *Hallucinogens and Shamanism*, Michael Harner, ed., London: Oxford University Press, pp. 125-150.

Harris, Lloyd J. 1980. *The Book of Garlic*, 3rd ed., revised, Berkeley, CA: Aris.

Harrison, R.K. 1963. 'Healing Herbs of the Bible', *Janus*, 50:2-54.

Hartwich, Carl von. 1911. *Die menschlichen Genußmittel*, Leipzig: Tauchnitz.

Haskins, James. 1984. *Witchcraft, Mysticism and Magic in the Black World*, Garden City, New York: Doubleday.

Hauschild, Thomas. 1981. 'Hexen und Drogen', in *Rausch und Realität*, G. Vögler, ed., Cologne: Rautenstrauch-Joest-Museum, Vol. 1, pp. 360-367.

1982. *Der Böse Blick*, Berlin: Mensch und Leben.

Hayter, Alethea. 1988. *Opium and the Romantic Imagination*, Wellingsborough, Northamptonshire: Crucible.

Heffern, Richard. 1974. *Secrets of Mind-Altering Plants of Mexico*, New York: Pyramid.

1976. *The Complete Book of Ginseng*, Millbrae, California: Celestial Arts.

Heiser, Charles B. 1969. *Nightshades: The Paradoxical Plants*, San Francisco: Freeman.

1987. *The Fascinating World of the Nightshades*, New York: Dover.

Henglein, Martin. 1985. *Die heilende Kraft der Wohlgerüche und Essenzen*, Munich: Schönberger.

Hermanns, M. 1980. *Mythen und Mysterien der Tibeter*, Stuttgart: Magnus.

Herrick, James W. 1983. 'The Symbolic Roots of Three Potent Iroquois Medicinal Plants', in *The Anthropology of Medicine*, L. Romanucci-Ross *et al.*, eds., Westport, Connecticut: Bergin & Garvey, pp. 134-155.

Hill, W.W. 1938. 'Navajo Use of Jimson Weed', *New Mexico Anthropologist*, 3(2):19-21.

Hirschberg, Walter. 1988. *Frosch und Kröte in Mythos und Brauch*,

Vienna, Cologne, Graz, Austria: Böhlau.

Hirschfeld, Magnus & Richard Linsert. 1930. *Liebesmittel*, Berlin: Mann.

Höfler, Max. 1990. *Volksmedizinische Botanik der Germanen*, Berlin: VWB (reprint of the 1908 edition).

Hofmann, Albert. 1964. *Die Mutterkornalkaloide*, Stuttgart: Enke.

1975. 'LSD und die mexikanischen Zauberdrogen', *Nordwestdeutsche Gesellschaft für ärztliche Fortbildung*, (lecture).

1979. *LSD — Mein Sorgenkind* , Stuttgart: Klett-Cotta.

1983. *LSD—My Problem Child: Reflections on Sacred Drugs, Mysticism, and Science*, Los Angeles: Jeremy Tarcher.

1986. *Einsichten — Ausblicke*, Basel: Sphinx.

1989. *Insight/Outlook*, Atlanta: Humanics New Age.

Höhle, Sigi, Claudia Müller-Ebeling, Christian Rätsch & Ossi Urchs. 1986. *Rausch und Erkenntnis: Das Wilde in der Kultur*, Munich: Knaur.

Holler, Johannes. 1989. *Das neue Gehirn*, Südergesellen, Germany: Bruno Martin.

Hu, Shiu Ying. 1976. 'The Genus *Panax* (Ginseng) in Chinese Medicine', *Economic Botany*, 30:11-28.

Huber, E. 1929. *Das Trankopfer im Kulte der Völker*, Hannover-Kirchrode: Oppermann.

Hudson, Charles M., ed. 1979. *Black Drink, A Native American Tea*, Athens: University of Georgia Press.

Huxley, Aldous. 1962. *Island*, New York: Harper.

Hyslop, Jon & Paul Ratcliffe. 1989. *a Folk Herbal*, Oxford: Radiation.

Jackson, Betty P. & Michael I. Berry. 1979. 'Mandragora - Taxonomy and Chemistry of the European Species', in *The Biology and Taxonomy of the Solanaceae*, J.G. Hawkes *et al.*, eds., London: Academic Press, pp. 505-512.

Jacq, Christian. 1985. *Egyptian Magic*, Chicago: Bolchazy-Carducci.

Jahn, Janheinz. 1986. *Muntu - die neoafrikanische Kultur*, Cologne: Diederichs.

Janiger, Oscar & Marlene Dobkin de Rios. 1973. 'Suggestive Hallucinogenic Properties of Tobacco', *Medical Anthropology Newsletter*, 4(4):6-11.

1976. 'Nicotiana an Hallucinogen?', *Economic Botany*, 30:149-151.

Jansen, Karl L.R. & Colin J. Prast. 1988a. 'Ethnopharmacology of Kratom and the *Mitragyna* Alkaloids', *Journal of Ethnopharmacology*, 23(1):115-119.

1988b. 'Psychoactive Properties of Mitragynine (Kratom)', *Journal of Psychoactive Drugs*, 20(4):455-457.

Jantzen, Friedrich. 1980. *Amors Pflanzenkunde*, Stuttgart: Kosmos.

Jimenez, A.C. 1977. 'Folklore médico y fitoalucinismo en el Perú', *Folklore*

Americana, 23:89-100.
Johnston, Thomas F. 1972. '*Datura fastuosa*: Its Use in Tsonga Girls' Initiation', *Economic Botany*, 26:340-351.
Jordan, Michael. 1989. *Mushroom Magic*, London: Elm Tree.
Junquera, Carlos. 1989. 'Botanik und Schamanismus bei den Harakm-bet-Indianern im südwestlichen Amazonasgebiet von Peru', *Ethnologia Americana*, 25/1, Nr. 114:1232-1238.
Kamal, Hassan. 1975. *Encyclopaedia of Islamic Medicine*, Cairo: GEBO.
Kappstein, Stefan. 1980. *Das Buch vom Ginseng*, Bern: Morzsinay.
Kapur, Sohaila. 1983. *Witchcraft in Western India*, Bombay: Orient Longman.
Katz, Fred & Marlene Dobkin de Rios. 1971. 'Whistling in Peruvian Ayahuasca Healing Sessions', *Journal of American Folklore*, 84(333):320-327.
Katz, Richard. 1982. *Boiling Energy*, Cambridge, Massachusetts: Harvard University Press.
Kennedy, Allison & Christian Rätsch. 1985. 'Datura: Aphrodisiac?', *High Frontiers*, 2:20,25.
Kepler, Angela Kay. 1983. *Hawaiian Heritage Plants*, Honolulu: Oriental.
Khlopin, Igor N. 1980. 'Mandragora turcomanica in der Geschichte der Orientalvölker', *Orientalia Lovaniensia Periodica*, 11:223-231.
Kimmins, Andrew, ed. 1975. *Tales of Ginseng*, New York: Morrow.
1977. *Tales of Hashish*, New York: Morrow.
Kluge, Heidelore. 1988. *Zaubertränke und Hexenküche*, Munich: Heyne.
Knab, Tim. 1977. 'Notes Concerning Use of Solandra Among the Huichol', *Economic Botany*, 31:80-86.
Knecht, Sigrid. 1966. 'Mexikanische Zauberpapiere', *Tribus*, 15:131-148.
1971. 'Rauchen und Räuchern in Nepal', *Ethnomedizin*, 1(1):209-222.
1985. 'Die heilige Heilpflanze *Tulasi...*', *Curare* (special volume), 3/85:95-100.
Knoll-Greiling, Ursula. 1959. 'Rauschinduzierende Mittel bei Naturvölkern und ihre individuelle und soziale Wirkung', *Sociologus*, 9(1):47-60.
Kolta, K.S. 1987. Der heilige Antonius als Heiler im Spätmittelalter', *Beiträge zur Geschichte der Medizin*, 31(38):97-101.
Krause, M. 1909. 'Die Gifte der Zauberer im Herzen Afrikas', *Zeitschrift für experimentelle Pathologie und Therapie*, 6:1-4.
Kreuter, Marie-Luise. 1982. *Wunderkräfte der Natur*, Munich: Heyne.
Kriss-Rettenbeck, Lenz & Liselotte Hansmann. 1977. *Amulett und Talisman*, Munich: Callway.
Kronfeld, Moritz. 1981. *Donnerwurz und Mäuseaugen: Zauberpflanzen und Amulette in der Volksmedizin*, Berlin: Zerling (reprint of the 1891

edition).
Laarss, R.H. 1988. *Das Buch der Amulette und Talismane*, Munich: Diederichs.
La Barre, Weston. 1970. 'Old and New World Narcotics', *Economic Botany*, 24(1):73-80.
1989. *The Peyote Cult*, Norman, Oklahoma: University of Oklahoma Press (fifth edition, enlarged).
Laing, Dave & John Hendra. 1977. *Beer and Brewing*, London: Macdonald Educational Ltd.
Langdon, E. Jean. 1979. 'Yagé Among the Siona: Cultural Patterns in Visions', in *Spirits, Shamans, and Stars*, D.L. Browman & R.A. Schwarz, eds., The Hague: Mouton, pp. 63-80.
Latorre, Delores L. & Felipe A. Latorre. 1977. 'Plants Used by Mexican Kickapoo Indians', *Economic Botany*, 31(3):340-357.
Lehane, Brendan. 1977. *The Power of Plants*, New York; Maidenhead, England: McGraw-Hill.
Lehmann, Arthur & James E. Myers, ed. 1989. *Magic, Witchcraft, and Religion: An Anthropological Study of the Supernatural*, Mountain View, California: Mayfield (second edition).
Lemoine, Jacques. 1989. 'Die Brücke - Ein wichtiges Element des Hmong- und Yao-Schamanismus', in *Opfer und Ekstase: Wege der neuen Schamanen*, G. Doore, ed., Freiburg i. Br., Germany: Bauer, pp. 95-107.
Leuenberger, Hans. 1970. *Im Rausch der Drogen*, Munich: Humboldt.
Leuner, Hanscarl. 1981. *Halluzinogene*, Bern: Huber.
Lewin, Louis. 1886. *Ueber Piper Methysticum*, Berlin: Hirschwald.
1929. *Gottesurteile durch Gifte und andere Verfahren*, Berlin: Stilke (Beiträge zur Giftkunde, Vol. 2).
1980. *Phantastica*, Linden, Germany: Volksverlag (reprint of 1927 edition).
1986. *Banisteria Caapi, eine neues Rauschgift und Heilmittel*, Berlin: EXpress (reprint of 1928 edition).
Lewis, Ioan M. 1971. *Ecstatic Religion*, Harmondsworth, England: Penguin.
1986. *Religion in Context*, Cambridge, England: Cambridge University Press.
Li, Hui-Lin. 1974a. 'The Origin and Use of *Cannabis* in Eastern Asia: Linguistic-cultural Implications', *Economic Botany*, 28:293-301.
1974b. 'An Archaeological and Historical Account of *Cannabis* in China', *Economic Botany*, 28:437-448.
1978. 'Hallucinogenic Plants in Chinese Herbals', *Journal of Psychedelic Drugs*, 10(1):17-26.
Lindstrom, Lamont, ed. 1987. *Drugs in Western Pacific Societies*, Lanham,

Maryland: University Press of America.
Litzinger, William J. 1981. 'Ceramic Evidence for Prehistoric *Datura* Use in North America', *Journal of Ethnopharmacology*, 4:57-74.
Lizot, Jacques. 1982. *Im Kreis der Feuer*, Frankfurt/Main: Syndikat.
Lockwood, Tommie E. 1979. 'The Ethnobotany of Brugmansia', *Journal of Ethnopharmacology*, 1:147-164.
Loewe, Michael & Carmen Blacker, ed. 1981. *Divination and Oracles*, London: Allen & Unwin.
Lohberg, Rolf. 1984. *Das grosse Lexikon vom Bier*, Stuttgart: Scripta.
Lowy, Bernard. 1972. 'Mushroom Symbolism in Maya Codices', *Mycologia*, 64:816-821.
1974. '*Amanita muscaria* and The Thunderbolt Legend in Guatemala and Mexico', *Mycologia*, 66(1):188-191.
1977. 'Hallucinogenic Mushrooms in Guatemala', *Journal of Psychedelic Drugs*, 9(2):123-125.
Luna, Luis Eduardo. 1986. *Vegetalismo — Shamanism Among the Mestizo Population of the Peruvian Amazon*, Stockholm: Acta Universitatis Stockholmensis, 27.
Lurker, Manfred. 1987. *Lexikon der Götter und Symbole der alten Ägypter*, Bern: Scherz.
Ma'ax, K'ayum & Christian Rätsch. 1984. *Ein Kosmos im Regenwald*, Cologne: Diederichs.
Madsen, William & Claudia Madsen. 1972. *A Guide to Mexican Witchcraft*, Mexico: Minutae Mexicana.
Majupuria, Trilok Chandra & D.P. Joshi. 1988. *Religious & Useful Plants of Nepal & India*, Lalitpur, Lahkar (India): Gupta.
Manniche, Lise. 1989. *An Ancient Egyptian Herbal*, London: British Museum.
Markale, Jean. 1989. *Die Druiden*, Munich: Goldmann.
Martin, Richard T. 1969. 'The Role of Coca in the History, Religion, and Medicine of South American Indians', *Economic Botany*, 23:422-438.
Martin, Rudolf. 1905. *Die Inlandstämme der malayischen Halbinsel*, Jena: Gustav Fischer.
Martinetz, Dieter, Karlheinz Lohs & Jörg Janzen. 1989. *Weihrauch und Myrrhe*, Stuttgart: Wissenschaftliche Verlagsgesellschaft.
Marzell, Heinrich. 1927. 'Alraun', in *Handwörterbuch des Deutschen Aberglaubens*, Berlin: de Gruyter, Vol. 1, pp. 311-323.
1964. *Zauberpflanzen Hexentränke*, Stuttgart: Kosmos, Vol. 241. Matsumoto, Kosai II.
1979. *The Mysterious Reishi Mushroom*, Santa Barbara: Woodbridge.
Maxwell, Nicole. 1990. *Witch-Doctor's Apprentice*, New York: Citadel

(introduction by Terence McKenna).
Mayagioitia, Lilien, José-Luis Diaz & Carlos M. Contreras. 1986. 'Psychopharmacologic Analysis of an Alleged Oneirogenic Plant: Calea Zacatechichi', *Journal of Ethnopharmacology*, 18(3):229-244.
Mayer, Karl H. 1977. 'Salvia Divinorum: Ein Halluzinogen der Mazateken von Oaxaca', *Ethnologia Americana*, 14(2):776-779.
McBride, L.R. 1988. *Practical Folk Medicine of Hawaii*, Hilo: Petroglyph.
McDowell, John Holmes. 1989. *Sayings of the Ancestors: The Spiritual Life of the Sibundoy Indians*, Lexington: University Press of Kentucky.
McGuire, Thomas, M. 1982. 'Ancient Maya Mushroom Connections', *Journal of Psychoactive Drugs*, 14(3):221-238.
McKenna, Dennis J., L.E. Luna & G.H.N. Towers. 1986. 'Biodynamic Constituents in *Ayahuasca* Admixture Plants: An Uninvestigated Folk Pharmacopoeia', *América Indígena*, 46:73-101.
McKenna, Dennis J. & G.H.N. Towers. 1984. 'Biochemistry and Pharmacology of Tryptamines and ß-Carbolines : A Minireview', *Journal of Psychoactive Drugs*, 16(4):347-358.
1985. 'On the Comparative Ethnopharmacology of Malpighiaceous and Myristicaceous Hallucinogens', *Journal of Psychoactive Drugs*, 17(1):35-39.
McKenna, Terence. 1989a. *Wahre Halluzinationen*, Basel: Sphinx.
1989b. 'Among Ayahuasquera', in *The Gateway to Inner Space*, Christian Rätsch, ed., Bridport, Dorset: Prism, pp. 179-211.
1989c. 'Plan, Plant, Planet', *Whole Earth Review*, 64:5-11.
1992. *Food of the Gods: The Search for the Original Tree of Knowledge*, New York: Bantam.
Mee, Margaret. 1988. *In Search of Flowers of the Amazon Forests*, Woodbridge, Suffolk: Nonesuch Expeditions.
Mehra, K.L. 1979. 'Ethnobotany of Old World Solanaceae', in *The Biology and Taxonomy of the Solanaceae*, J.G. Hawkes *et al.*, eds., London: Academic Press, pp. 161-170.
Meier, P. Joseph. 1913. 'Die Zauberei bei den Küstenbewohnern der Gazelle-Halbinsel, Neupommern, Südsee', *Anthropos*, 8:1-11,285-305,688-713.
Meijer, Willem. 1974. '*Podophyllum peltatum* — May Apple', *Economic Botany*, 28:68-72.
Melzer, Dietmar H. 1984. *Märchen der Guaraní-Indianer*, Friedrichshafen, Germany: D. Melzer.
1985. *Indio Guaraní — vergessenes Volk am Rio Paranö*, Friedrichshafen, Germany: D. Melzer.
1987. *Dschungelmärchen*, Friedrichshafen, Germany: idime.

Mercatante, Anthony. 1976. *The Magic Garden*, New York: Harper & Row.

Metzner, Ralph. 1986. *Opening to Inner Light*, Los Angeles: Tarcher.

1987. 'Transformation Processes in Shamanism, Alchemy, and Yoga', in *Shamanism*, Sh. Nicholson, ed., Wheaton, Illinois: The Theosophical Publishing House, pp. 233-252.

1988. 'Hallucinogens in Contemporary North American Shamanic Practice', *Proceedings of the Fourth International Conference on the Study of Shamanism and Alternate Modes of Healing*, Berkeley, CA: Independent Scholars of Asia, pp. 170-175.

1989. 'Molecular Mysticism: The Role of Psychoactive Substances in the Transformation of Consciousness', in *The Gateway to Inner Space*, Christian Rätsch, ed., Bridport, Dorset: Prism, pp. 73- 88.

Meyer, Clarence. 1986. *Herbal Aphrodisiacs (from World Sources)*, Glenwood, Illinois: Meyerbooks.

Meyer, Marvin W., ed. 1987. *The Ancient Mysteries*, San Francisco: Harper & Row.

Miller, Richard Alan. 1983. *The Magical & Ritual Use of Herbs*, New York: Destiny.

1985. *The Magical & Ritual Use of Aphrodisiacs*, New York: Destiny.

Mitrovic, Alexander. 1907. 'Mein Besuch bei einer Zauberfrau in Norddalmatien', *Anthropophyteia*, 4:227-236.

Mitsuhashi, Hiroshi. 1976. 'Medicinal Plants of the Ainu', *Economic Botany*, 30:209-217.

Moerman, Daniel E. 1986. *Medicinal Plants of Native America*, Ann Arbor: University of Michigan, Museum of Anthropology, Technical Reports, No. 19.

Moore, Jerry D. 1989. 'Pre-Hispanic Beer in Coastal Peru: Technology and Social Context of Prehistoric Production', *American Anthropologist*, 91:682-695.

Morningstar, Patricia J. 1985. '*Thandai* and *Chilam*: Traditional Hindu Beliefs About the Proper Uses of Cannabis', *Journal of Psychoactive Drugs*, 17(3):141-165.

Mortimer, W. Golden. 1974. *Coca — The Divine Plant of the Incas*, San Francisco: And/Or.

Moser-Schmitt, Erika. 1981a. 'Sozio-ritueller Gebrauch von Betel in Indien', in *Rausch und Realität*, G. Vögler, ed., Cologne: Rautenstrauch-Joest-Museum, Vol. 1, pp. 320-323.

1981b. 'Sozio-ritueller Gebrauch von Cannabis in Indien', in *Rausch und Realität*, G. Vögler, ed., Cologne: Rautenstrauch-Joest-Museum, Vol. 1, pp. 542-545.

Mount, Guy. 1988. *The Peyote Book: A Study of Native Medicine*, Arcata, California: Sweetlight (second edition).
Müller-Ebeling, Claudia. 1987. 'Die Alraune in der Bibel', in *Die Sage vom Galgenmännlein im Volksglauben und in der Literatur*, Alfred Schlosser, ed., Berlin: EXpress, pp. 141-149.
Müller-Ebeling, Claudia & Christian Rätsch. 1986. *Isoldens Liebestrank: Aphrodisiaka in Geschichte und Gegenwart*, Munich: Kindler.
1987. 'Kreisrituale', *Sphinx*, 6/86:42-47.
1989a. *Heilpflanzen der Seychellen*, Berlin: VWB.
1989b. '"Mentale Anarchie" - Wild und Heilig', in *Vom Wesen der Anarchie & vom Verwesen verschiedener Wirklichkeiten*, Bernd Kramer, ed., Berlin: Kramer, pp. 107-121.
Münch, Burchard Friedrich. 1785. *Practische Abhandlung von der Belladonna und ihrer Anwendung*, Göttingen: Dieterich.
Munizaga A., Carlos. 1960. 'Uso actual de *Miyaya* (Datura stramonium) por los araucanos de Chile', *Journal de la Société des Américanistes*, 52:4-43.
Münzel, Mark. 1977. *Schrumpfkopf macher?*, Frankfurt/Main: Museum für Völkerkunde.
Musés, Charles. 1989. 'The Sacred Plant of Ancient Egypt', *The Gateway to Inner Space*, Christian Rätsch, ed., Bridport, Dorset: Prism, pp. 143-159.
Nahas, Gabriel G. 1982. 'Hashish in Islam 9th to 18th Century', *Bulletin of the New York Academy of Medicine*, 58(9):814-831.
Naranjo, Claudio. 1969. 'Psychotherapeutic Possibilities of New Fantasy-Enhancing Drugs', *Clinical Toxicology*, 2(2):209-224.
Naranjo, Plutarco. 1974. 'El cocaísmo entre los aborígenes de Sud América', *América Indígena*, 34(3):605-628.
1983. *Ayahuasca: Etnomedicina y Mitología*, Quito: Libri Mundi.
Nemec, Helmut. 1976. *Zauberzeichen*, Vienna: Schroll.
Ohnuki-Tierney, Emiko. 1980. 'Ainu Illness and Healing: A Symbolic Interpretation', *American Ethnologist*, 7(1):132-151.
Ott, Jonathan. 1976a. *Hallucinogenic Plants of North America*, Berkeley: Wingbow.
1976b. 'Psycho-Mycological Studies of Amanita - From Ancient Sacrament to Modern Phobia', *Journal of Psychedelic Drugs*, 8(1): 27-35.
1979. *Hallucinogenic Plants of North America*, Berkeley: Wingbow (revised edition).
1985. *Chocolate Addict*, Vashon, Washington: Natural Products Co.
Ott, J. & J. Bigwood, eds. 1978. *Teonanacatl: Hallucinogenic Mushroom*

of North America, Seattle: Madrona.
Ownbey, G. 1961. 'The Genus *Argemone* in South America and Hawaii', *Brittonia*, 13:91-109.
Papyrus Ebers. 1973 *Das Älteste Buch über Heilkunde*, Berlin: de Gruyter.
Pattee, Rowena. 1989. 'Ekstase und Opfer', in *Opfer und Ekstase: Wege der neuen Schamanen*, G. Doore, ed., Freiburg i. Br., Germany: Bauer, pp. 32-53.
Pelt, Jean-Marie. 1983. *Drogues et plantes magiques*, Paris: Fayard.
Pelton, Ross & Taffy Clarke Pelton. 1989. *Mind Food and Smart Pills*, New York: Doubleday.
Penzer, N.M. 1952. *Poison-Damsels and other Essays*, London: Private Printing.
Perez de Barradas, José. 1957. *Plantas magicas americanas*, Madrid: Inst. 'Bernardino de Sahagun'.
Perger, K. Ritter von. 1864. *Deutsche Pflanzensagen*, Stuttgart, Oehringen: August Schaber.
Peterson, Nicolas. 1979. 'Aboriginal Uses of Australian Solanaceae', in *The Biology and Taxonomy of the Solanaceae*, J.G. Hawkes et al., eds., London: Academic Press, pp. 171-189.
Peuckert, Will-Erich. 1960. 'Hexensalben', *Medizinischer Monats-spiegel*, 8:169-174.
Pinkava, Donald J. & Howard Scott Gentry, eds. 1985. 'Symposium on the Genus Agave', in *Desert Plants*, 7(2).
Pinkson, Tom. 1989. 'Purification, Death, and Rebirth: The Clinical Use of Entheogens within a Shamanic Context', in *The Gateway to Inner Space*, Christian Rätsch, ed., Bridport, Dorset: Prism, pp. 91-118.
Plato. 1980. *Symposium*, K.J. Dover, ed., New York: Cambridge University Press.
Plies, Rainer & Herman de Vries. 1987. *die steppenraute harmal, peganum harmala l., und ihre medizinische verwendbarkeit neue erkenntnisse einer alten heilpflanze*, Eschenau: MS.
Polia Meconi, Mario. 1988. *Las lagunas de los encantos: medicina tradicional andina del perü septentrional*, Piura, Peru: CEPESER.
Pollock, Steven H. 1975a. 'The Psilocybin Mushroom Pandemic', *Journal of Psychedelic Drugs*, 7(1):73-84.
1975b. 'The Alaskan Amanita Quest', *Journal of Psychedelic Drugs*, 7(4):397-399.
1977. *Magic Mushroom Cultivation*, San Antonio: HMRF.
Pope, H.G. 1969. '*Tabernanthe iboga* — an African Narcotic Plant of Social Importance', *Economic Botany*, 23:174-184.
Prance, Ghillean T. 1970. 'Notes on the Use of Plant Hallucinogens in

Amazonian Brazil', *Economic Botany*, 24:62-68.

Prance, G.T., D.G. Campbell & B.W. Nelson. 1977. 'The Ethnobotany of the Paumarí Indians', *Economic Botany*, 31:129-139.

Preuss, K.Th. 1899. 'Die Zaubermuster der ôrang Sêmang in Malâka', *Zeitschrift für Ethnologie*, 22:137-197.

Pursey, Helen L. 1977. *Die wundersame Welt der Pilze*, Zollikon, Switzerland: Albatros.

Quezada, Noemi. 1975. *Amor y magia amorosa entre los aztecas*, Mexico: UNAM.

Quijada Jara, Sergio. 1982. *La Coca en las costumbres indigenas*, Huancayo, Peru: Imprenta Rios.

Rätsch, Christian. 1985. *Bilder aus der unsichtbaren Welt*, Munich: Kindler.

1986a. *Chactun — Die Götter der Maya*, ed., Cologne: Diederichs.

1986b. *Ethnopharmakologie und Parapsychologie*, Berlin: EXpress.

1986c. 'Alchemie im Regenwald - Dichtung, Zauberei und Heilung', *Salix*, 2(2):44-64.

1987a. 'Die Alraune heute', in *Der Alraun: Ein Beitrag zur Pflanzensagenkunde*, Adolf Taylor Stark, ed., Berlin: EXpress, pp. 87-109.

1987b. Psychedelische Diagnostik im ethnographischen Kontext', paper held at the Second Symposium on Psychoactive Substances, June 12-14, Kandern, Germany.

1987c. 'Mexikanische Prophetien - Träume und Visionen', *Grenzgebiete der Wissenschaft*, 36(2):116-134.

1987d. 'Das Zepter der heroischen Medizin', in *Das Scheiss Buch*, Löhrbach, Germany: Der Grüne Zweig, 123:80-83.

1987e. 'Der Rauch von Delphi', *Curare*, 4/87, 10:215-228.

1987f. *Indianische Heilkräuter*, Cologne: Diederichs.

1988a. 'Tarot und die Maya', *Ethnologia Americana*, 24(1), Nr. 112:1188-1190.

1988b. 'Das Bewußtsein von der Welt: Mensch und "Umwelt" im lakandonischen Kosmos', in *Die Neuen 'Wilden'*, Peter E. Stüben, ed., Giessen, Germany: Focus, pp. 166-171.

1989a. 'Die Pflanzen der Götter auf der Erde', *Imagination*, 4(1):18-20.

1989b. *Gateway to Inner Space*, ed., Bridport, Dorset: Prism.

1990a. *Pflanzen der Liebe*, Bern: Hallwag.

1990b. 'Sich lieben, sinnlos mit allen Sinnen: Tristan und Isoldes Liebestrank aus ethnopharmakologischer Sicht', *Imagination*, 5(1):17-19.

1990c. 'Und Moleküle bohren sich durch die Nase: Von psychedelischen Schnupfpulvern', in *Ene Mene Mopel — Die Nase & Der Popel*,

Werner Pieper, ed., Löhrbach, Germany: Der Grüne Zweig, 139:111-118.

1991. *Von den Wurzeln der Kultur: Die Pflanzen der Propheten*, Basel: Sphinx.

in pr. 'Mexikanische Drogen in Europa', Afterword to Friedrich Freiherr von Gall, *Medizinische Bücher..*, Berlin: VWB.

Rätsch, Christian & Andreas Guhr. 1989. *Lexikon der Zaubersteine aus ethnologischer Sicht*, Graz, Austria: Akademische Druck-und Verlagsanstalt (ADEVA).

Rätsch, Christian & Heinz J. Probst. 1985. 'Xtohk'uh: Zur Ethnobotanik der Datura-Arten bei den Maya in Yucatan', *Ethnologia Americana*, 21/2, Nr. 109:1137-1140.

Rahner, Hugo. 1957. *Griechische Mythen in christlicher Deutung*, Zürich: Rhein-Verlag.

Regardie, Israel, ed. 1968. *Roll Away the Stone*, St. Paul, Minnesota: Llewellyn.

Reichel-Dolmatoff, Gerardo. 1971. *Amazonian Cosmos*, Chicago University Press.

1975. *The Shaman and the Jaguar*, Philadelphia: Temple University Press.

1978. *Beyond the Milky Way*, Los Angeles: UCLA.

Reis Altschul, Siri von. 1967. 'Vilca and its Use', in *Ethnopharmacological Search for Psychoactive Drugs*, Daniel H. Efron, ed., Washington, D.C.: U.S. Department of Health, Education, and Welfare, pp. 307-314.

Reko, Blas Pablo. 1945. *Mitobotánica Zapoteca*, Tacubaya, Mexico: Private Printing.

'1947. 'El arbol del papel en el México antiguo', *Sociedad Botanica de México Boletín*, 5:12-19.

Reko, Victor A. 1986. *Magische Gifte*, Berlin: EXpress.

Remann, Mickey. 1984. *Der Globaltrottel*, Berlin: Rotbuch.

1989. *SolarPerplexus*, Basel: Sphinx.

Resch, Andreas. 1987. 'Exotisches Psi - Paranormales in anderen Kulturen. Basler Psi-Tage 1986', *Grenzgebiete der Wissenschaft*, 36(1):14-38.

Riedlinger, Thomas J., ed. 1990. *The Sacred Mushroom Healer: Essays for R. Gordon Wasson*, Portland, Oregon: Dioscorides.

Riva, Anna. 1974a. *Voodoo Handbook of Cult Secrets*, Toluca Lake, California: Occult Books.

1974b. *The Modern Herbal Spellbook*, Toluca Lake, California: Occult Books.

Robertson, James D. 1978. *The Great American Beer Book*, Ottawa, Illinois: Caroline House.

Robicsek, Francis. 1978. *The Smoking Gods: Tobacco in Maya Art, History and Religion*, Norman, Oklahoma: University of Oklahoma Press.

Rohde, Eleanour Sinclaír. 1971. *The Old English Herbals*, New York: Dover.

Roldan, Colores. 1975. *Teonanacatl (carnita divina)*, Mexico: Editorial Orion.

Römpp, Hermann. 1950. *Chemische Zaubertränke*, Stuttgart: Kosmos.

Rose, Jeanne. 1972. *Herbs & Things*, New York: Grosset & Dunlap.

Rosenbohm, Alexandra. 1991. *Halluzinogene Drogen im Schamanismus: Mythos und Ritual im kulturellen Vergleich*, Berlin: Dietrich Reimer.

Roth, Lutz, Max Daunderer & Kurt Kormann. 1984. *Giftpflanzen — Pflanzengifte*, Munich: ecomed.

Rouhier, Alexandre. 1986. *Die Hellsehen hervorrufenden Pflanzen*, Berlin: EXpress.

Rowell, Margery. 1978. 'Plants of Russian Folk Medicine', *Janus*, 65:259-282.

Rubel, Arthur & Jean Gettelfinder-Krejci. 1976. 'The Use of Hallucinogenic Mushrooms for Diagnostic Purposes Among Some Highland Chinantecs', *Economic Botany*, 30:235-248.

Ruben, Walter. 1952. *Tiahuanaco, Atacama und Araukaner*, Leipzig: Harrassowitz.

Rubin, Vera & Lambros Comitas. 1976. *Ganja in Jamaica*, Garden City, New Jersey: Anchor.

Ruck, Carl A.P. 1982. 'The Wild and the Cultivated: Wine in Euripides' Bacchae', *Journal of Ethnopharmacology*, 5:231-270.

Ruiz de Aalarcon, Hernando. 1984. *Treatise on the Heathen Superstitions That Today Live Among the Indians Native to This New Spain*, 1629, J. Richard Andrews & Ross Hassig, trans. and eds., Norman, Oklahoma: University of Oklahoma Press.

Sami-ali. 1971. *Le haschischen égypte*, Paris: Payot.

Sandermann, W. 1980. 'Berserkerwut durch Sumpfporst-Bier', *Brauwelt*, 120(50):1870-1872.

Sandford, J.H. 1972. 'Japan's "Laughing Mushrooms"', *Economic Botany*, 26:174-181.

1973. *In Search of the Magic Mushroom*, New York: Potter.

Sarianidi, W. 1988. 'Die Wiege des Propheten', *Wissenschaft in der USSR*, 5:118-127.

Sauer, J. & L. Kaplan. 1969. 'Canavalia Beans in American Prehistory', *American Antiquity*, 34(4):417-424.

Scanziani, Piero. 1972. *Amuleti Talismani Gahmahez*, Milan: Elvetica Edizioni.

Schadewaldt, Hans. 1968. *Der Medizinmann bei den Naturvölkern*, Stuttgart: Fink.
Scheerer, Sebastian & Irmgard Vogt, eds. 1989. *Drogen und Drogenpolitik*, Frankfurt/Main: Campus.
Scheidt, Jürgen vom. 1972. 'Drogenrausch und parapsychische Phänomene', *Zeitschrift für Parapsychologie*, 14(4):244-251.
Schenk, Gustav. 1954. *Das Buch der Gifte*, Berlin: Safari.
Schildkrout, Enid, ed. 1989. *Wild Spirits — Strong Medicine*, New York: The Center for African Art, Seattle: University of Washington Press.
Schindlbeck, Markus. 1978. 'Jagdzauber der Sawos in Gaikorobi, Mittlerer Sepik, Papua-Neuguinea', *Verhandlungen der Naturforschenden Gesellschaft in Basel*, 89:25-40.
Schlichting, Michael & Hanscarl Leuner, eds. 1988. *Psychoactive Substanzen und veränderte Bewuötseinszustände*, Report on the Second Symposium, Göttingen: ECSB/ECSC.
1989. *Psychoactive Substanzen und veränderte Bewuötseinszustände*, Report on the Third Symposium, Göttingen: ECSB/ECSC.
Schlosser, Alfred, ed. 1986. *Die Sage vom Galgenmännlein im Volksglauben und in der Literatur*, Berlin: EXpress.
Schmidbauer, Wolfgang. 1968. 'Die magische Mandragora', *Antaios*, 10:274.
1984. 'Mandragora', in *Handbuch der Rauschdrogen*, Wolfgang Schmidbauer & Jürgen vom Scheidt, eds., Frankfurt/Main: Fischer.
Scholz, Dieter & Dagmar Eigner. 1983. 'Zur Kenntnis der natürlichen Halluzinogene', *Pharmazie in unserer Zeit*, 12(3):75-79.
Schopen, Armin. 1978. *Das Qat*, Wiesbaden: Steiner.
1981. 'Das Qat in Jemen', in *Rausch und Realität*, G. Vögler, ed., Cologne: Rautenstrauch-Joest-Museum, Vol. 2, pp. 496-501.
Schöpf, Hans. 1986. *Zauberkräuter*, Graz, Austria: Akademische Druck- und Verlagsanstalt (ADEVA).
Schröder, Ekkehard, ed. 1985. 'Ethnobotanik — Ethnobotany', *Curare*, (special volume), 3/85:1-447.
Schrödter, Willy. 1981. Pflanzengeheimnisse, Kleinjörl, Germany: Schroeder.
Schulte, Dirk F. n.d. ... ein Männlein steht in Walde...der Fliegenpilz & sein gebrauch, Verlag im Nachtschatten.
Schultes, Richard Evans. 1967. 'The Botanical Origins of South American Snuffs', in *Ethnopharmacological Search for Psychoactive Drugs*, Daniel H. Efron, ed., Washington, D.C.: U.S. Department of Health, Education, and Welfare, pp. 291-3.
1976. *Hallucinogenic Plants*, Racine, Wisconsin: Western.

1977. 'A New Hallucinogen from Andean Colombia: Iochroma fuchsioides', *Journal of Psychedelic Drugs*, 9:45-49.

1979. 'Solanaceous Hallucinogens and Their Role in the Development of New World Cultures', in *The Biology and Taxonomy of the Solanaceae*, J.G. Hawkes et al., eds., London: Academic Press, pp. 137-160.

1988. *Where the Gods Reign: Plants and Peoples of the Colombian Andes*, Oracle, Arizona and London: Synergetic Press.

Schultes, Richard Evans & Albert Hofmann. 1979. *Plants of the Gods*, New York; Maidenhead, England: McGraw-Hill.

1980. *The Botany and Chemistry of Hallucinogens*, Springfield, Illinois: Charles C. Thomas (second edition).

Seefelder, Matthias. 1987. *Opium — Eine Kulturgeschichte*, Frankfurt/Main: Athenäum.

Seitz, George J. 1967. 'Epena, the Intoxicating Snuff Powder of the Waika Indians and the Tucano Medicine Man, Agostino', in *Ethnopharmacological Search for Psychoactive Drugs*, Daniel H. Efron, ed., Washington, D.C.: U.S. Department of Health, Education, and Welfare, pp. 315-338.

Selden, Gary. 1979. *Aphrodisia*, New York: E.P. Dutton.

Sharon, Douglas. 1978. *Wizard of the Four Winds*, New York: Free Press.

1982. 'Botanik, Chemie und ritueller Gebrauch des San-Pedro-Kaktus in den mittleren Anden', in *Rausch und Realität*, G. Vögler, ed., Cologne: Rautenstrauch-Joest-Museum, Vol. 2, pp. 444-467.

Siegel, Ronald K. 1989. *Intoxication*, New York: E.P. Dutton.

Siegel, R.K., P.R. Collings & J.L. Diaz. 1977. 'On the Use of *Tagetes lucida* and *Nicotiana rustica* as a Huichol Smoking Mixture', *Economic Botany*, 31:16-23.

Sigerist, Henry E. 1963. *Der Arzt in der mesopotamischen Kultur*, Esslingen, Germany: Robugen.

Skeat, Walter William. 1967. *Malay Magic*, New York: Dover.

Smet, Peter A.G.M. de. 1985. *Ritual Enemas and Snuffs in the Americas*, Amsterdam: CEDLA.

Smet, Peter de & Nicholas M. Hellmuth. 1986. 'A Multidisciplinary Approach to Ritual Enema Scenes on Ancient Maya Pottery', *Journal of Ethnopharmacology*, 16(1-2):213-262.

Smith, Elvin D. 1985. 'Argyreia nervosa', *Psychedelic Monographs and Essays*, 1.

Smith, Terence A. 1977. 'Tryptamine and Related Compounds in Plants', *Phytochemistry*, 16:171-175.

Spilmont, Jean-Pierre. 1984. *Magie*, Munich: Heyne.

Spranz, Bodo. 1961. 'Zauberei und Krankenheilung im Brauchtum der

Gegenwart bei Otomí-Indianern in Mexico', *Zeitschrift für Ethnologie*, 61:61-67.

Stafford, Peter. 1983. *Psychedelics Encyclopedia*, Los Angeles: Tarcher.

Stamets, Paul. 1978. *Psilocybe Mushrooms and Their Allies*, Seattle: Homestead.

Starck, Adolf Taylor, ed. 1986. *Der Alraun: Ein Beitrag zur Pflanzensagenkunde*, Berlin: EXpress.

Stark, Raymond. 1980. *The Book of Aphrodisiacs*, New York: Stein and Day.

Staufenbiel, Gerhardt. 1981. 'Die Teezeremonie in Japan', in *Rausch und Realität*, G. Vögler, ed., Cologne: Rautenstrauch-Joest-Museum, Vol. 2, pp. 576-581.

Stern, Bernhard. 1903. *Medizin, Aberglaube und Geschlechtsleben in der Türkei*, Berlin: Barsdorf.

Stewart, Omer C. 1987. *Peyote Religion: A History*, Norman, Oklahoma: University of Oklahoma Press.

Storl, Wolf-Dieter. 1986. *Vom rechten Umgang mit heilenden Pflanzen*, Freiburg i. Br., Germany: Bauer.

1988. *Feuer und Asche — Dunkel und Licht: Shiva — Urbild des Menschen*, Freiburg i.B., Germany: Bauer.

Stutley, Margaret. 1980. *Ancient Indian Magic and Folklore*, Boulder, Colorado: Great Eastern.

Swiderski, Stanislav. 1965. 'Le Bwiti', *Anthropos*, 60:541-576.

Taberner, Peter V. 1985. *Aphrodisiacs: The Science and the Myth*, Philadelphia: University of Pennsylvania Press.

Tabor, Edward. 1970. 'Plant Poisons in Shakespeare', *Economic Botany*, 24(1):81-94.

Taussig, Michael. 1987. *Shamanism, Colonialism, and the Wild Man*, Chicago: University of Chicago Press.

Taylor, Norman. 1966. *Narcotics — Nature's Dangerous Gifts*, New York: Dell.

Tercinet, L. 1950. *Mandragore Qui-es-tu?*, Paris: Private Printing.

Thamm, Berndt Georg. 1986. *Andenschnee*, Basel: Sphinx.

Thiel, Josef F. 1986. *Was sind Fetische?*, Frankfurt/Main: Museum für Völkerkunde.

Thompson, C.J.S. 1968. *The Mystic Mandrake*, second edition, New York: University Books.

1989. *Magic and Healing*, New York: Bell.

Thorwald, Jürgen. 1962. *Macht und Geheimnis der frühen Ärzte*, Munich: Knaur.

Tierny, Gail D. 1974. 'Botany and Witchcraft', *El Palacio*, 80(2):44-50.

Touw, Mia. 1981. 'The Religious and Medicinal Uses of *Cannabis* in China, India and Tibet', *Journal of Psychoactive Drugs*, 13(1):23-34.

Trehane, Piers. 1989. *Index Hortensis*, Wimborne, Dorset: Quarterjack.

Trupp, Fritz. 1984. *Die letzten Indianer Kulturen Südamerikas*, Wörgl, Austria: Perlinger.

Urchs, Ossi. 1986. 'Die Lust wächst wild', *Playboy*, (German edition), 4(April)/86:117-118, 180-191.

Uyldert, Mellie. 1987. *Verborgene Kraft der Pflanzen*, Munich: Hugendubel.

Valdes, Leander J., III, William M. Butler, George M. Hatfield, Ara G. Paul & Masato Koreeda. 1984. 'Divinorin A, a Psychotropic Terpenoid, and Divinorin B from the Hallucinogenic Mexican Mint Salvia divinorum', *Journal of Organic Chemistry*, 49(24):4716-4720.

Valnet, Jean. 1980. *Aromatherapy: The Treatment of Illness with the Essences of Plants*, England: Daniel.

Van Bruggen, Theodore. 1983. *Wildflowers, Grasses & Other Plants of the Northern Plains and Black Hills*, Rapid City, South Dakota: Badlands Natural History Association.

Verrill, A, Hyatt. 1939. *Wonder Plants and Plant Wonders*, New York: Appleton.

Vestal, Paul. 1952. *Ethnobotany of the Ramah Navaho*, Cambridge, Massachusetts: Papers of the Peabody Museum XL, 4.

Vetterling, Bernhard. n.d. *Halluzinogene Pilze bei uns*, Löhrbach, Germany: Grüne Kraft (Der Grüne Zweig 65).

Villoldo, Alberto & Erik Jendresen. 1990. *The Four Winds: A Shaman's Odyssey into the Amazon*, San Francisco: Harper & Row.

Villoldo, Alberto & Stanley Krippner. 1984. *Healing States*, New York: Simon & Schuster.

Vinci, Leo. 1980. *Incense: Its Ritual Significance, Preparation and Use*, New York: Weiser.

Viola, Severino. 1979. *Piante medicinali e velenose della flora italiana*, Milan: Edizioni Artistiche Maestretti.

Völger, Gisela, ed. 1981. *Rausch und Realität*, Cologne: Rautenstrauch-Joest Museum (two volumes).

Voltz, Michel. 1981. 'Hirsebier in Westafrika', in *Rausch und Realität*, G. Vögler, ed., Cologne: Rautenstrauch-Joest-Museum, Vol. 1, pp. 174-181.

Von Hagen, Victor W. 1944. *The Aztec and Maya Papermakers*, New York: Augustin.

1979. *Die Wüstenkönigreiche Perus*, Bergisch-Gladbach, Germany: Bastei-Lübbe.

Vrchotka, Jaroslav. 1974. *Mandragora: Illustrovaná Kniha Vèdecká 15.-*

17. Století, Prague: Katalog vystavy Národní muzeum v Praze.

Vries, Herman de. 1984. *natural-relations I — die marokkanische sammlung*, Stuttgart: Mueller-Roth.

1985. 'die steppenraute, ihr gebrauch in marokko als heilpflanze und psychotherapeutikum', *Salix*, 1(1):36-40.

1989. *natural relations — eine skizze*, Nuremberg: Verlag für moderne Kunst.

1991. 'über die sogenannten hexensalben', *Integration*, 1:31-42.

Wagner, Hildebert. 1985. *Pharmazeutische Biologie*, third edition, Stuttgart, New York: Gustav Fischer.

Wagner, Rudolf G. 1981. 'Das Han-shi Pulver - eine ''moderne'' Droge im mitteralterlichen China', in *Rausch und Realität*, G. Vögler, ed., Cologne: Rautenstrauch-Joest-Museum, Vol. 1, pp. 320-323.

Wallnöfer, Heinrich. 1968. *Zauberdrogen — Ärzte — Menschenopfer*, Stuttgart: Fink.

Walton, James W. 1969. 'Muinane Diagnostic Use of Narcotics', *Economic Botany*, 23:187-188.

Warburg, Otto. 1897. *Die Muskatnuß*, Leipzig: Engelmann.

Wassen, S. Henry. 1967. 'Anthropological Survey of the Use of South American Snuffs', in *Ethnopharmacological Search for Psychoactive Drugs*, Daniel H. Efron, ed., Washington, D.C.: U.S. Department of Health , Education, and Welfare, pp. 233-289.

1979. 'Was Espingo (Ispincu) of Psychotropic Importance for the Shamans in Peru?', in *Spirits, Shamans, and Stars*, D.L. Browman & R.A. Schwarz, eds., The Hague: Mouton, pp. 55-62.

Wasson, R. Gordon. 1971. 'Ololiuqui and the Other Hallucinogens of Mexico', in *Homenaje a Roberto J. Weitlaner*, Mexico, D.F.: UNAM, pp. 329-348.

1972. *Soma — Divine Mushroom of Immortality*, New York: Harcourt Brace Jovanovich.

1974. 'The Role of "Flowers" in Nahuatl Culture', *Journal of Psychedelic Drugs*, 6(3):351-360.

1979. 'Traditional Use in North America of Amanita muscaria for Divinatory Purposes', *Journal of Psychedelic Drugs*, 11(1-2):25-28.

1980. *The Wondrous Mushroom*, New York: McGraw-Hill.

Wasson, R. Gordon, Albert Hofmann & Carl A.P. Ruck. 1978. *The Road to Eleusis: Unveiling the Secret of the Mysteries*, New York: Harcourt Brace Jovanovich.

Wasson, R. Gordon, Stella Kramrisch, Jonathan Ott & Carl A.P. Ruck. 1986. *Persephone's Quest: Entheogens and the Origin of Religion*, New Haven: Yale University Press.

Weck, Wolfgang. 1986. *Heilkunde und Volkstum auf Bali*, BAP Bali, Jakarta: Intermasa.

Wedeck, Harry E. 1963. *Dictionary of Aphrodisiacs*, New York: Philosophical Library.

1966. *A Treasury of Witchcraft*, New York: Citadel.

1989. *Dictionary of Aphrodisiacs*, New York: Philosophical Library.

Wedemeyer, Inge von. 1972. 'Mais, Rausch- und Heilmittel im alten Peru', *Ethnomedizin*, 2(1-2):99-112.

Weil, Andrew. 1972. *The Natural Mind: A New Way of Looking at Drugs and the Higher Consciousness*, Boston: Houghton Mifflin.

1975. 'The Green and the White', *Journal of Psychedelic Drugs*, 7(4):401-413.

1976. 'The Love Drug', *Journal of Psychedelic Drugs*, 8(4):335-337.

1977. 'Some Notes on Datura', *Journal of Psychedelic Drugs*, 9(2):165-169.

1980. *The Marriage of the Sun and Moon*, ed., Boston: Houghton Mifflin.

1988. *Health and Healing*, Boston: Houghton Mifflin (revised and updated).

Weil, Andrew & Winifred Rosen. 1983. *From Chocolate to Morphine*, Boston: Houghton Mifflin.

Weiner, Michael A. 1972. *Earth Medicine — Earth Goods*, New York: Collier.

Wilbert, Johannes. 1979. 'Magico-Religious Use of Tobacco Among South American Indians', in *Spirits, Shamans, and Stars*, D.L. Browman & R.A. Schwarz, eds., The Hague: Mouton, pp. 13-38.

1987. *Tobacco and Shamanism* in South America, New Haven: Yale University Press.

Winkelman, Michael & Marlene Dobkin de Rios. 1989. 'Psychoactive Properties of !Kung Bushman Medicine Plants', *Journal of Psychoactive Drugs*, 21(1):51-60.

Wlislocki, Heinrich von. 1891. *Volksglaube und religiöser Brauch der Zigeuner*, Münster, Germany: Aschendorffsche Bucandlung.

Wolff, Fritz. 1910. *Avesta — Die heiligen Bücher der Parsen*, Strassburg: Trübner.

Yarnell, Richard A. 1959. 'Prehistoric Pueblo Use of Datura', *El Palacio*, 66(5):176-178.

Zech, Paul. 1982. *Die grüne Flöte vom Rio Beni: Indianische Liebesgeschichten*, Frankfurt/Main: Fischer.

Index of Plants According to Their Botanical Names

The column on the left lists the plants discussed in this book in order of their botanical names; the column on the right gives the entry where that plant can be located in the text.

Argemone spp.	*Prickly Poppy*
Argyreia nervosa	*Woodrose*
Argyreia spp.	*Woodrose*
Argyreia tuberosa	*Woodrose*
Artemisia abronthanum	*Artemisia*
Artemisia absinthium	*Artemisia*
Artemisia frigida	*Artemisia*
Artemisia keiskiana	*Artemisia*
Artemisia ludoviciana	*Artemisia*
Artemisia mexicana	*Artemisia*
Artemisia scopulorum	*Artemisia*
Artemisia spp.	*Artemisia*
Artemisia tilesii	*Artemisia*
Arundo donax	*Reed*
Aspidosperma quebracho-blanco	*Quebracho*
Astralagus spp.	*Locoweeds*
Atropa belladonna	*Belladonna*
Banisteriopsis caapi	*Ayahuasca*
Banisteriopsis rusbyana	*Ayahuasca*
Banisteriopsis spp.	*Ayahuasca*
Boletus satanas	*Mushrooms*
Brugmansia candida	*Angel's Trumpet*
Brugmansia sanguinea	*Angel's Trumpet*
Brugmansia spp.	*Angel's Trumpet*
Brugmansia suaveolens	*Angel's Trumpet*
Brunfelsia spp.	*Manaca*
Caesalpina bonduc	*Yun-Shih*
Caesalpinia sepiaria	*Yun-Shih*
Calea zacatechichi	*Zacatechichi*
Calonyction muricatum	*Lakshmana*
Canavalia maritima	*Beans*
Canella alba	*Canella*
Canella winteriana	*Canella*
Cannabis indica	*Hemp*
Cannabis sativa	*Hemp*
Catha edulis	*Qat*
Cedra libani	*Cedar*
Cedrella mexicana	*Cedar*
Cinnamomum camphora	*Camphor*

Claviceps purpurea	*Ergot*
Clidemia setosa	*Orchids*
Coffea arabica	*Coffee*
Cola acuminata	*Cola*
Cola nitida	*Cola*
Cola spp.	*Cola*
Coleus blumei	*Coleus*
Coleus pumilus	*Coleus*
Conium maculatum	*Hemlock*
Copelandia cyanescens	*Jambur*
Corynanthe pachyceras	*Yohimbe*
Corynanthe yohimbe	*Yohimbe*
Crocus sativus	*Saffron*
Cymbidium devonianum	*Orchids*
Cynanchum caudatum	*Ikema*
Cytisus canariensis	*Genista*
Datura alba	*Thornapple*
Datura ceratocaula	*Thornapple*
Datura discolor	*Thornapple*
Datura fastuosa	*Thornapple*
Datura ferox	*Thornapple*
Datura inoxia	*Thornapple*
Datura leichardti	*Pituri*
Datura metel	*Thornapple*
Datura spp.	*Thornapple*
Datura stramonium	*Thornapple*
Datura tatula	*Thornapple*
Dendrobium linawianum	*Orchids*
Duboisia hopwoodi	*Pituri*
Elaphomyces cervinus	*Mushrooms*
Ephedra americana	*Ephedra*
Ephedra californica	*Ephedra*
Ephedra distachya	*Ephedra*
Ephedra fragilis	*Ephedra*
Ephedra nevadensis	*Ephedra*
Ephedra sinica	*Ephedra*
Ephedra spp.	*Ephedra*
Ephedra vulgaris	*Ephedra*
Ephemerantha macraei	*Orchids*

Erythrina americana	*Colorines*
Erythrophloeum judicale	*Mwamfi*
Erythroxylon coca	*Coca*
Fabiana imbricata	*Pichi-Pichi*
Ferraria glutinosa	*Gaise Noru Noru*
Ferula asafoetida	*Asafoetida*
Ficus spp.	*Amate*
Ganoderma lucidum	*Ling-Chih*
Goodenia lunata	*Pituri*
Goodyear pubescens	*Orchids*
Hamamelis virginiana	*Witch Hazel*
Heimia salicifolia	*Sinicuiche*
Helleborus officinalis	*Hellebore*
Hydrocotyle asiatica minor	*Fo-Ti*
Hyoscyamus albus	*Henbane*
Hyoscyamus faleslez	*Henbane*
Hyoscyamus niger	*Henbane*
Hyoscyamus niger var. *chinensis*	*Henbane*
Hyoscyamus physaloides	*Henbane*
Hyoscyamus spp.	*Henbane*
Ilex cassine	*Black Drink*
Ilex guayusa	*Guayusa*
Ilex paraguariensis	*Maté*
Ilex vomitoria	*Black Drink*
Inocybe spp.	*Mushrooms*
Iochroma fuchsioides	*Guatillo*
Ipomoea pandurata	*Morning Glory*
Ipomoea rubrocaerulea	*Morning Glory*
Ipomoea spp.	*Morning Glory*
Ipomoea tricolor	*Morning Glory*
Ipomoea violacea	*Morning Glory*
Ipomoea violacea var. *Pearly Gates*	*Morning Glory*
Juniperus drupacea	*Cedar*
Juniperus oxycedrus	*Cedar*
Juniperus phoenicea	*Cedar*
Juniperus recurva	*Juniper*
Juniperus spp.	*Cedar; Juniper*

Nicotiana trigonophylla	*Tobacco*
Nicotiana velutina	*Pituri*
Nuphar luteum	*Water Lily*
Nuphar luteum variegatum	*Water Lily*
Nymphaea alba	*Water Lily*
Nymphaea ampla	*Water Lily*
Nymphaea caerula	*Water Lily*
Nymphaea lotus	*Lotus; Water Lily*
Nymphaea spp.	*Water Lily*
Ocimum sanctum	*Tulasi*
Oncidium cebolleta	*Orchids*
Orchidaceae	*Orchids*
Orchis maculata	*Orchids*
Orchis sp.	*Orchids*
Oxytropis lambertii	*Locoweeds*
Oxytropis sericea	*Locoweeds*
Panax ginseng	*Ginseng*
Panax quinquefolium	*Ginseng*
Paneolus papilianaceus	*Laughing Mushroom*
Papaver somniferum	*Poppy*
Paullinia cupana	*Guaraní*
Pedilanthus itzaeus	*Pedilanthus*
Pedilanthus tithymaloides	*Pedilanthus*
Peganum harmala	*Syrian Rue*
Peucedanum decursivum	*Fang-Kuei*
Peucedanum japonica	*Fang-Kuei*
Phallus impudicus	*Mushrooms*
Phallus spp.	*Mushrooms*
Phasaeolus vulgaris	*Beans*
Phoenix dactylifera	*Date Palm*
Phoradendron flavescens	*Mistletoe*
Physostigma venenosum	*Calabar Bean*
Phytolacca acinosa	*Shang-Lu*
Phytolacca esculenta	*Shang-Lu*
Pinus cedrus	*Cedar*
Pinus spp.	*Copal*
Piper betle	*Betel*
Piper methysticum	*Kava-Kava*
Pithecolobium diversifolium	*Jurema*

Vaccinium uliginosum	*Vaccinium*
Vanda tesselata	*Orchids*
Vanilla planifolium	*Orchids*
Veratrum album	*Hellebore*
Verbena officinalis	*Vervain*
Viscum album	*Mistletoe*
Vitis vinifera	*Wine*
Voacanga dregei	*Voacanga*
Voacanga spp.	*Voacanga*
Withania somnifera	*Jangida*
Zea mays	*Maize*
Zingiber officinarum	*Ginger*

Glossary

abortifacient. Agent for inducing an abortion (miscarriage). Agent for aborting or killing a fetus. Many magical plants, especially the hallucinogens, have abortifacient effects and thus may not be used or may only rarely be used by women. It is possible that midwives and witches made use of this fact to purposefully induce abortions.

androgyny. The merging of male and female traits into a unity.

anthropomorphic. Having human form; graphic representations in which human traits become manifest. Some magical plants receive their power as a result of their anthropomorphic appearance.

antidote. Antitoxin: a substance which counteracts the effects of a poison or neutralizes or destroys the poison. A number of magical plants have been used as universal antidotes.

aphrodisiac. An agent which increases sexual desire, the erotic experience, and physical pleasure. A large number of magical plants are used as aphrodisiacs.

apotropaic. Capable of warding off that which is evil or negative or threatening. Many magical plants are considered to be apotropaic when they are used or worn as amulets.

decoction. An extract prepared by boiling a medicinal or magical plant.

diuretic. An agent which increases the urge to urinate or stimulates kidney activity. Many magical plants have diuretic effects.

divination. Fortunetelling or prophesying via a divine medium. Divination is often carried out in conjunction with the ingestion or use of magical plants.

ejaculation. The act of ejecting semen.

epiphyte. A plant which grows upon another nonparasitically.

estrogen. Female sex hormone. Several of the magical plants which are used for love or fertility magic contain estrogenic substances.

hallucinogen. An agent which makes the human mind susceptible to having visions; an agent which evokes hallucinations (sensory experiences that exist only within the mind). Most magical plants are hallucinogens.

hermetic. Pertaining to the magical teachings of Hermes Trismegistus.

ithyphallic. Pictorial representation of a male being with an erect penis; such representations were usually considered apotropaic.

maceration. An extract of a medicinal or magical plant obtained by adding the plant to cold water or another cold liquid (such as beer or wine).

metabolism. The processes by which the organs of the body chemically alter ingested substances.

necromancer. A magician who contacts the world of the dead or the souls of the deceased. Often, this occurs in conjunction with the use of magical plants.

panacea. A wondrous cure-all. Many magical plants are said to be panaceas.

psychedelic. Consciousness expanding, vision producing. Most magical plants have psychedelic effects.

psychoactive. Activating the psyche or the mind; plants of this type typically make unconscious psychic material available to the conscious mind. Almost all magical plants have psychoactive effects.

psychotropic. Changing the psyche or consciousness. Psychotropic effects may be psychedelic, psychoactive, or sedative; the term also encompasses stupefying or confusing effects.

rhizotome. One who digs roots. Because rhizotomes often dig magical roots, they may easily be suspected of witchcraft.

sedative. An agent which soothes or calms. Some magical plants have sedative effects.

substitute. A substance which is used in place of something else.

synergistic. Working together; combining two types of effects with one another in order to attain a new effect. In magical drinks, various agents are often combined for their synergistic effects.

toxic. Poisonous; having poisonous effects.